D1557012

BOOKS BY HOWARD MOSS

Poems

Notes from the Castle
A Swim off the Rocks
Buried City
Selected Poems
Second Nature
Finding Them Lost
A Winter Come, A Summer Gone
A Swimmer in the Air
The Toy Fair
The Wound and the Weather

Criticism

Whatever Is Moving
Writing Against Time
The Magic Lantern of Marcel Proust

Edited, with an Introduction

New York: Poems
The Poet's Story
The Nonsense Books of Edward Lear
Keats

Satire

Instant Lives

Plays

Two Plays

For Children

Tigers & Other Lilies

Whatever Is Moving

HOWARD MOSS

Whatever

Little, Brown and Company

I s   M o v i n g

Boston/Toronto

FIRST EDITION

Library of Congress Cataloging in Publication Data

Moss, Howard, 1922–
  Whatever is moving.

   1. Literature, Modern — 19th century — History and
criticism — Addresses, essays, lectures. 2. Litera-
ture, Modern — 20th century — History and criticism —
Addresses, essays, lectures. I. Title.
PN761.M64 809'.03 81-12352
ISBN 0-316-58571-8 AACR2

Lines from ELIZABETH BISHOP: THE COMPLETE POEMS
Copyright © 1969 by Elizabeth Bishop; lines from MORNING OF
THE POEM by James Schuyler Copyright © 1976, 1978, 1980 by
James Schuyler, reprinted by permission of Farrar, Straus and
Giroux, Inc.

The Author is grateful to the Estate of L. E. Sissman and to the
Atlantic Monthly Press for allowing him to use the title "Dying: An
Introduction" from the poem and collection of the same title by L. E.
Sissman, published in 1967 by Little, Brown and Company in associ-
ation with the Atlantic Monthly Press.

Additional Acknowledgments on page 278.

MV

Designed by Rosalie H. Davis

*Published simultaneously in Canada
by Little, Brown & Company (Canada) Limited*

PRINTED IN THE UNITED STATES OF AMERICA

For Daniel D'Arezzo

CONTENTS

I

II

III

CONTENTS

IV

PART ONE

WALT WHITMAN

A Candidate for the Future

CERTAIN writers belong not only to the history of literature but to History itself, and Whitman is one of them. He was crucially positioned: the American colonies had declared their independence exactly forty-three years before his birth in 1819, and the Revolution was still a vivid event in the minds of the adults around him. Psychically, his life stretched from the Revolution through the Civil War to the era of the Robber Barons. Truly an American poet of change, the man and the work tend toward the heroic, the mythological. One of the great virtues of Justin Kaplan's *Walt Whitman — A Life* is his ability to rescue the man from the giant without diminishing his stature. Separating the genius from the diamond in the rough isn't easy, for Whitman was several men in one: Brahman, Bohemian, spokesman for a new democratic society, dandy, creator of an original kind of American poetry — a self-educated and self-intoxicated

3

peasant of the ecstatic. Even the photographs, many never seen before, reinforce the kaleidoscopic sense of an ever-shifting personality. Mr. Kaplan, letting the various Whitmans speak, allowing for ambiguities, comes to no ringing conclusions.

A child of Long Island's "bare unfrequented shore," Whitman became, in time, a printer, newspaperman, teacher, and editor. The son of a dour housebuilder of English stock and a Quaker mother of Dutch descent, his childhood was marred by instability. The record of insanity, intemperance, and failure in the Whitman family makes dismal reading. Living in the country provided no roots; moving from West Hills to Brooklyn and back, the Whitmans occupied a dozen different houses before the poet was eleven. At that age, he stayed behind in Brooklyn, as a printer's apprentice, on his own. There, and in Manhattan, "the blab of the pave" mingled with the "Howler and scooper of storms, capricious and dainty sea" to become strands in an original verbal amalgam that makes "Song of Myself" — the key poem of *Leaves of Grass* — so remarkable.

The first, 1855 edition of that book bore no author's name; an engraved daguerrotype of a gypsylike workman — one of Whitman's guises — adorned the frontispiece. Its poems untitled, the book opened with what is now "Song of Myself." In truth, a song of everyone *but* myself — "of every rank and estate am I / of every hue and religion" — it speaks for a consciousness beyond any individual ego, one made up of many. In taking on its various personas, Whitman's ability to be androgynous and anonymous, his gifts of identification and sympathy are those of a great poet. They developed into an uneasy egotism later in life, as if the many characters of

4

a literary work had filtered into the person who created them. Whitman's notion of himself *as* America, at first the mark of a passive generosity of spirit, grew overbearing, and narrowed into mere ambition. Empathy in the artist was reduced to role-playing in the man; the myth-maker and the self-server became interchangeable.

Whitman's homosexuality complicated his role as an American spokesman, just as his "mysticism" added an eerie note to his social views, those of a freethinker brought up on Quakerism, Carlyle, George Sand, and Margaret Fuller. Divorced from any traditional faith, his spiritual illuminations are closer to the sutras of the Oriental contemplative religions than to the visions of Christian saints. Denial and self-excoriation — the desert and the hair shirt — were alien to him. Divine irrationality, the kind we associate with Blake, Christopher Smart, and Rimbaud, is closer to the mark. Moreover, these illuminations had to be accommodated to the nineteenth-century notion of progress. Queen Victoria and Whitman were born in the same year. "Sex was a major disorder," and Whitman, the only writer of nineteenth-century America completely at odds with Puritanism, was — in his trust in an expansive commercialism, his "pursuit of health as a supreme good" — a true product of the Victorian age. No matter how original his thought, it wove in and out of commonly held beliefs. Phrenology, for instance, was an accepted science in Whitman's time — Horace Mann, Henry Ward Beecher, Ralph Waldo Emerson, Edgar Allan Poe, and Daniel Webster all believed in it — and so was "animal magnetism." "I sing the body electric" was more a literal than a figurative reference. Life was seen as voltage and wattage. People were little wireless posts at the mercy of internal

5

shocks and outgoing currents. Mr. Kaplan sums it up: "Whitman was a sort of storage battery or accumulator for charged particles of the contemporary."

In "Song of Myself" we hear for the first time Whitman's unique blend of biblical cadence (particularly the Psalms), primitive chant, and the ongoing catalogue — devices eventually to be at the service of a cosmic universe made up of American particularities, a secular Bible of sorts, full of contradictions and oddities. No other major poem I know sets itself such contrary tasks: to reveal the oneness of things, to praise the freedom of the individual, to celebrate the multitude in song. The overall title of *Leaves of Grass* is brilliantly fitting: the mass individuated in the unique leaf, the leaf one with the general green. The musical side of the poem sprang from Whitman's love of voices. Aroused as a youth by fiery preachers and professional orators, he savored, as his taste matured, the delights of the theater. Italian opera became a passion. The works — and the singers — opened up, and were exemplars of, a whole hidden emotional life. Sensitive to voices, he was totally responsive to their grandest manifestation. Opera introduced Whitman to the fusion of sound and action, the projection of emotion through virtuosity. Thematic repetition in Whitman is conscious but has a characteristic sounding board. Many of the poems are best approached as long arias, and even the natural music of bird song has the calculated effect of a musical motif entering a score.

In 1848, Whitman, then editor of the *Brooklyn Eagle*, was fired after a political squabble with its owners. Invited to edit the *New Orleans Crescent*, he traveled with his brother Jeff on a two-week journey south and west by train, stagecoach, and steamboat. Whitman's only reference points had been Long Island, Brooklyn, and Manhattan. Words had been his only form of travel. His view of America expanded. A sense of the continent broadened the base and scope of *Leaves of Grass*. And New Orleans, with its French and Spanish heritage, was sensuous and fruitful. "By the time he returned to Brooklyn . . . he had travelled five thousand miles, and seen democratic vistas of city and wilderness, river and lake, mountain and plain." The cosmic intentions of *Leaves of Grass* were accumulating a large continental underpinning.

In his notebook, Whitman kept clarifying his thoughts, perfecting his design: "Make no quotations and no references to other writers. Take no illustration whatsoever from the ancients or classics. . . . Make no mention or allusion to them whatever, except as they relate . . . to American character, or interests." Again, "[to make] the poems of emotions, as they pass or stay, the poems of freedom, and the exposé of personality — singing in high tones democracy and the New World of it through These States." The words after the dash are the kind of sentiments that put many readers off by their air of fake grandiosity. The grandeur was partly temperamental, partly defensive: Mr. Kaplan says, ". . . there were hints that a less robust spirit had once prevailed, a spirit covert, hesitant, perturbed, lonely, and always unrequited. ('It is I you hold and who holds you,' he addressed his reader, becoming his own book, 'I spring from the pages into your arms.')" He was "cautious" and "artful" and told Edward Carpenter, one of his many English admirers, "I think there are truths which it is necessary to envelop or wrap up."

One of them was obvious — but to some not obvious enough. After the publication of the "Calamus" poems,

Whitman found himself in a position for which he had no taste: an international (but unwilling) advocate of homosexual love. John Addington Symonds was relentless in his pursuit of explications. What Symonds really wanted was for Whitman to declare himself. (There was a side to Whitman Symonds could never have imagined. Referring to an essay Symonds had written called "Democratic Art, with Special Reference to Walt Whitman," Whitman said, "I doubt whether he has gripped 'democratic art' by the nuts, or L of G either.") A whole colony of English homosexuals trooped to Whitman's flag. His brother George could never understand why Oscar Wilde would travel all the way to Camden, hardly a pleasure spot, just to see "Walt." It was in a letter replying to Symonds that the six illegitimate children first appear. A "mulatto mistress" was a later embellishment. This story was taken seriously by scholars for years even though no one ever came forward to claim the famous name or the possibly lucrative literary rights.

Whitman was attracted to ferryhands, drivers, and mechanics, enjoying their naturalness, their savvy, their lingo. Peter Doyle, a horse-car conductor he met in his Washington days, was the most satisfactory companion of his life. But even here he pressed too far:

. . . give up absolutely, & for good, from this present hour, this feverish, fluctuating, useless undignified pursuit of 16.4 — too long (much too long) persevered in — so humiliating.

In Whitman's notebooks, "16" stands for "P" and "4" for "D" — the cryptography of a child. It becomes clear from Mr. Kaplan's book that Whitman's intense emotional affairs were all with men. Ellen O'Connor, the wife of Whitman's friend and critic William O'Connor, fell madly in love with him, and Anne Gilchrist, an English widow, wrote him passionate letters offering her hand in marriage. Whitman tried to put her off to no avail. She came over and lived in America with her children for several years, only to return to England, in the end, disappointed. Not quite able to deny himself any form of idolatry, Whitman welcomed women cautiously, proffering them his person in place of his love. He became a familiar figure in the O'Connor household in Washington and the Gilchrist ménage in Philadelphia. In fact, he liked nothing better than to "join" an already established domestic circle, adopting, and being adopted by, one family after another. In these establishments, he was the overgrown prodigal son come home to roost, or that friendly but remote familiar, the genius-uncle.

Leaves of Grass went through nine editions in Whitman's lifetime, its author striving in each successive recasting for the proper arrangement of the poems, readjusting sections and shifting sequences to accommodate additions to an ever-expanding work, which grew from the twelve poems of the 1855 edition to the three hundred eighty-three of the so-called Deathbed edition that bears Whitman's imprimatur. Lines and phrases were always being revised, stanzas tightened, and, as new poems were added, old ones were jettisoned to make room for them. Juvenile outpourings were discarded. Poems superseded others.

Leaves of Grass was full of prescriptions for the future. Emerson's clever description of it as a "combination of the 'Baghavad-Gita' and 'The New York Herald,'" meant as a putdown, would today be considered a compliment — but only because *Leaves of Grass* is already in place to show the way. (Emerson's comment was a far cry from his first spontaneous reaction to the poem, emblazoned forever in a famous letter: "I am not blind to the worth of the wonderful gift of 'Leaves of Grass.' I find it the most extraordinary piece of wit and wisdom that America has yet contributed. . . . I find incomparable things said incomparably well. . . . I greet you at the beginning of a great career" — the most generous unsolicited response of one writer to another in the history of American letters. Without it, the poetry, which had few takers, might have been lost forever. Whitman sent the letter to the *New York Tribune* and incorporated it into the second edition of *Leaves of Grass* — in both cases without permission from Emerson — two acts of insensitivity in Whitman's long career of self-advertisement. A poet–prophet–public-relations man, he wrote three anonymous reviews of his own book, modestly characterizing it, in one, as "the most glorious of triumphs in the known history of literature. . . .")

The true miracle of *Leaves of Grass* is that, with all its excesses, its extravagant claims, its endless catalogues, it is, at its very best, a poem of pure feeling — feeling that seeps through phrase after phrase, poem after poem. It is so loving that the transformation of its emotions into words on so vast a scale is astonishing. A long love affair with the future, broken in speech sometimes, eloquent beyond anything one remembers, remarkable in the minting of its language, it is a sad poem, a love poem to some "you" never found, some "you" not only personal, intimate, and sexual, but connected with an epic largeness of democratic vistas, as if the poet were in love with future Americans not yet born, or always yet to come. No one has yet explained, including Mr. Kaplan — and certainly not Whitman — where it sprang from. Whitman encouraged the view of the "transformation miracle" — the "journalist-loafer" turned into the great poet and prophet, as if at the touch of a wand. His followers, sodden with worship, helped the idea along. Actually, Whitman worked on it for years. It was *almost* a miracle, but a flawed one, for there is always the problem in Whitman of the false prophecy, the naïve dream, the wished-for fulfillment seen as accomplished fact. Its unevenness is too obvious to be commented on.

Leaves of Grass did more than change opinions; it altered the intellectual climate of the world. (And the moral climate, too. "Free love?" Whitman once asked. "Is there any other kind?") Van Gogh, working on *Starry Night* in Arles, was affected by it; Gerard Manley Hopkins took it to heart; LaForgue translated the "Children of Adam" poems; it was crucial to D. H. Lawrence and Hart Crane. People as wildly different as Thomas Eakins and Tennyson, Gertrude Stein and Henry James felt its impact. In our time, the Black Mountain School, the Beats, and the New York School of Poets emerged from it.

When the Civil War started, *Leaves of Grass* had been through three editions. "Out of the Cradle Endlessly Rocking," the "Children of Adam," and the "Calamus" poems had all been added. Its message of brotherly love became literal. Just as one brother, Jeff, had been party to Whitman's expanding conception of America, it was concern for another, George, that led Whitman to the battlefields of the South. In a garbled casualty report, Whitman learned that George had been wounded. No news followed. Whitman left Washington for Virginia in search of him, found him, and saw at first hand what the war was really like.

He dealt with it the only way he knew — as a healer. He returned to Washington to become a "wound-dresser" at Armory Square Hospital. Seventy thousand sick and wounded crowded every inch of it.

Whitman came into the wards like "a rich old sea captain, he was so red-faced and patriarchal-looking and big." He entertained the wounded, recited Shakespeare and Scott, told stories, wrote letters for the illiterate and the disabled, attended the feverish young, assisted at the grisly amputations, and comforted the dying. The suffering was indescribable: ". . . by the end of the war Whitman figured he had made over six hundred hospital visits and tours, often lasting several days and nights, and in some degree ministered to nearly a hundred thousand of the sick and wounded on both sides. . . ."

Yet there were compensations: the alleviation of pain, the sense of being part of a great design, of contributing. Paternal concern, brotherly companionship, mothering compassion were mixed up with emotions sometimes dangerously close to obsession. In the end, he was undone not only by the physical and mental suffering of the patients, and the fatigue of the work, but by his barely controllable feelings. Here is a letter from Whitman to Thomas P. Sawyer, one of the soldiers:

Dear Comrade, you must not forget me, for I never shall you. My love you have in life or death forever. I don't know how you feel about it, but it is the wish of my heart to have your friendship. . . . If you should come safe out of this war, we

should come together again in some place where we could make
our living, and be true comrades and never be separated while
life lasts. . . . My soul could never be entirely happy, even in
the world to come without you, dear comrade. . . . Goodbye,
my darling comrade, my dear darling brother, for so I will call
you, and wish you would call me the same.

Here is Sawyer's reply:

I fully appreciate your friendship as expressed in your letter and
it will afford me great pleasure to meet you after the war will
have terminated or sooner if circumstances permit.

The generalized "you," the beloved addressed in Whitman's poems, had, like Plato's universals, an idealized counterpart in President Lincoln. As a poet of the body, Whitman believed "The scent of these armpits is aroma finer than
prayer / This head is more than churches or Bibles or
creeds"; but as a poet of the soul, having eschewed Christi-
anity, he needed a god of his own. ". . . Lincoln [became]
his personal agent of redemption, a symbolic figure who
transcended politics, leadership, and victory." His mother
was the only other person in Whitman's life who had had
this idealized aura. The "Drum-Taps" poems came out of
the war and were dutifully added to *Leaves of Grass*. Their
price was high: "The perfect health Whitman was so proud
of broke in the hospitals along with a delicate structure of
denial and sublimation. Love became irreversibly linked with
disease, mutilation, death, absence." In 1865, Lincoln was
assassinated; in 1873, Whitman's mother died. Long before,
he had written a line that now seemed perfectly appropriate:
"Agony is one of my changes of garment."

The year Whitman's mother died, he became partially paralyzed. Strokes were to cripple Whitman the rest of his life. After living with the family of his brother George in Camden for several years, he bought a small house of his own. Some of Mr. Kaplan's most charming pages are devoted to Whitman's last years. Confined more or less to an upper-front bedroom-workroom, he recovered only to be laid back again by another bout of illness. "It was not until old age," according to John Burroughs, the naturalist, who knew Whitman for over twenty years, "that Whitman's presence and ambience became fully achieved. . . . He created an overall impression of sunniness, equanimity, and contemplative leisure." Whitman, still fiddling with *Leaves of Grass*, stirred the mass of papers at his feet with his cane. Everything natural, found, or man-made was source material for the mesmeric catalogues of the poem. The house had the air of a ship's cabin, landlocked and foundering in debris, in spite of the sailor's widow who kept house for him. Whitman was a collector of people and things, but, in both cases, the choices had nothing to do with market values or current fashion. Like a bird building a nest, he knew exactly what he needed (not much) for his comfort, and what he had to have (everything) for his poem. Whitman needed help to get around and always found it; he was surrounded by people who revered him to the point of idolatry. In 1893, he was finally laid to rest in the elaborate tomb in Harleigh Cemetery that had cost him more than the Camden house. By the time the reader comes to Whitman's death, he can almost take "My foothold is tenoned and mortised in granite / I laugh at what you call dissolution" as the literal truth.

Whitman's life is enigmatic not only by virtue of genius; it is steeped in the deliberately muddy waters of destroyed evidence and manipulated fact. Putting a coherent Whitman together is an exercise in conjecture; the more insistent the claim the more suspicious its truth. Mr. Kaplan never insists; he merely presents. If he is sometimes long on Freud and short on philosophy, his is still the best all-around portrait we have of a man whose influence can only increase. Whitman bears a relation to Lincoln not unlike Shakespeare's to Elizabeth I and Michelangelo's to the Medici. In each instance, as the years pass, the more obvious it becomes that the representative figure of the age, like a negative gradually developing in time, is not the ruler but the artist.

Great Themes, Grand Connections

No recent visitor has had a good word to say for present-day Alexandria. Caesar and Cleopatra would be offended, it seems, by its crowded streets, and Euclid and Plotinus would wrinkle up their noses at its garbage-strewn alley-ways. Alexandria is over two thousand years older than the United States, but hardly a stone is left to remind its Arab citizens of its Ptolemaic splendors. An echo chamber of Greek, Jewish, Roman, and Christian voices — pasts within pasts — its fabled nature remains invisible. Because it does, other cities vibrate inside the real one — cities of the imagination, hidden but waiting to be discovered — and they have excited philosophers and writers through the ages: most recently, Lawrence Durrell, in the *Alexandria Quartet*, and E. M. Forster, who wrote the city's most authoritative guidebook, *Alexandria: A History and a Guide*. In it, Forster says, "Then, as now, [Alexandria] belonged not so much to Egypt as to the Mediterranean, and the Ptolemies realised this. Up in Egypt they played the Pharaoh. . . . Down in Alexandria, they were Hellenistic." And so it is not surprising that the truest Alexandrian voice of all should belong to a native son and a member of the Greek diaspora — Constantine Cavafy, born in 1863. Nondescript except for his extraordinary eyes, vastly intelligent, he worked as a civil servant in Alexandria's Third Circle of Irrigation for over thirty years, lived with his rather silly mother and slew of brothers in genteel poverty, and escaped at night to the seediest part of town to sleep with boys. For all these reasons, or for none, he became one of the most fascinating poets Greece has offered the world — the Greek language, not the state, for Cavafy never set foot in Greece until he was thirty-eight, and then only briefly.

Robert Liddell's biography *Cavafy* begins with a genealogy almost as complex as that of the Ptolemies. Odd facts complicated Cavafy's life. His father, who had worked in England, became a British national, conferring automatic British citizenship upon his son. Cavafy was Greek by inheritance, an Egyptian by residence, and a British citizen. There were nine children in all — two dead in their first year, and one of those the only girl. Constantine, her replacement, was his mother's favorite, and she kept him in frocks and curls as long as she could. Of the others, his next two older brothers were important to the poet: Paul, with whom he lived for many years, and John, the closest to Constantine in temperament and understanding. Paul, debtridden, alcoholic, and homosexual, finally ran off to the Riviera to spend his declining years. John wrote poems and translated some of his brother's. Commerce (including embezzlement in one case) was always a stronger thread than artistry in the Cavafy family, but after the father died the Cavafys, once notable and rich, were poor; they lived the sort of life led by "well-bred" people who have lost their money — a fading luxuriance up front, and a tightening of belts behind doors.

At the time of his father's death, Constantine was seven. His mother remained in Alexandria for the next two years. Then the English connection asserted itself, and the family began one of those pilgrimages that must seem biblical to a child, stopping off at Marseilles, Paris, and London, and finally settling in Liverpool. The oldest son engaged in "unhappy speculations," the second lost his shirt in sugar and United Bonds. The tiny Cavafy inheritance dwindled to a pittance. The sense of shadowy cities and of a dynasty ending may have communicated itself to Constantine; he never forgot that he was the son of an extravagant man. The family moved from Liverpool to London, remaining fixed there for a year; reversing course, they returned to Paris and Marseilles. Five years after they started out, they were back in Alexandria. The poet was fourteen, and, except for three forced years of exile in Constantinople (after the Arab "troubles" and the British bombardment) and a trip or two to Europe, he lived in Alexandria for the rest of his life. It was in Constantinople, according to Liddell, that Cavafy had his first homosexual experience.

Liddell follows Cavafy from birth to his death, in 1933, but what there is to follow is meager. Rémy de Gourmont's remark about Flaubert is true of Cavafy: "Apart from his books, he is of very little interest." Sensible and forthright, Liddell's biography does all it can with the available facts, exhausting the Greek sources and providing the necessary checks and balances. It rescues Cavafy from the Freudians, working up from below, and the Marxists, determined to turn everything into a poster.

Before 1911, Cavafy was, by and large, a sentimental poet, writing what he later called "trash." It would have taken a clairvoyant rather than a critic to see the promise of a major poet in the first work. Cavafy was always grateful that he hadn't published early. In fact, he never published at all in any conventional sense: no volume of his poems came out during his lifetime. Poems in manuscript or broadsheet were sent to a select list of people — elected subscribers — and later, Cavafy included reprints and offsets of magazine publications. Two pamphlets appeared, in 1904 and 1910; a bound booklet in 1917. These slowly accreting works filled folder after folder with what Cavafy's translators, Philip Sherrard and Edmund Keeley, refer to as "the canon," a group of a hundred and fifty-three poems. Sherrard and Keeley have added to the original canon twenty-two "unpublished" poems, some among Cavafy's finest, in their edition of the *Collected Poems* — a hundred and seventy-five poems in all, only thirty-five of which come from the period before 1911. The time between a poem's composition and its "publication" could stretch to as long as a quarter of a century. The intervening years left open the possibility of endless revision and the repositioning of poems once Cavafy had come to see his work in terms not of single poems but of a sequential order as complex as the huge territory and time that became his subject.

In a well-known poem, "Days of 1909, '10, and '11" (the

"Days of 19 . . ." poems are part of a series, which has been picked up and revoiced by James Merrill in *his* "Days of 19 . . ." poems), Cavafy sees a boy in an ironmonger's shop, a boy willing to sell his body in order to buy a few cheap pieces of clothing. Under his "cinnamon-brown suit [and] mended underwear," the naked boy is perfection, at one with the beauty of ancient Greek statues, the heads of the favored stamped on precious coins. It was through images such as these that Cavafy began to connect a banal marketplace with a major seam in Greek civilization. What was at first a guilty burden became in the end the means of discovering great themes and grand connections. Cavafy was moved by correspondences, and saw in them the true gestures of history. And thus it was through the erotic that the historical came to life. But though correspondences were moving, they were also ironic, because power — Caesar, Sparta, the Roman Empire — could exist only to be swept away, and had little effect, ultimately, on the repetition of human patterns, the endless tale of construction and pillage. Correspondences were not metaphors to Cavafy — his poems are almost completely free of them in any literal sense — but ongoing dramas, and so the poems are usually monologues, the speaker a fictitious or real person in history, the tone contemporary but the voice timeless.

The historical poems tell their stories in a disinterested way: their savor is the dry accumulated wisdom of someone who has taken the measure of two thousand years of imperial struggle, if not always the measure of himself. They have, as the poet says in "Dareios," "a certain insight into the vanities of greatness . . . [its] arrogance and intoxication." Scene after scene adds up to a play whose dimensions dawn on the reader only slowly. Edmund Keeley, in his completely knowledgeable critical study, *Cavafy's Alexandria*, a model of compression and concentration, lists as an appendix the principal settings of Cavafy's poems in the ancient world of Hellenism: Athens, Eleusis, Argos, Thermopylae, Macedonia, Ithaca, Delphi, Rhodes, Sparta, Rome, Poseidonia, Sicily, Syracuse, and so on. They read like a roll call of what we never knew, or have long forgotten. Sometimes we are in Libya, sometimes in Persia. And, using only Cavafy's titles, I would add a few dates to suggest the grand strategy of the poems: "Of Dimitrios Sotir (162–150 B.C.)," "Of the Jews (A.D. 50)," "Young Men of Sidon (A.D. 400)," "For Ammonis, Who Died at 29, in 610," "Days of 1903." These are poems of statement, forbidding at first in their lack of color, their wide frame of reference, their historical data. The extraordinary thing about them is not Cavafy's ability to see the ancient world alive with character but the accumulated sweep of the whole. Reading them, one feels that history is a vast reality one can dip into at any particular moment. The past being perpetually present, and alive, history becomes permanent. These poems do one of the big things poems should do: they make one aware of time. Cities whose names appear in the newspapers every day make Cavafy's point over again — Beirut, Sidon, Jerusalem, Cairo — and though "historical" suggests the textbook, the opposite effect is at work here: these poems are the products of sensibility, not of scholarship. The method is that of ironic reversal: Claudius justifying his role in *Hamlet*; an invasion of barbarians who are conceived as rescuers rather than destroyers. Young men looking for the main chance — say, in Sidon in 300 B.C. — appear as if they were familiar strangers glimpsed at a bus stop. If one could imagine a contemporary American poet standing on a balcony — as Cavafy stood on his in the Rue Lepsius — resurveying the entire history of the American continent, including its Indian past, one would have some notion of Cavafy's accomplishment.

But that accomplishment seems to me peculiarly patchy, for the great poems stand out — poems like "Waiting for the Barbarians"— and the love poems tend to diminish the cumulative effect of the whole, even though they are the source of its vitality. A worldliness that sometimes brings to mind its supreme example, *Antony and Cleopatra*, alternates with a provincialism that is purely emotional, as if we had in the same person and the same works greatness and a diminishment of it. Most writers of Cavafy's stature save that kind of immaturity for life, but because his life *was* the poems it has entered into the bloodstream of the texts themselves. Impeccable in tone, scrupulous in having rid themselves of every shred of rhetoric, they manage nevertheless to suggest lost opportunities. Cavafy divided his work into three categories: historical, erotic, and philosophical. He is superb in the first, risks sentimentality in the second, and is weakest in the third. Intelligence is not philosophy, any more than insight is psychology. The depth of thought in these poems is not always equal to the genius of the sensibility that created them. When we compare Cavafy with Eliot — a perfectly reasonable comparison, considering the period, the roles they cast themselves in, and their ultimate achievement — we find in Eliot components missing in Cavafy: philosophical reach, an awareness of traditions other than Hellenism, and a feeling for the natural world that provides a balance between personal history and the historical record.

The urban voice is distinguished from the nature poet's by more than consciousness and irony. The nature poet is usually religious and seeks a god, the city poet mythological and seeks a hero. (Certain works — *Moby Dick*, for one — though ostensibly belonging to the first category belong to the second. The crew of the *Pequod* are the inhabitants of a small city at the mercy of an evil essentially man-made, though in the form of a natural monster. The whale is more Ahab's creation than God's.) Nature is conspicuously absent from Cavafy's poems; he is moved less by the pastoral conventions and the cycle of the seasons than "by seeing something of this city I love, a little movement in the streets, in the shops." And he uses the city in unexpected ways. It is not only the past in the present but the tangle of mortal and god that gives these poems their impact. The heroic is humanized but never condescended to. In what is possibly Cavafy's most famous poem, "The God Abandons Antony," a shift in emphasis reveals both his devotion to the city and his mining of a tradition. After the defeat at Actium, Antony is abandoned to his death. In Plutarch it is Dionysus who abandons him, in Shakespeare it is Hercules, but in Cavafy it is Alexandria herself. By association, the city has taken on a triple quality: the god, the hero, and the civilization for whom they exist.

Cavafy was one of the first modern poets openly to acknowledge his homosexuality. He made good use of it, for it connected him with the "Alexandrian mode," which Keeley defines as

first of all to search for the hidden metaphoric possibilities, the mysterious invisible processions, of the reality one sees in the literal city outside one's window. If one is Cavafy, the mode is then to dramatize and expand these discovered possibilities until they carry a broad mythic significance. Cavafy's use of the mode begins with his choosing to move from personal metaphors to communal and historical metaphors, and from there to the projection of a self-contained mythical world that serves to represent both his special view of Greek history and his image of the perennial human predicament.

Homosexuality is invisible, and so is the Alexandrian past. One develops its secret negative in the dark, the other is a library of countless lost photographs. The homosexual has certain built-in advantages as a spokesman for the city. The search for the hero is not merely literary, and if alienation and loneliness are the marks of the city-dweller, the homosexual is set apart simply by being sexually categorized. (One would become more aware of this if the distinguishing characteristic of a person's nature were to be described as being heterosexual.) In most homosexual lives, the search for a partner to go to bed with and/or love cuts across artificial social barriers; the bellboy and the ambassador, the governor and the mechanic may be found in each other's company sub rosa. Exploring byways of the city usually, but not always, outside the bourgeois domestic circle, the homosexual gets to know the city in ways most people don't — strange places at strange hours. Secrets contain within themselves a hidden spring — the compulsion to reveal them — and this compulsion has something in it of the quality of history: the story not yet revealed, the truth under the appearance of it, the onion skin of façade endlessly waiting to be peeled away. It isn't hard to understand why the only occupation imaginable to Cavafy other than the poet's was that of the historian.

In *Cavafy's Alexandria*, Keeley traces the poet's development through various projections of the city itself, and his chapter headings are a precise guide to his method: "The Literal City," "The Metaphoric City," "The Sensual City," "Mythical Alexandria," "The World of Hellenism," "The Universal Perspective." It is the method of the stone thrown in the water, making ever-expanding ripples.

To me, there are striking similarities between Cavafy and Proust, and homosexuality centered in a mother with whom a relationship lasts intact through middle age is the least of them. The chief bond is how each of them rescued himself from frivolity by converting sexuality into an obsession with the past. The tinkle of salon music is a never-distant menace in both cases. Each managed ultimately to resist that peculiar mother-derived nicety of necktie and manner characteristic of the social lives of "good" families — the whole upper-bourgeois apparatus of balls and carriages, the meaningless events to which so many lives are dedicated. Preoccupied with younger men, Proust and Cavafy both contrived to emerge from the palm court onto the plains of myth, if myth is history transformed into a body of work one can permanently refer to, which grows out of and transcends the limits of its creator and touches perimeters so wide that the generic begins to take the place of the specific: the Cavafy voice speaking through many heroes, the Proustian tone and intelligence shedding light on everything. In each case, the history of a people came to the rescue as a force and focusing agent: it would be utterly impossible to read Cavafy without Greece and the Hellenic world in view at all times, and completely mistaken to read Proust without knowing that the

Guermantes are — no matter how flawed and stupid in their immediate versions — the means of leading back through the great genealogical family names of France to the roots of a language and a culture.

Yet Proust's and Cavafy's attitudes toward homosexuality couldn't be more different. For Cavafy it was the release and abandonment of the pagan, for Proust the guilty secret of Christian and Jewish morality — though he regretted, if Gide quotes him correctly, having put in only his "bad" homosexual experience and left out all that was charming. For all their resemblances, Proust and Cavafy were on opposite sides of the fence: Proust found in love a form of bondage, and Cavafy in sex a means of connection. There is a moral tone in Cavafy, whereas in Proust there is always a certain Mosaic ring. Cavafy is closer to Whitman, who, by one of those historical coincidences that seem preordained, had just published the "Calamus" poems in 1863, the year of Cavafy's birth.

Cavafy was one of the first "modern" writers in his fidelity to his own experience, his disdain for rhetoric and decoration, his use of demotic Greek as well as the high style, and he belongs to a tradition whose outlines are now clear. By apprehending the present and the past as simultaneous realities, the major figures of twentieth-century literature have worked private worlds into epic proportions, reinventing the image of the self (Proust), a city (Joyce), a country (Yeats), or a tradition (Eliot and Pound) as the reflected image of a civilization. In Cavafy's case, as in Joyce's, the mythological city is forged out of disparate elements: the commonplace life of the streets and the splendor of ancient tales and legends, in which the ordinary man of the first could become the unwitting hero of the second. The process was, we now know, reversible: at the time that Joyce was turning Bloom into Ulysses, Cavafy was, so to speak, turning Ulysses into Bloom.

Goodbye to Wystan

Thank You, Fog contains Auden's last poems. The book is posthumous and, as his literary executor explains in a short preface, half the ghost of what it might have been. Writers, being human, are not in a position to choose their monuments. This one is more Audenesque than Auden, hardly fitting as the final words, the summing up of a man who set his mark on an age. As he developed into a superb writer, he became something more: an intellectual and moral touchstone for three generations of Englishmen and Americans. None of the obvious sources, as a leftist of the thirties, as a High Church Anglican of the sixties — or even the work itself — quite account for it. History and genius worked in magical combination: Auden was in Spain in 1937, in China in 1938, in Germany in 1945. He was, after Pound and Eliot, the only international poet of the English language. (One can write poetry and be an international figure without being an international poet.)

Auden's poetry was a conductor of history — "conductor" in its electrical, its travel-guide, and perhaps even its musical sense. He was our supreme journalist of the imagination, not only the recorder and the interpreter of the event but the conscience that gave it perspective. History is hard on people who feel its impact fully at any particular time, and Auden himself had harsh words to say about poems like "Spain" and "September 1, 1939." The role of the automatic moralizer, the too-easy invoker of love was one he came, naturally, to distrust. And because so many poems sprang from the immediate occasion he may have lost something in depth to what he gained in range. Though I don't think anyone doubts Auden composed masterpieces, it is not so easy to say, as it is in Eliot's or Stevens's case, exactly what — which — they are. First, the number of poems is astounding; they form a kind of cumulative masterpiece. And then, for poets of my generation, those born in the twenties, Auden was so formative, so influential that the early poems seem more like natural objects or remembered childhood landscapes than like works of art. Is "Look, stranger, on this island now" a masterpiece? Is "Doom is dark and deeper than any sea dingle"? I cannot imagine the history of poetry without them. To mention "In Praise of Limestone" or "The Sea and the Mirror" is only to begin the list.

Though an addict of the north, Auden was still southern enough to adore Ischia, to have had a cottage on Fire Island, to admire the Goethe of the "Italian Journey." (How fitting, then, that his farmhouse in Austria should have been bought with the proceeds of an Italian literary prize!) He wrote plays, libretti, the narration for documentary movies; inspired a ballet; devised masques, charades; and turned out cabaret songs, popular lyrics, and even a hymn for the United Nations. He had an ear, as any great poet would have to, as finely tuned (at least in the early poems) as the brain it was tuned for was intelligent. Only painting seemed not to interest him very much, though Breughel inspired one of the anthology pieces of our time, "Musée de Beaux Artes," and Hogarth the libretto for *The Rake's Progress.* The range of interests is large and singular: lead mining, opera, theology, detective stories, food, gossip, science, espionage, psychoanalysis, politics, literary criticism, philosophy, mountain climbing, medicine.

After Marx proved to be an untrustworthy guide, was it Freud or Kierkegaard who dominated his thinking? Different as his positions might be at various times, part of the Auden magic was the ability to synthesize practically everything; in the long run none of his views seemed inconsistent. They had a unifying theme: behind the theoretical façades, he waged a long battle against hokum. And when a view of his own began to take on the stale smell of hot air Auden changed it — not to be fashionable but for the sake of the reasonable. Like all men in his position — men who have become public through the practice of what originally seemed a private art — views were ascribed to him long after he had abandoned them, and notions he never subscribed to were laid at his door. There were paradoxes, shifts, reversals, and sometimes plain shockers — show-off ideas he probably only half-believed himself. Not that he lied. In fact, the steady beam that kept being broadcast for almost half a century proclaimed the opposite: he was, if anyone was, our best antidote to lying. At the end, truth became an obsession and, like most obsessions, was taken too literally and too far (he thought Yeats, for instance, had "lied" in saying that "once out of nature" he would never take his bodily form from any natural thing, "but such a form as Grecian goldsmiths make" — "Nobody wants to be a golden bird," Auden once said to me). There was a feeling when he died quite unlike the feelings occasioned by the deaths of Eliot or Moore, to take obvious examples — a voice one had counted on, a voice oddly personal, was gone forever. It was more than an authoritative voice; it was a voice that had helped establish what was to be taken as authoritative. Eccentric but rational, it spoke up for the Good. And it remained youthful even when it was no longer certain of what it was to be young. The phrase "freaked out," for instance, appears in "Nocturne," the finest poem in *Thank You, Fog.* It is a symptom of the wrong kind of vitality. But it is also a sign of how Auden listened.

In "A Thanksgiving," a rather automatic poem, he names the important influences: Hardy, Thomas (Edward), Frost, Yeats, Graves, Brecht — he even thanks Hitler and Stalin for forcing him to think about God — and then goes on to Kierkegaard, Williams, Lewis (C.S.), Horace, and Goethe. What a crew! Auden, by being his own man, went Hegel one better. He was kind but had an exact sense of who he was. There was something endearing about him, and something forbidding; he had the royal air and the common touch: austere Horatian, camp gossip, English gentleman, messy schoolboy. And there *was* something peculiar about being with him. No matter how many times one might say "Wystan" this or "Wystan" that, still there would be the sudden awareness that one was talking to *Auden.* No other famous writer — at least in my experience — evoked quite the same reaction. It was like having lunch with Byron, or meeting Sir Thomas Wyatt at a party.

Auden innocently gave rise to the ultimate snobbishness. Is there anything more exclusive than immortality? After a certain point — say, the early fifties —hardly anyone could doubt he was in the presence of one of English literature's monuments, someone who had already taken his place in the Pantheon. I don't think Auden had the slightest doubt about it either. That Westminster Abbey hurried to make the endorsement official doesn't mean that Auden's life was any easier. He worked incredibly hard; he was — after Edna St. Vincent Millay — the only self-supporting poet in this country, and it couldn't have been fun to go around wearing clothes, no matter how dirty, stained, or unpressed, or write notes, no matter how short, that were already collector's items. A certain air of unreality clung to Auden's efforts to be earthbound. A sign of how unreal he could be in stating a position is the rather pathetic official notice that appeared in *The New York Times* requesting his correspondents to burn his letters. (The subsequent bonfire has yet to be lighted.) And this is the same Auden who valued Keats's letters over his poems, and reviewed Chekhov's letters in *The New Yorker*!

At any one time, there must be five or six supremely intelligent people on the earth. Auden was one of them. How lucid the introduction to *The Greek Reader* remains. How marvelously original the introduction to *The Oxford Book of Light Verse*. How extraordinary his comments on romantic poetry in *The Enchafèd Flood*. Almost everything he touched — with the exception of his own light verse, and that includes the two unfortunately resurrected lyrics from *The Man of La*

32

Mancha — was of an excellence few writers ever come close to attaining. The gifts were prodigious, including the energy. But he might have become something else —a geologist like his older brother, or a doctor like his father, or even a clergyman like his two grandfathers. No matter the role, the brain would — and did — inform everything: fascinating, fascinated, unique. He was an impatient man, compulsive about time, and he could on occasion be more dazzle than substance. As he was during his Shakespeare lectures at the New School in the forties, where the commentary was so brilliant that one forgot, half the time, that its relationship to a particular play was quite often tangential. Or at a dinner party when he said, "You can tell a man is going to pieces when he starts being late for appointments, and a woman when she stops caring about her looks" — a perfectly legitimate, even provocative remark — followed by "Time belongs to men and space to women," a dubious one. Auden's high-wire performances wound down in quality, naturally, as he got older, but the voice can still be heard, recorded or in memory, a speech more individually characteristic than almost any I can think of — a kind of speech defect, really — a mumbling, childlike (childish?) kind of tumbling forth of words, a moist kind of gabbling, as if the instrument were not quite quick enough for what it was intended to convey.

But in spite of his brilliance, something always seemed to me to be missing. Though the poems belie it, his presence had no animal force — I don't mean anything to do with physical attractiveness — but as if some gut intuition, some inherent instinctive sense of things, were absent, as if the intelligence took up too much room to allow for something

33

else — a coordination of physical elements, a grace, an ease of manner, an awareness, say, of the pleasures and dangers commonly met at any moment by the least of us. As if he were not, in short, quite comfortable in his own skin. How much of this is simply a wrong impression, how much the result of a studied way of protecting himself I don't know.

The important thing is that he restored to poetry what it had for a long time lacked, a relevant human voice. After the Victorian and the Edwardian poets had had their say, the problem was somehow to construct a style out of the real that was neither banal nor elevated. It became the great task of this century's poetry, a labor that often produced the humdrum at one end of the scale and the rhetorical at the other. It also produced those marvels, William Carlos Williams and Wallace Stevens. It was a style that had to be come at through the back door — is that why two separate versions of it emerged full-blown from a pediatrician (Williams) and the vice-president of an insurance company (Stevens)? Auden arrived at it in some way through the language of science and through the peculiar fact of his being the only important poet writing in English to fall in love with the north and the German rather than the Mediterranean and the French —not the Provençal troubadors of Pound but the Icelandic sagas — not the sensuous or the visionary but the rational and the divine, and particularly that version of it struggling with either the animal or the absurd, a line one can trace through Freud, Lewis Carroll, and the mystics that interested Auden: Simone Weil and Dag Hammarskjöld.

It is also a line one can trace through Auden, for intelligence, no matter how high, is not the hallmark of the poet. The true sounds one hears in Auden's best poems derive

from the disappointments of the animal and the landscape of
his youth. In what may be the most haunting love poem of
this century, the loved one's head is merely *human*, the narrator's arm, enclosing him, is *faithless*, and "Time and fevers
burn away / Individual beauty from / Thoughtful children,
and the grave / Proves the child ephemeral . . ."

Auden brought a new language into poetry, his own. He
was in love with words, all kinds of words, and what he did
with language and grammar is too complex and original to be
dealt with in a short essay. It was part of his originality to
revivify the adjective, that most maligned part of English
speech, by projecting psychological states into what had been
merely colorful or evocative: "Underneath the abject wil-
low," "Fish in the unruffled lakes," or, from poems in *Thank
You, Fog*, "the modest conduct of fogs," and "the vagrant
moods of the weather." Sometimes a verb would convey this
human characteristic — "May with its light behaving,"
"Time crumbs all ramparts" — an example, too, of Auden's
mating of the imperial and the cozy — sometimes an adverb
was refreshed by its context: "The entirely beautiful."

This conspicuous but singular personification animated a
world of private myth and public statement. The primitive
fairy story and folk tale that form a background for the early
poems gave way to the social postures of the thirties, and
they, in turn, to orthodoxy. First the hobgoblin and the troll,
then exhortation and moral pleading, and finally the worldly
saint and the City of God. But just as Auden's Marxism was
never thoroughgoing but a more stimulating antidote to bourgeois passivity, so his Protestantism seems less religious piety
than a return to a formal tradition. As Auden came to distrust the Big, the social and the evolutionary narrowed down

35

to the domestic. Who could be a spokesman for a world no longer capable of being understood, and no longer even desirable except in its immediate surround: the habitat, the old friend, the familiar? The grand pronouncement and the general gave way to praise for the local and the near. And even they tend to close in further — many of the later poems have as their subject the self or the body.

But strangely, as the world Auden dealt with became more specific, his language became more abstract. The great effectiveness of the early poems comes from many sources, but one of them was the poet's ability to take a familiar noun and qualify it with a reference from an unfamiliar world; the language of one kind of discourse modifies another. Who, before Auden, had ever heard of "uncritical islands," "florid music," "aloof peaks," "whorled, unsubtle ears," or "baroque frontiers"? The early poems — the world of the great evolutionary-revolutionary Uncle, the oppositions of We and They — have an immediacy of diction, a musical attraction, or an absolute originality of phrasing the later poems lack. Distrusting the too-ready attitudinizing of the thirties poems, Auden turned against even the poems that had preceded them, where the musical genius of the language is most apparent. And perhaps as he began seriously to write libretti, he decided to leave the composing to others. Whatever the case, he devised a new prosy kind of meditative poem — as if musical effects, in language at least, were simply another form of lying — sometimes extraordinary in the freshness of its thought, or the quirkiness of its wording, sometimes dull because the language has lost its vividness as well as its relation to song.

Auden was generous, self-involved, petulant, and sometimes peevish. There were oracular moments, and moments of simple boyish sweetness. And, as he grew older, he became, like most people, more eccentric. At the end, he had the look of a man who is always catching trains. It seems (from other sources) that all he really wanted to do was to go home and go to bed.

I saw him last at the big send-off at the Coffeehouse just before his return to Oxford. Looking around the room, one could see the interesting collection of people who had been singled out for this last American shindig. It was typical of Auden that the faces should range from the very famous to the absolutely unknown, should include as many women as men, should scale up (or down?) from the very old to the very young, and include friends he was loyal to whom he might long ago have forgotten. And that, at a table raised a little above the height of the others, there should have been a last-minute difficulty about who was to sit next to him. It was impossible to say whether the position was being shied away from or oversubscribed. He seemed then, as he had so many times before, quite alone.

ELIZABETH BISHOP

✿

The Canada-Brazil Connection

Miss Bishop comes from the north and, like a lot of north-
ern people, she went south; but the title of her first book,
North & South, tells us only part of the story. Its north is
New York City, and its south Key West; yet the limits it
suggests have wider boundaries, earlier and later counterparts: a more distant north, Canada, and a farther south,
Brazil. And so, in the later poems, the earliest Canadian
landscape is revived, and Brazil replaces Florida. That the
two connections are similar we have no doubt; that they are
different explains why a poem like "The Moose" — a late
poem — restates and enriches several Bishop themes: a journey, a rediscovery, the magical appearance of an animal, the
sudden awareness of a particular kind of consciousness.
Though its setting is New Brunswick, one can cross the bor-
der quickly into Nova Scotia, where the poet grew up, an
area with pastoral views, snow, and an insistence on *its*
Anglo connection. There is in Miss Bishop's Nova Scotia

something odd, as if the South Pole had been settled by an English middle class. It is exotic, and, at the same time — to use a word she uses so tellingly in "Filling Station" — "comfy."

One figure, not middle class, appears early, and he focuses a concern of Miss Bishop's throughout: the off-creature, the person not part of the comfortable world she found herself in — a comfortable world that had its attendant horrors. (One doesn't become a poet for nothing.) And that figure is the blacksmith, who plays such an important role in "In the Village." A counter to a world that has suddenly become impossible (the mother's scream, her madness are facts, feelings a child cannot take in, or, if taken in, cannot bear), he is interesting in himself: he makes something, horseshoes, and he works in the natural world, his ultimate clients being horses. A native and a craftsman — two good Bishop things to be — he is also an outsider, in the sense of being exotic to the child's world at the time. His peculiarity is to normalize the situation; that is, through his oddity, he makes things all right. And this sense of normality and oddness in tandem appears many times in the poems, notably in "Faustina, or Rock Roses," in "Anaphora," which ends with a beggar on a bench in a park, and in "Robinson Crusoe," a perfect subject: the homely and the fantastic are inherent in it. And since the poet is concerned with the domestic *in* the exotic (a primitive oil lamp, say, contrived from an old Milk of Magnesia bottle and an oil drum), some distancing is required. It is supplied by an obvious source, travel, but also by a more subtle one, perspective. If one is in Key West, New York takes on special aspects, and the same is true of Nova Scotia and Brazil. The imagination, of course, has its own cameras, and if any example were needed of what Miss Bishop can do without traveling six thousand miles, "The Monument" would be a good one. But her particular imagination is excited by new places, or old ones that become new by the switch in viewpoint great distances provide. "Questions of travel" are never resolved by literal answers, yet distance at least provides optical shifts and refreshments of thought.

The blacksmith is the key to a preoccupation and a method. He is a staple of the town's life; yet he is surrounded by flames and the clanking of iron, and performs miracles of fire and water. His magic derives from his storybook quality rather than his usefulness; yet they cannot quite be separated. Something peculiar — and awful — has just happened: the scream. Something odd — and restorative — is posed against it. Could it be that ordinariness hides within it what is magical and at the same time helpful — the mysterious leaven of a cure? This notion of "something shining through the leaves," this prince inside the frog, crops up often, and even in the choice of subject: it is to be found in the factories of "Varick Street," where there are "on certain floors / certain wonders"; in a hired seamstress who may be one of the Fates; in "Jerónimo's House," which is a "gray wasps' nest / of chewed-up paper / glued with spit," but also a "fairy palace" with "writing-paper / lines of light." "Twelfth Morning; or What You Will" is a particularly fine specimen of this kind of transcendence, neither prettifying nor sentimental. These poems — genuine acts of sympathy — skirt dangerous territory; it's hard to think of another poet who could so consistently use servants as subjects, or a squatter as the hero (or anti-hero) of a big poem, without slipping into snobbishness or whimsy.

Sympathy is a form of empathy, and a way of entering another world by way of transference. Where other poets change coats, Miss Bishop sheds skins. "The Riverman" presents us with a totally formed universe felt from the inside, as if knowledge had been transformed into feeling. And the lures of anthropology are present everywhere, because in primitive cultures phenomena are reduced and made clear; the combination of the practical and the occult, of the humdrum and the godlike, is taken for granted. And the poet searches for that fusion in places where it has never existed before — in subjects not considered to be the stuff of poetry ("Filling Station," "The Gentleman of Shalott," "Trouvée"), or in well-known themes made new ("The Sandpiper," "Florida"). Reading a new Elizabeth Bishop poem always evoked a special kind of anticipation; one was surprised to be led not only to a change of viewpoint but to a widening of perception in general. Who else would have connected a sandpiper and William Blake? Or Baudelaire and marimba music?

In these poems, the world works better through dissimilarity than through conformity. Moreover, the poems prove, in the precision of their descriptive details and the special nature of their perceptions, that the world isn't conforming by nature. If it consists of the odd, the wonderful, and the strange, we get to know them through their opposites: the banal, the commonplace, and the known. "The Bight," for instance, is "littered with old correspondences" — in both senses of the word: One corresponds via letters, and correspondences are metaphors. Thus, the unnoticed is teased into illumination. No better example could be mentioned than "News Story," in which a battlefield emerges from an ashtray. But since ash is a key notion here, there is, in spite of a feat of the imagination, a literal correspondence.

There is another way the common and the extraordinary are put into play: by viewing differences so clearly, the actuality of sameness is brought into doubt. How useful is a word as general as "bird," for instance, if "unseen hysterical" ones "rush up the scale / every time in a tantrum"? Tanagers are flashy, pelicans clown. It's odd how clearly these words bring to mind their creatures almost instantly. And what about a fish whose "eyes . . . were far larger than mine / but shallower"? No one before, I think, has revealed that fact: the largeness of fish eyes compared to human. *Certain* fish eyes, that is. As soon as we think of that image, we search for its accuracy in life, but also for its contradiction. We test an image by its reality, and by its reality we test the truthfulness of the writer. It is by what one chooses to see and *how* one chooses to see it that this underground proving takes place. Not only does the image lead us to comparisons and, therefore, to thought; but those eyes, in a second, put both the viewed and the viewer onto the scale.

By its accuracy, by its choice of what is to be put in and left out, Miss Bishop's world begins to take on moral properties. They involve manners in particular and judiciousness in general: there is no scope in these poems that is not measured by a true balancing of weights. And when enlargement occurs, say, in "Roosters," in the introduction of the figure of Saint Peter, we move from the chicken coop to the Vatican, to "old holy sculpture" where "a little cock is seen / carved on a dim column in the travertine," without jarring the imagination or shifting the tone. We move quickly, but with absolute grace, from nature to art, and from there to perceptions that have ethical force. And we believe the lines that explicitly make their points — "There is inescapable hope, the pivot" or "cock-a-doodles yet might bless / his dreadful rooster come to mean forgiveness" — because we have been led to them by a process as natural as it is artful. It is not difficult to lend one's assent, finally, to the statement "that 'Deny deny deny' / is not all the roosters cry."

The henhouse leads us by steps to the New Testament; the blacksmith is commonplace, but begins to take on mythical proportions. If "mythical" seems too broad a word, then "fictional illumination" might be more accurate. The point is: he is much more than he first appears to be. He is ordinary and mysterious, like a living room in which the furniture is dotted with antimacassars but in which there is also a compass lying on an end table. The living room in "First Death in Nova Scotia" is claustrophobic, but the poem ends with the image of a road. In these poems, we are always going someplace (one of the primary conditions for having a good time), and the images, figures, and characters travel, literally and by analogy. The blacksmith is repeated in other characters of a similar transcendence: in Faustina, in Cootchie, or — to get away from servants — even in the nice policewoman with blue eyes who gets off the tender in "Arrival at Santos." I suppose the apotheosis of all these figures is Manuelzhino, but not far behind him are the native in "The Riverman" and the fugitive in "The Burglar of Babylon."

Miss Bishop's cool eye for detail is also a dramatic lens, and her feeling for character is shaded but pronounced. Her little dramas — even the family that makes its greasy appearance in "Filling Station" — suggest the theater; in fact, they suggest that strange combination of talents I have mentioned elsewhere: those of the painter and of the playwright. I do not disparage Miss Bishop's infallible ear when I say she is closer to the painters than to the composers in most of the poems. Abstraction is not particularly interesting to this poet, and music is not famous for dealing with particulars. What can be handled, looked at, examined, walked around, reperceived, turned in different lights, hung up, or laid down — that is of much more interest.

Character is specific, at least what is interesting about it. General qualities, we have come to believe, obscure what could, under more penetrating examination, be separated out. Miss Bishop, a great disbeliever in the general, comes to character often, and most often through landscape, oddly, for it is moot whether the subject of these poems is places or people. On the face of it, place would seem the greater concern. Even titles as general as *North & South* and *Geography Three* are more modest than categorical. The tendency in the poems is not to generalize but to point to and specify. Character either possesses landscape or is possessed by it; the binoculars trained on "The Burglar of Babylon" reveal an entire slum. The traditional "character study" is absent. The attendant world, falling into place before and behind, gives the poems their interest, their power, and their wit. The personal has little to do with it. The subtitle of "The Bight," not the text of the poem itself, tells us it is the poet's birthday. As for wit, in "Filling Station," after saying "somebody waters the plant," Miss Bishop slyly adds, "Or oils it maybe." That's funny, but it also makes its own crazy, revealing comment about a world in which oilcan after oilcan

44

spells out "Esso -so -so -so." (And isn't there a possible play here on "so-so"?) Once more we are in a double world, with a taboret, oilcans, wicker, doilies, and a rubber plant — a bourgeois nest in a gas station — a world tailor-made for the Bishop eye. And only the Bishop eye would have seen it.

In a line in "Manuelzhino" — "The world's worst gardener since Cain" — we have a small biblical echo reminiscent of the larger one in "Roosters." Part of Manuelzhino's charm is his inability to handle specifics — not a problem for his creator. Yet they have something in common. Account books turn out to be dream books, numbers wander slantwise across the page, impossible to add or subtract. And slantwise is the way this poet looks at character: from a side, obliquely. As if she had caught it in its natural habitat without its being aware. There is an assumption of character in creatures, in her moose, her fish, her roosters, the boy leading the horse in "Twelfth Morning," even the little toy horse of "Cirque d'Hiver." These are characters, at least of a sort, because insight is not this poet's thing; the world revealed is everything — its immediacy, its exactitude; but not necessarily its significance. The historical and the confessional rarely crop up in these poems. And one would have to search hard for psychological interest of the kind we have become used to: the inner life, neurotic conflict, Baudelaire's "wing of madness." Yet, by plainly presenting character, human, animal, or metaphysical (I refer to the sailor asleep on the top of the mast in "The Unbeliever," to the surprising number of poems in which some religious or biblical reference is invoked, the passing metaphor in "Manuelzhino," the extended one in "Roosters," the extraordinary "The Prodigal," and the grand design of "Complete Concordance") — by presenting character and giving it its eccentricities right up front at the footlights, by some miraculous process of foreshortening or enlargement, it makes a permanent imprint. Who would have thought of the Prodigal Son hiding pints of whiskey under the floorboards? But it makes perfect sense; it makes prodigality real. If one could think of a playwright fascinated by drama and incongruity but rather indifferent to personality, one might have something analogous: the whole surround intensely filled with single objects, and directed and lit by an expert.

This gift is partly a matter of clarity, of wakefulness, and it is informative, I think, to go over the poems and note how many of them begin at dawn or at daybreak: "Earliest morning, switching all the tracks"; "At six o'clock we were waiting for coffee"; "Paris, 7 A.M."; "At four o'clock / in the gunmetal blue dark / we hear the first cry of the first cock"; "Each day with so much ceremony / begins"; "Dawn an unsympathetic yellow"; and so on. And, conversely, sleep and dream are mentioned often, as if they were conditions opposed to wakefulness — conditions from which it is necessary to be roused. With the exception of "The Weed," dream in its literal sense is rarely invoked, but it runs a thread through the fabric of the poems — important in itself, but more important, I think, as a contending force: not the place where knowledge is to be found, but that state of being that precludes physical observation.

These characters and animations, joined by new servants and creatures in the later poems — the depressing seamstress in "House Guest," the headless chicken in "Trouvée" (another poem beginning at dawn) — have qualities in common: they are humorous and unappeasable, and, with the exception of the chicken, survivors. Manuelzhino, one feels, will outwit, in the end, the poet's landowner-friend, whose voice we hear throughout — will outwit her by persistence and inscrutability. What more effective armor is there than a shrewd dreaminess? What these portraits suggest is sympathy, kindness, judgment — behind them all, a set of moral standards is shifting gears — but neither intimacy nor love, though one line explicitly says, "I love you, I guess. . . ." That guess is as far as Miss Bishop goes; yet an understated love poem like "The Shampoo" moves one by its restraint, its minimal claims.

Strength and independence under the façade of weakness arouse the poet's interest. It is not a matter of dissimulation but of simultaneous perception of power and vulnerability, a doubleness manifested over and over again, culminating, perhaps, in "The Armadillo," where all the armor the animal possesses is not proof against fire. And also in the choice of servants as subjects, because a second character is always implicit: servants, after all, are hired and, in one way or another, play roles. They present the poet with a person *and* a persona observable at close range without the risk of presumption. Familiar but aloof, being around so often, they allow for the sureness of external fact and a tacit affection. And around each of them, a world, unlike that of the poet's but peculiarly congenial to her talents, materializes. One would not imagine, for instance, a Rio society hostess being the subject of an Elizabeth Bishop poem. Or even a nice middle-class Canadian lawyer.

This duality is also manifested in the canny manipulation of odd couplings of words, particularly adjectives and nouns, where a tension is set up between them that creates a kind of verbal magnetic field: "awful but cheerful," "the uncontrolled, traditional cries," "commerce and contemplation," "a grave green dust," "the blurred redbud," "the somnambulist brook," etc.

In fact, in spite of the clarity of vision, this two-faceted perception may be the key to what makes these poems work so beautifully, enhancing their surfaces with an electric undercurrent. A deep division — reserve at war with the congenial — undercuts the authority of the poems; more telling than geographical polarities is the implied disparity of "master" and "servant," the yoking together of such dissimilar notions as "awful" and "cheerful." A New England iron in the manner — or, I should say, in the *lack* of manner — in conflict with an easygoing willingness to accept life as it is, its perkiness and variety, is everywhere present. Critical judgment in these poems is more likely to suspend itself for what is harmless, or distant, or struggling, or moving in its persistence, than it is for the suffering or conflicts of peers. No drug addicts, drunks, or suicides make an appearance; no poets, academics, or white-collar workers are alluded to. Infused with a compassion that knows by instinct where true feeling ends and false sentiment begins, the poems are remarkably trustworthy on human terms, considering how descriptive they are generally taken to be. It is as if we discovered in a landscape painter not a psychologist but the surprising gift of portraiture. And when social protest becomes explicit, as it does in "Squatter's Children," or in "Going to the Bakery," there is no sudden tearing of fabric or gnashing of teeth. A style has been arrived at that allows for wider circles of emotion and more direct social comment than is at first apparent. This effect depends, partly, on the

personification of objects and ideas: Love's a boy; the high-
way leading from the country to the city is a clown with
"long, long legs"; "The Man-Moth" is a case completely in
point; the weed opens its mouth to say, "I grow / but to di-
vide your heart again"; a cloud is equally articulate: "I am
founded on marble pillars," it says; in "Quai d'Orléans,"
"light and nervous water hold / [an] interview"; an insect
becomes a gladiator; a lighthouse stands "in black and white
clerical dress" and "lives on his nerves"; the moon, in "In-
somnia," "if deserted by the universe," would "tell it to go to
hell"; in "Going to the Bakery," "the round cakes look about
to faint — / each turns up a glazed white eye."

Part of the effect of lower depths and widening circles
stems from a sub rosa notion steaming away under a grating:
if Miss Bishop wanted to, she could tell us more, because we
always feel that more slides have been taken than are going
to be projected. It comes, too, from the existence of hardly
noticeable actors. I have read "The Monument," for instance, many times; but it takes a close examination, or a
very good memory, to realize that a conversation is going on
while the poem proceeds, that an artist-prince is a minor
character, that, in saying "Watch it closely" — the poem's
three last words — movement, the choices of animate life,
grow sketchily alive. And sometimes a figure, suddenly lit,
will transform what has been, up to that point, merely descriptive. In "Little Exercise," the sleeper at the bottom of
the rowboat is that figure. In "Love Lies Sleeping," the gen-
eralization of "queer cupids of all persons getting up" zooms
in on an individual. He may be "one, or several," but still
the effect is cinematic, a narrowing down that paradoxically
allows the poem to expand in unexpected directions by a

sudden infusion of emotion. Here are the last two stanzas of
"Love Lies Sleeping":

> *for always to one, or several, morning comes,*
> *whose head has fallen over the edge of his bed,*
>   *whose face is turned*
>   *so that the image of*
>
> *the city grows down into his open eyes*
> *inverted and distorted. No. I mean*
>   *distorted and revealed,*
>   *if he sees it at all.*

Why is that last line so moving? It is so simple — a series
of the most ordinary of monosyllables. It suggests death or
sleep, but whatever it suggests separates the subject viewed
from the viewer. *She* sees it, but the protagonist doesn't. And
that is a true distance, and a lonely one, that the poems present to us without a word of protest — or caution — and
without pointing a finger. One is brought up short in feeling
more than a description of morning arriving in a city seems
to warrant. It is ways such as these that the poems take in
more territory than first meets the eye. Even a portrait as
negative as the one in "House Guest" has a shimmer of feeling because the heart was wrung, even if the mind was irri-
tated or the social sense outraged. And, again, there is a lift-
ing up, a surprise, at the poem's conclusion — a "bony foot"
on the treadle of the sewing machine, and we are in the
presence, perhaps, of one of the three Fates, Clotho, that
literal and figurative *spin*ster.

In "Under the Window: Ouro Preto," something more
dazzling occurs, something new, a finer grasp of local char-

acter, of the razor-thin but most effective use of dialogue, the one-line label that brings to mind a person or an entire world. We get it in " 'Women.' *'Women!'* " where the italicization speaks for itself; in " 'When my mother combs my hair it hurts' "; in that macho legend painted on the bumper of a new Mercedes truck, "HERE AM I FOR WHOM YOU HAVE BEEN WAITING"; or the line of the "gallant driver" of the wreck of a car with its "syphilitic nose," "NOT MUCH MONEY BUT IT IS AMUSING." That line might stand as a splendid epitaph for the writing of poetry in America. Wryness and true feeling are a lot to achieve when world-weariness and bathos could so easily have been offered in their place. And in a poem so steeped in local color, to rise to the extraordinary ending is a particular Bishop miracle:

> *Oil has seeped into*
> *the margins of the ditch of standing water*
>
> *and flashes or looks upward brokenly,*
> *like bits of mirror — no, more blue than that:*
> *like tatters of the* Morpho *butterfly.*

The poems, then, seem to me to explore emotions more profoundly than is usually acknowledged. They reject many alternatives — one need merely turn a page or two in *The Collected Poems* to come across the Bishop translation of Andrade's "Don't Kill Yourself, Carlos" to be startled. It's a marvelous poem, but the sudden rise in temperature produces a different kind of weather. Having been pigeonholed for so long as a cool customer, Miss Bishop is ladylike but tough; but also much warmer, much more involved in life, than a mere mapmaker or tour guide. If passion is missing from these poems — and I don't think it is — so is self-absorption. Their seeming casualness belies their extraordinary concentration — a concentration reminiscent of Emily Dickinson at her best. The discarded temptations of the printed Bishop canon have made it a small one, and its smallness has given rise too easily to the word "minor." What we find in these poems is elegance and withheld power. What else does "restraint" mean? One has to have something to restrain, and these poems, so easy to read, give up their secrets slowly. Shedding moral light, affection in these works extends itself more easily to the victor who has battled and won than to the loser who merely survives. Admiring action, Bishop's poems may conceal a fear of passivity in itself: the reduction of the status of the observer to that of the excluded. It would be hard to station the writer behind a movie camera in these poems, to say with assurance from just what angle the movie was being shot. The object is everything; the viewer, the viewer's position — except by inference — the merest assumption. Yet how remarkably consistent that lens is, how particularly keen the eye behind it! There is a great deal to be said for scope, but more to be said, I think, for the absolutely achieved. These poems strike me as ageless; there are no false starts, no fake endings. None of the provincial statements of youth, none of the enticements of facility are allowed to enter. Starting with "The Map," we are in the hands of an artist so secure in the knowledge of what makes and doesn't make a poem that a whole generation of poets — and remarkably different ones — has learned to know what a poem is through her practice. She has taught us without a shred of pedagogy to be wary of the hustling of emotions, of the false allurements of the grand. Rereading these poems, how utterly absent the specious is! There is no need to revise them for future editions, the way Auden revised, and Marianne Moore revised, and Robert Lowell revised. Nothing need be added, nothing taken away. They constitute a body of work in which the innovative and the traditional are bound into a single way of looking. From a poet's point of view, these poems are the ones, more than all her contemporaries', that seem to me most to reward rereading.

JAMES SCHUYLER

Whatever Is Moving

Because he has been ill, on and off, for many years, James
Schuyler doesn't give poetry readings, attend literary confer-
ences, or direct writers' workshops — and that is why one of
the most original poets in America is known, so far, only to
a small audience. He is a poet of the immediate: of views out
of train and restaurant windows, of lawns and plants, of up-
state New York and New York City. He is interested in love
and painting, and old buildings and nature, and one can say
things that simple about him because he is not a poet of great
ideas, of grand gestures, or of psychological insight (except
in passing). In *The Morning of the Poem*, he has written a sixty-
page poem (the one from which the book takes its title) as if
on a dare — a dare because he could be mistaken for a min-
iaturist embarking on the *Iliad* — and the miracle is that it is
rarely boring. Schuyler has no obvious eccentricities of manner and writes in a mode familiar to many poets, yet what

54

would ordinarily be a difference in degree becomes a difference in kind. The narrow-gauge railroad track takes care of the style ("Write skinny poems," he advises Frank in "Dining Out with Doug and Frank"), and his subject matter, ostensible and real, is the flux of everyday life. But what are merely grocery lists in other hands are transformed into sacred objects in his. By writing so well, he justifies a subject and a method — this-is-my-life, and I'm-telling-it-like-it-is. It is no secret by now that, taken in tandem, they can be one of the great gifts to tedium devised by the human mind. Though Schuyler belongs to a convention, he lets us know what it is by transcending it.

His world comes alive through precision of detail, a trait he shares with the late Elizabeth Bishop, and that precision is tutored by, and is at the service of, the immediate surround. Schuyler trusts immediacy itself to bring to light — through memory and association — experiences that warrant an intensity not justified by mere physical surroundings, often the jumping-off place from which a poem begins. A chronicler of the haphazard, Schuyler depends on the literal aspects of the actual for inspiration: what particular birds alight on a weekend in the country, the real buildings along the route on a walk in the city. Faithful to the scene, fidelity takes its cue from whatever is presented. His work is a poetry of chance sparked by the spontaneous encounter and nourished on the luckily given, and it is not a poetry fixed on the individual line. The fleeting moment is arrested in the very process of movement, and the reader's eye follows the thrust of the syntax down the page as it presses forward. The general effect is fluid, even rapid. Schuyler's randomness (and possibly the ongoing speed of his voice) are in conflict

with a love of the stable, the familiar, and the domestic.
When the ordinarily unnoticed gets down on paper, it can be
something as trivial and flat as

> . . . To get up
> to this morning view
> and eat poached eggs
> and extra toast with
> Tiptree Gooseberry Preserve
> (green) — and coffee,
> milk, no sugar. . . .

More often, the animate and the inanimate illuminate
each other in a moment of true perception:

> The Istrian stone with the silver-pink cast to
>   it of George Arends that
> After a rainstorm enflames itself: no: that's
>   the bricks (Istrian
> Stone and bricks contrasted) that become petals
>   of roses, blossoming
> Stone. Black gondolas glide by, the sure-footed
>   gondoliers bending and
> Leaning on their poles, wearing green velvet
>   slippers. On Diaghilev's
> Tomb a French count left his calling
>   card: more suitable
> Than withering flowers. I left only a glance
>   and a thought.
> But Europe — split, twisted, shivering-leaved
>   olive trees,

Grapevines strung high in swags between
poplar trees — Europe isn't
Home. . . .

The scrupulous observation of the minute fact can lead to inconsequentiality: a poetry of trade names can always be said to be accurate. Schuyler is not completely out of the woods in this regard: his freshness depends in part on being childlike, and the childlike can quickly descend to childishness and sometimes silliness. To be childlike is engaging, except when it is not appropriate. Certain relationships, for instance, remain superficial: very little of the person Schuyler refers to as "the most important in my life" comes through on paper — an ex-lover, married, who left him and gave no reason for doing so. Of this person, we get something of the body but little of the mind. What is enigmatic to Schuyler is cryptic to the reader. This shadowiness may be a matter of tact or it may spring from a habit of reference: Schuyler deals only with people who are real, people you can look up in a phone book. If John Ashbery is around, or Schuyler is staying with Jane and Joe Hazen in Water Mill, their names appear undisguised. And perhaps this lover, though real, is touched by an ideality that renders him ultimately unnameable (though he appears, to us, as "Bob"). Because of a compulsion to spell out the facts, the literal truth is the ethical touchstone of the poems, which are, by the same token, descriptive rather than metaphorical. This literalness is not an incapacity to dramatize but a singular and childlike trust in truthfulness. What could be taken as a failure of the imagination is, rather, a belief in a kind of magic: if even one fact or name were faked, the apparatus on which the poems depend — the connection between the naming of things and the reality of the world — might be in danger of collapsing.

As a whole, the poems are less contemplative meditations than attempts to snare the source of action — emotion and thought are susceptible to whatever is moving, usually within a small compass. Schuyler's fondness for ferryboats (which move but do not go very far) produces a small elegy for New York City's ferries in the middle of "Dining Out with Doug and Frank," a deceptively simple poem because it is doing many things at once (one of which is to keep going). When Schuyler, a born storyteller, free-associates, what we usually get instead of images or metaphorical connections is a story — a memory relevant in some special way to the matter in hand. In "Dining Out," for instance, Doug and Frank are "young and beautiful"; their relationship is the theme, however submerged, for a set of variations, one being the story of Schuyler and Bill Aalto, his "first lover." And just as sitting at a bar and restaurant on the West Side of New York brings to mind the romantic notion of moonlit rides on Hudson ferryboats, so the same setting makes Schuyler aware of the sado-masochistic bars along the riverfront, which, in turn, activate ideas of violence, sex, and death. And this "liebestod" notion reminds Schuyler of the actual deaths of Peter Kemeny, a friend who committed suicide by throwing himself in front of a subway train, and Aalto, who died of cancer. In between, almost by happenstance, there is the story of Billy Nichols, who went bird-watching in Central Park, and had his head beaten in because someone wanted his binoculars. Covered with blood, Nichols made it to Fifth Avenue. Several taxis refused to pick him up. At Roosevelt Hospital he waited for hours before he received medical attention. We are told these facts and we believe them because their truth depends less on a roman-à-clef knowledge of the figures involved than on Schuyler's veracity of detail elsewhere — his description, for instance, of the salvaged and revitalized interior of McFeely's Bar at the Terminal Hotel, the setting of "Dining Out":

> . . . *The ceiling is*
> *florid glass, like the cabbage-rose*
> *runners in the grand old hotels*
> *at Saratoga: when were they built?*
> *The bar is thick and long and*
> *sinuous, virile. Mirrors: are*
> *the decorations on them cut*
> *or etched? I do remember that*
> *above the men's room door the*
> *word Toilet is etched*
> *on a transom. Beautiful lettering,*
> *but nothing to what lurks*
> *within: the three most*
> *splendid urinals I've ever*
> *seen. Like Roman steles. . . .*

Throughout, a caressing attention to minutiae is coupled with a gift for swift narrative; Schuyler can sketch in a whole story in one quick breath. A panorama of events races by as we take in the complicated ingredients of "Dining Out with Doug and Frank": a tribute to friendship, an elegy for New York (or a time and view of it), the stories of three deaths ("Terminal Hotel" exudes its own punning, mortuary air), and the ongoing tale of the narrator himself, who has moved to 74th and Broadway but has not yet ventured into Central Park (the Billy Nichols episode, the only one of outer-directed violence, acts as a warning). In "Dining Out with Doug and Frank," parentheses perform their usual grammatical function, but they also bear the burden of a unique task: they become enclosures, safety pockets of memory, each of which is a burial ground: there lies Bill Aalto, and there Peter Kemeny, and there Billy Nichols. These memorial parentheses are sad, of course, being the archaeological debris of time and age, but the dig as a whole is successful: the poem itself is buoyant, exuberant, and full of life and charm.

The nostalgic ferry rides reveal something else: though Ischia and Capri and various Italian towns are mentioned, Schuyler's world is one in which intimacy — and safety — are more important than knowledge. The familiar routes of a ferry are now, it seems, the only form of travel he would enjoy. The known and the loved, renewing themselves, are more salutary than the exotic and the new. The swinging alacrity, the no-nonsense yet feeling attributes of "Dining Out with Doug and Frank" make it remarkable — these stories, elegies, relationships simply happen on the page, as if by a turn of conversation. That is Schuyler's gift: a magical fusion of romance and fact, the enchanting, telling, but offhand reference. He is singular in his effervescence, in his verbal excitement, even when he is dealing, as he so often is, with the seemingly small scale, or the potentially tragic. The overall tone can include them both. "The Payne Whitney Poems" — the second section of the book — which deal with Schuyler's stay in a mental hospital, are a triumph of will over circumstance, and if they sometimes have the air of poems one forced oneself to write, still they prove — again —

that Schuyler can be gorgeous without being pretentious, simple without being stupid, and can move from the comic-strip laconic to the grandiloquent with scarcely a tremor.

He shares with Elizabeth Bishop (once more) the knack of making the lyrical dramatic. Schuyler's theatrical effects come from surprise — a form of suspense, however rarefied. We are kept waiting, in these poems, not for the withheld but for the next turn of the screw, one we could not imagine for ourselves. Some slight distortion of vision (affording even greater clarity, the way certain drugs are supposed to make visible the ordinarily invisible) lends a hand to the effect, the distortions being close enough to rational thought to keep the reader engaged. At the heart of this is a peculiar blend of the cosmopolitan and the native, the innocent and the worldly, perfect for poems but uncomfortable, perhaps, in life, where the secret of dealing with feelings so widely spaced apart is to keep them separate. In Schuyler's work, these double feelings sometimes merge into a single focus, or one is used to illustrate the other. The voice one hears is that of an informed innocent. A frame of reference, at odds with innocence but flavoring it, underlies and intensifies perception, giving it an undercurrent and a reality it might not otherwise have — as if a child were to delight us with naïve observations only to reveal a moment later, that he is the author of a comedy of manners. The poems are energized by an alternating current that flows between natural utterance and civilized speech. In the very best ones, what might have been incongruous voices are forged into a single tone.

Incongruity of another kind works for Schuyler in phrases like "Silver day / how shall I polish you?" or "water so cold it's / like plunging into a case of knives," where the natural

and the domestic play into each other's hands. But incongruity isn't necessary when Schuyler hits on a descriptive notion
that is inherently emotional: ". . . I turned / my back and
this small green world went shadowless." Because, one day,
we will cast no shadow? Schuyler doesn't say that; he doesn't
even hint at it. He simply darkens the scene, and drama,
feeling, and prior knowledge come suddenly into being.

Schuyler's command of visual effects, particularly in
poems that rarely resort to metaphor, is evident everywhere.
What might not be noticed so readily is the subtlety of his
ear. Purely a matter of talent, this innate musicality is without strain or pressure. And the sounds are particularly magical when the range is small. His feeling for duration and
stress is instinctive. In "Song," with its exquisite beginning,
he is as delicate as Haydn:

> *The light lies layered in the leaves.*
> *Trees, and trees, more trees.*
> *A cloud boy brings the evening paper:*
> The Evening Sun. *It sets.*

Or, in "Growing Dark":

> *The grass shakes.*
> *Smoke streaks, no,*
> *cloud strokes,*
> *The dogs are fed.*
> *Their licenses*
> *clank on pottery.*

What we are listening to — we think — in most of the
poems is natural speech filtered through an imagination that

allows the canvas and the score equal power. Just as in the theater dialogue is not conversation but must sound like it, so in Schuyler's poems the "poetic" effects seem as natural as breakfast:

> *You know da Vinci's painting of*
> *The Virgin sitting in her mother's lap,*
> *Bending and reaching toward the child:*
> *Mary, Jesus, and St. Anne: beautiful*
> *Names: Anne, from a Latin name from*
> *The Hebrew name Hannah. The sun shines*
> *Here and out the window I see green, green*
> *Cut into myriad shapes, a bare-foot-*
> *Caressing carpet of fresh-grown grass (a*
> *Gift from Persia, courtesy of D. Kermani),*
> *Green chopped into various leaves: walnut, maple,*
> *Privet, Solomon's-seal, needles of spruce:*
> *Green with evening sunlight on it,*
> *Green going deep into penetrable shade: . . .*

Good as the poems in the first two sections of the book are, we do not take Schuyler's measure until we read the title poem. It has a double fascination: the voyeurism elicited by someone else's diary or journal, and the excitement good poetry affords — in this case, enhanced by the spice of a virtuoso performance. Whether sixty pages of life as it occurs, with flashbacks, asides, set pieces, digressions on travel, nature engravings, and so on, would have been more impressive if they had been exploited in the service of a great idea, an overall large conception, is moot. In place of philosophical speculation or historical sweep, we get hard-earned truths: a special mixture of country wisdom and the savvy of the city.

The poem, more than any other Schuyler has written, demonstrates his uncanny control of tone.

The poem's essential device is a doubling of viewpoint: Schuyler is in East Aurora, a small town in western New York State, staying with his mother in a white-clapboard house he knew as a child. At the same time, the poem is addressed to a specific "you" (though many other "you"s appear in it), Darragh Park, the painter, who is at work in his studio on West 22nd Street in Chelsea, in Manhattan. The poem switches back and forth between Schuyler in East Aurora and Park in Chelsea, but on the way we visit Italy, Zurich, Geneva, Great South Bay, Nantucket, Paris, Maine, New Brunswick, Long Island, and Germany. The constantly shifting landscape — always swinging back to East Aurora — allows Schuyler to test to the limit his free-wheeling ability to catch the atmosphere of places, and his genius for run-on improvisation.

A continuing sexual motif weaves in and out — men Schuyler has been attracted to, described lovingly, fleetingly, and, most often, frustratedly: a muscular, handsome man who leans out a window after a snowstorm in New York City; a moving man; a soldier; the lost lover; a man in a grocery store; a gray-haired German the narrator actually went to bed with, who turns out, later, to have been a "bore." The lost lover is a floating "you" in the poem, a parallel to Park, about whom Schuyler says, in an early passage, "How easily I could be in love with you, / who do not like to be touched." So the poem is, sub rosa, a love poem, whose objects of devotion are offshoots of "Bob," the lost and great love. The sexual frankness of the poem is devoid of the musky odors of the confessional — and even the erotic — the context being expansive enough to absorb Schuyler's recurring sexual preoccupations. Schuyler is never "mythological" or "symbolic" — we are being given the straight stuff. But though he is the plainest of poets he is also one of the most mysterious because, though straightforward and realistic, the effects — like those, say, of Magritte — can be hallucinatory and surreal. The language is rarely distinguished if one separates out a phrase or a sentence. But how extraordinary it is in an extended passage or taken as a whole! What we have, really, in "The Morning of the Poem," is a poetry diary on the order of MacNeice's "Autumn Journal," at least in its method. And because the poem is addressed to a specific person, it has something of the flavor of a letter, a letter being written by an emperor or poet in exile who is writing to a confidant back in the capital. Though once in a while Schuyler falters — asking too many naïve questions, for one, questions that could be answered by making a phone call or opening an encyclopedia — the overall performance is amazingly successful.

It is not without interest that both Ashbery in "Self-Portrait in a Convex Mirror" and Schuyler in his title poem chose a painter (one dead, one alive) as the chief figure in the design of a long work that is basically a self-portrait. And painting is crucial in Schuyler's case because it brings with it one of the essential components of his verse — light. It also allows for correspondences of many kinds: Schuyler uses Park as one factor in an opposition that might read art/city versus nature/country, and the exchange between them has something of the quality of an extended metaphor.

We switch between Schuyler and Park through the poet's favorite device, the colon, and the colon also introduces passages at random — memories, related incidents, the appearance of chance characters, checkpoints of nostalgia. The immediate scene — the mother, the TV set, the view out the window and down the road — always swings back into focus. The transitions are generally smooth, though occasionally we get the jerky effect of an old movie projector. Parts of the collage arrive from a great distance, but they are always pasted in and made to fit the grand design, whose center is Schuyler himself in East Aurora.

The best nature poems seem to be written by people who have had a long experience of the city — perhaps they have the largest stake in the natural. Schuyler is as quirky a nature poet as we have produced, and in the accretion of physical data in his long poem, a view of nature creeps into the work, barefoot, on its own. A version of the pastoral is being promulgated: value is essentially native, home-grown, and surprisingly traditional. The weed as well as the flower, the restored interior of McFeely's bar as well as the Italian Monument — these are the permanent properties, values that attest not only to the age-old continuity of man but to the connection between the child and the adult. Currents of feeling, pulsations of nervous response are aroused by talismanic objects, natural, architectural, and sexual. The natural world is comforting, almost maternal, yet its variety is celebrated with romantic intensity. Love, or let's say sex, has an adolescent aura in the poems, and also a certain camp flavor; the sexual impulses are mainly voyeuristic or masturbatory; the true satisfactions of the flesh are all of the past. The homosexual longing is frank, promiscuous, and runs through the poems as a whole. It neither diminishes nor enhances the character of the narrator; everything is seen in the light of a dispassionate compassion, which is useful even to himself.

We credit, we do not discount, we may even regret — having handed ourselves over so completely to the writer — the adolescent sexuality (and, if it needs to be said, not adolescent because it is homosexual), but it has no negative impact. There is nothing exhibitionistic about it; the deeply felt friendships celebrated throughout the book make a far more lasting impression, and the natural world in which everything is steeped acts as a counterbalance. Nature is sensual; the weed accidentally come upon and the studied specimen are equally well observed. In love with gardens, Schuyler is passionate about wildflowers:

> Canadian columbine, rusty red
> (Or rather orange?), spurred,
> Hanging down, drying, turning
> Brown, turning up, a cup
> Full of fine black seeds
> That sparkle, wake-robin,
> Trillium, a dish of rich
> Soft moss stuck with little
> Flowers from the woods —
> Bloodroot, perhaps
> Rose pogonia, sea lavender
> And, best of all, bunches
> And bunches and bunches of
> New England asters, not blue,
> Not violet, certainly not
> Purple: bright-yellow-
> Centered, so many crowded
> Into vases and bowls that
> The house seems awash
> With sea and sun. . . .

Behind Schuyler's pastoral backdrops, a moral world begins to take shape. That world is not easy to define, but its outlines may be suggested in Schuyler's portrait of his mother. A churchgoer and TV watcher, she starts out as a "parent," a person of false values, conventional, middle class, the usual white-collar mother. But by the end of the poem, she has become a character of strength and integrity, assuming a role somewhat akin to Proust's grandmother, the central moral figure of *A la Recherche du Temps Perdu*, who, through a simple quality, natural goodness (and its corollary, uncritical love), develops into an unswerving force. The portrait of Schuyler's mother is marked by clarity and surety; without slurring her negative qualities (from the son's point of view), she assumes a positive aspect. (A similar process of moral illumination occurs in Schuyler's treatment of Lottie, the alcoholic wife, in that small masterpiece of a novel *What's for Dinner?*) Though Schuyler's mother sometimes irritates him, the loving colors in which she is presented, in spite of all the outward facts being stacked against her, hold the key to Schuyler's moral view, more apparent in tone than in stated attitude, in the way a character is handled than in a character's intrinsic merit. Remaining true to oneself is, for Schuyler, the greatest of moral virtues. He can be cruel and childish, but he is in touch with parts of himself not usually available for examination and not often handled by most writers. This can become excessive — as if all truths were of equal importance. A line like "Funny, I haven't beat my meat in days — why's that?" seems to me a question hardly worth asking. And his mother's ingrown toenail may help establish the genre — the no-holds-barred journal entry — but the fine line between the necessary fact and the pointless detail is blurred.

These poems, no matter where they range in space or time, are poems of loneliness, and an unwritten irony spells itself out underneath them — though the world is often chastened, it is still viewed with a puzzled affection. The poems hew close to the bone; the ordinary delicacy that divides life and letters seems not only irrelevant but a form of evasion. The title poem, in particular, is the work of a persistent romantic, and as American as apple pie; in fact, it sometimes reads like a perverse underground commentary on *Our Town*. Schuyler's poems lack the historical sweep, the philosophical perspective one finds in the work, say, of Brodsky and Walcott. But they ring true, translating life into the action and imagery of a poetry that is never telegraphic, journalistic, or confessional. How Schuyler manages to be absolutely truthful and an obsessed romantic at the same time is his secret.

PART TWO

The Poet's Voice

How much the reputation of a writer depends on critical attention! And how little attention is paid to writers who are either too popular or too "obvious" to merit close reading or explication. What pleasure is there in writing criticism that reveals what everyone can see for himself? By the nature of the beast, criticism is attached to the enigmatic. And the enigmatic is assumed to be new just as the new is assumed to be important. About certain writers — no matter how good — practically nothing is said. For every piece on E. M. Forster there are a hundred on Virginia Woolf, for every essay on Tolstoy two hundred on Joyce. The plainer the writer the less there is to explain, or so it seems at first glance. "Modernism" has spawned a backyard of critics eager to untangle the intricacies of this or that new phenomenon for an abashed public or admiring colleagues. To imagine a critical establishment with nothing to unravel is like imagining a processing factory with nothing to process. So the difficulty, the *unavailability*, of a work spawns — in numerical proportion — interpreters: shedding light, showing the way, and re-creating the work while creating its reputation. There are fashions in difficulty as there are in hats. Fashions do not detract from genius; they merely allow copiers an opportunity for reproduction at bargain prices. Yesterday's avantgarde — Eliot, Joyce, Stravinsky, Picasso — all seem now remarkably congenial. The process has even been speeded up: except to a very few, John Ashbery was ten years ago an inaccessible writer; he may soon be in danger of becoming a household word.

And so it comes as a surprise to find Richard Poirier, in *Robert Frost: The Work of Knowing*, tackling a poet who has up to now been considered self-evident. Used as a model to counter the difficulties of Eliot, Yeats, and Stevens, Frost has been taken for granted as a dispenser of recognizable wisdoms and acknowledged truths — good, maybe great, but needing no gloss. Randall Jarrell in two essays, "The Other Frost" and "To the Laodiceans," began the complicated task of rescuing Frost from his admirers by examining the texts in the way they deserved, separating the extraordinary writer from the public man. Frost played the Yankee rustic deep in the verities; except in scattered statements on poetry, his critical intelligence was masked. As early as 1917, he wrote in a letter to Louis Untermeyer, "All the fun is . . . saying things . . . that almost but don't quite formulate. I should like to be so subtle at this game as to seem to a casual person altogether obvious."

Why the notion of Frost as a one-dimensional grand old man of American letters developed — and why it is wrong — is Mr. Poirier's subject. In his close reading of representative poems, he sees Frost's work as "a perpetual debate between, on the one side, the inherent necessity for form in language and in nature, which requires a dialogue of accommodation, and, on the other, the equally inherent human need for excursion beyond form." The argument involves method as well as theme: the grand sonorities of traditional English poetry scored against vernacular New England speech, and the idea of "home" — a place of rest, love, and enclosure — in opposition to the desire for flight from it. Frost used Thoreau's word "extra-vagance" to imply more than excess — to stand for the need to go beyond the strictures of the formed, whether they were to be found in the domestication of marriage or in the metrical pattern of the poem itself. Since form was the basic subject and putting it into form the method, a poem became a secret commentary on itself. As Mr. Poirier explains, Frost's speculative "walks" were both real actions and metaphoric devices, the theme of a poem and the way to write it. ("He would have known that 'stanza' means 'room' — so that when he walks out into the woods, he takes his 'room' with him.") Frost often cast himself as a meditative wanderer temporarily off base, searching for freedom yet regretting its restrictive loneliness, or hankering for security only to find it limiting and dull. These two states were not mutually exclusive. Ambivalence enriches implications, and Mr. Poirier discovers unexpected meanings in texts long familiar:

"Stopping by Woods on a Snowy Evening" is about a central human experience — the enchantments that invite us to surrender ourselves to oblivion; "Mending Wall" is about the opposite impulse, which is to fence yourself in, to form relationships that are really exclusions. But at the same time and in the same terms both poems propose that these human dilemmas are also poetic ones, in the one case the possibly destructive solicitations of the sublime and in the other the claustrophobias of mechanical forms. The poems are about the will to live asserting itself against invitations either to surrender or to constraint, and these, it is intimated, issue as much from the convention of poetry as from conventions of feeling.

These might be overreadings if the context were not so intelligent that Frost becomes something altogether new; the effect is like listening to a symphonic chestnut revitalized under the baton of a gifted young conductor. Beneath the easy surfaces of the poems, tensions between speech and eloquence, commitment and rebellion, and heaven and earth struggle for resolution. The frequent use of the words "stars" and "walls" suggests a connection between — and the distance that separates — the earthbound and the sublime. Frost worked in the mine field of the middle ground: a realist who believed in instinct and a rationalist drunk on the romantic. A spokesman for altitude, but only up to "a certain height" — his notion of freedom was hedged in by reservations.

Frost's preoccupation with the natural world overlay two concurrent obsessions: love as a vital force surrounded by mythic rituals (or sometimes merely formal conventions), and poetry as a natural gift in need of shaping and pruning. Nature, love, poetry: a triple strand, each thread spun of something native and something civilized, is interlaced in poem after poem. Mr. Poirier's most original teasing out of inner meanings is in tracing the inherent sexuality of Frost's poems. Frost himself said that the subject of "The Subverted Flower" was "frigidity in women," and only allowed the poem to be published after his wife's death. Yet in spite of this kind of corroboration from his subject, the critic is persuasive but not wholly convincing. Sexuality in Frost may be "a submerged metaphor," but the reticence that led to its immersion in the first place remains a barrier to the reader's experience of it.

Although Mr. Poirier never makes a claim he doesn't try to demonstrate, something in Frost thwarts the complexity of his interpretation, as if the very grandeur and rightness of phrasing the poet achieved in his best poems — "Design," "The Silken Tent," "Home Burial," "Provide, Provide," "After Apple-Picking" — armed them with skins so tough they repel complication. And in his exhaustive technical analyses, Mr. Poirier oddly makes no mention of Frost's use of monosyllabic words — crucial, it seems to me, to his mastery of common speech in formal verse. No other poet I know uses them to the same extent, and often in a final line wholly made up of monosyllables that serves as the dramatic conclusion of an action or the summing up of an idea — "In Hardwood Groves," "Never Again Would Birds' Song Be the Same," "Waiting," "A Dream Pang," etc.

Mr. Poirier makes claims for Frost equal to those made for Yeats and Eliot. And it may be that Frost resists greatness less than readers like myself, brought up under the influence of Eliot, resist his being great. But though there is no lack of emotion in Frost, there is a lack of emotional range — a refusal to be either naked or gorgeous — and the insistent absence of the city narrows the field of vision. Sometimes the scale seems too inhumanly local. Who would ever guess from reading Frost that he was born in San Francisco and spent his first eleven years there? A touch of the borrowed personality enters into the moralizing sageness of his work — possibly the "cuteness" and "smugness" the critic himself so dislikes. No matter: Mr. Poirier has broken fresh ground everywhere, and, in a single book, has repositioned Frost, a writer already considered major, so that he remains in a tradition but is differently placed and more truly seen. A metaphysical cloak has replaced the rustic mantle. To illustrate how a reputation is deserved but developed for the wrong reasons and then to supply plausible correctives is one of the most difficult undertakings imaginable, the kind of rescue operation that artists need from time to time but rarely get. Mr. Poirier has done for Frost what Ralph Kirkpatrick did for Scarlatti and Eliot for the seventeenth-century metaphysical poets. Seen in a new light, the music and the poems were brought back to life. And in Mr. Poirier's wonderfully fresh readings of the texts, particularly of "Home Burial" and "A Star in a Stone-Boat," he has made it impossible to approach Frost again in a simpleminded manner. Moreover, by being a defense in the particular, his book is an attack in general on the notion that only the experimental is new.

The premise of David Kalstone's *Five Temperaments* is simple: poetry reflects life. Therefore: how do five very different American poets manage to use autobiographical material in their work? The poets are Elizabeth Bishop, Robert Lowell, James Merrill, Adrienne Rich, and John Ashbery. Where Mr. Poirier probes, praises, and dismisses, Mr. Kalstone appreciates. We are given the ordered observations and asides of a man who has thought carefully and deeply about his subject, a learned man, but one who is willing to be seduced by the magic of words, casual or mandarin. And always something new turns up. In his essay on Bishop, Mr. Kalstone connects the scream of the mother in the autobiographical story "In the Village" with Aunt Consuelo's scream in the dentist's office in "In the Waiting Room" — a remarkably revealing insight, for the latter poem is the one where Bishop first becomes aware of the unwanted burden of consciousness, of *being* someone:

> But I felt: you are an I,
> you are an Elizabeth,
> you are one of them.

And so we become aware that in Bishop consciousness is directly related to the experience of pain, and that the meticulousness of her perceptions may be a form of wariness. Mr. Kalstone is the first person I know to suggest that the poems in *Geography III*, the poet's last book, are visitations to the earlier poems, as if they were places of travel. In "The Moose," we encounter again the childhood Canada of her first book, *North & South*. And, in the late "Poem," a primitive landscape is drawn by the same great-uncle who "scribbled hundreds of fine black birds / hanging in *n*s in banks" in "Large Bad Picture," a poem from the forties.

In discussing the change of style between Lowell's second and third books, the most influential shifting of gears in the last thirty years of American poetry, Mr. Kalstone lets the author speak for himself:

I was in San Francisco, the era and setting of Allen Ginsberg, and all about very modest poets were waking up prophets. I became sorely aware of how few poems I had written. . . . Their style seemed distant, symbol-ridden and willfully difficult. . . . I felt my old poems hid what they were really about, and many times offered a stiff, humorless and even impenetrable surface. I am no convert to the "beats." . . . Still, my own poems seemed like prehistoric monsters dragged down into the bog and death by their ponderous armor. I was reciting what I no longer felt. . . . I felt that the best style for poetry was none of the many poetic styles in English, but something like the prose of Chekhov or Flaubert.

Mr. Kalstone is particularly canny in spotting key subjects and ways of dealing with them: Merrill's conviction that "life was fiction in disguise," his use of houses — each enclosing the scene of a continuing drama — to fix and transfix the past, his "slides" lit up from within, "as if a poem required a kind of scrim among its resources, before or behind which action may be seen in new configurations as new beams of light are introduced." Mr. Kalstone sees *Divine Comedies* as the culmination of Merrill's interest in narrative and nothing less than a contemporary reconstruction of its singular predecessor — Dante emerging from a Ouija board. Or Adrienne Rich's "burning impatience with the way writing fixes experience . . . her preference for the provisional . . . [her interest] in American life as registered and suffered by those not in power, those not directly responsible for it, and especially women. . . ." Or this, on Ashbery:

A great deal of [his] writing is done in an atmosphere of deliberate demolition. . . . In his images of thwarted nature, of discontinuity between present and past, Ashbery has turned his agitation into a principle of composition. . . . [He] is not simply reminding us that poetry has access to the inner life; he is emphasizing the unique power of language to reveal how much of external life the inner life displaces.

There is in *Five Temperaments* a warmth rare in criticism — Mr. Kalstone enjoys what he's talking about — and one weakness: the list of poets he has chosen to illustrate his argument seems dictated less by his thesis than by taste and, to use his word, temperament. One could make a list of five other poets who might more convincingly demonstrate a link between poetry and biography: Ammons, Merwin, Plath, Ginsberg, and Sexton, say. But it may be that the sometimes strained disparity between the work he admires and what it is meant to demonstrate led to the kind of increased awareness a detective might develop on discovering that his wife is the chief suspect.

In the middle of Mr. Poirier's book, we come upon the following: "Voice is the most important, distinguishing, and conspicuously insistent feature of Frost's poetry and of his writing about poetry. There is scarcely a single poem which does not ask the reader to imagine a human character equivalent to the movement of voice." Taken together, these two books suggest that the poetry of the past fifty years has discovered its central theme, but it is a theme so involved with the difficulty of writing poetry itself that seeing it plain isn't easy. In the pull between speech and eloquence, the low style and the high, gutter talk and the King's English, how to speak in the name of something real without being merely commonplace led to the subject to be spoken about. And that turned out to be: *who is speaking*. The problem of *how* turned into the problem of *what*. The tone of voice became the key factor. The human voice, like the fingerprint, is characteristically identifiable. The major question was one of truth or falsity — or, if not falsity, then the façade that Literature and society and civilization have put in the way of speaking the truth. Art is civilized, we have been led to believe by reading, looking at, and listening to more than twenty centuries of it. How could it be natural? The question was naïve but of absolute significance, for most of the efforts to get around it are visible in thousands of galleries, are whispered or shouted at a hundred poetry readings every night, and can be heard hammered out in our concert halls. The insistence on not being formal, or stuck-up, or mannered, the freedom to use any kind of language, the emphasis on being real and spontaneous are all to the good, but they are also symptoms. People who are natural do not ask themselves how to be natural. Art isn't nature. In the attempt to make it so, more than one artist raced in the opposite direction from the one in which he thought he was heading, like an arrow propelled backward from the bull's-eye to the bow. He adopted fashion where style was required — and by style I mean something as native to the individual writer as it is to the individual person. Marianne Moore, for instance, had style, because the way she wrote was hers alone. And by fashion I mean the sense of the word as it pertains to clothes. Its main feature is its impermanence; in order to exist, fashion must be deliberately changed. The shifting hemline and haircut made Paris, a city of art, into a center of fashion. It was in painting that fashion first asserted itself (because, of all the arts, painting is the most closely allied with money), and it has spread to every art in every corner, so that the distinction between what is truly style and what is merely fashion has become increasingly muddy. In discussing the abrupt shift in method between *Lord Weary's Castle* and *Life Studies*, Lowell explained why "Skunk Hour" — the most famous and characteristic poem in *Life Studies* — is dedicated to Elizabeth Bishop: "Because re-reading her suggested a way of breaking through the shell of my old manner." And, in regard to style and fashion, it is Elizabeth Bishop, in the end, who is the most illustrative and exemplary. She was herself from the beginning.

The First Line

In my case, the first line of a poem is crucial and is usually the given thing that comes out of the blue without conscious maneuvering, when the mind is released from the habitual. Most often it comes when I am in motion, when no fixed mooring allows habit to keep from consciousness what the imagination may be evoking. I mean "motion" literally: in subways, taxis, cars, buses, trains, planes, ships — and in dreams, for I take dreams to be forms of transportation. Lines that come from dreams, however, have to be written down when they occur — they tend to evaporate — or require the use of mnemonic devices in order for the aroused dreamer not to wake up completely, turn the lights on, get out of bed — or all three. Even so, I've lost lines I felt certain I would remember; associative reminders — words, things in the room, colors, clues embedded (you would think) unforgettably — have not been enough to keep them fixed in the mind. What poet hasn't had the feeling, sometime during the day, that a line, an idea, a title that sprang to mind the night before was lost forever? In the moment of knowing it has been experienced, there is also the experience of knowing it is gone. (There are, of course, occasional recapturings.)

The first line may turn out, in the end, not to *be* the first line, and, if it is not, it is usually the last. It can, on rare occasions, be a line in the middle of a poem around which the rest of the poem clusters, but most of the time, it is the opening wedge, the beginning of . . . what? Writing a poem is finding out what the given line leads to, or, to put it another way, what the line has hidden behind it. Sometimes it takes years to discover that; sometimes it follows as the night the day. It doesn't matter whether the poem is written quickly or takes months to revise, as long as the original "gift"— notion, words, phrase, sentence — is spontaneous. Sometimes the line leads nowhere. I call these false poems, like false pregnancies. That is not necessarily the fault of the line. It can be a failure of the imagination, a sickness of will, a bad period in anyone's life that stifles the messages the imagination is sending out. A broadcasting station with no atmosphere through which electromagnetic impulses can travel.

What does a first line do? It can seem to do nothing, be deceptive, like the beginnings of novels that are quiet, that do not arrest the attention very much, in which the lulling voice lures the reader on with a children's story told to a tea table, very quietly, an aside. I will a tale unfold, it says, but you can hardly hear it. "One afternoon, in the year 1889, a young woman got into a carriage in Amsterdam." And we are already launched. So many things are bubbling in the pot. Who is she? Where does she come from? Why is she getting into the carriage? There is the Holland sky. There are, perhaps, cobblestones? Boots? Horses? And a few trees?

The first line of a poem does more than that: it intrigues the ear — some way, no matter how quietly. And how hard it is, now, to think of all those famous first lines being put down on paper for the first time! They intrigue the ear *and* the mind. "April is the cruellest month, breeding. . . ." (The hand is poised above the typewriter? What will come next?) "I wonder, by my troth, what thou and I. . . ." (The pen hesitates?) "Lay your sleeping head, my love. . . ." "The saris go by me from the embassies. . . ." "Each day with so much ceremony. . . ." I would say that the best are musical and contain an embryonic concept: in the Eliot, the paradox of spring and cruelty; in the Donne, questioning and swearing at the same time; in the Auden, asking someone asleep to perform an action; in the Jarrell, being a passive witness to something exotic *and* official; in the Bishop, the implied irony of each day being a ceremonious occasion — yes, maybe, but not in any ordinary reader's life (including the poet's). So the line contains within it a seed of expectation. Or, if it is merely descriptive, it has to have something arresting — something implicitly dramatic, perhaps — no matter how subtly toned down. This can be the drama of syntax: "Anyone lived in a pretty how town. . . ." Or the delayed verb, of which Merrill is a master. Like the opening notes of a musical composition, it has to *allow* for the possibility of going further, of going *on*, has to be a springboard but also to sound inevitable. Who would think, after hearing the announcement of the first theme in the "Pastoral" Symphony, of going on in a different way, a way different from

Beethoven's? The theme has already taken on the authority of nature, as if it were a form found rather than a form invented. One would no more think of revising a rock. Well, if one has a first line like that, one is very lucky. And, of course, first lines are never *like* that, except in retrospect. Nothing is inevitable until it is concluded. Until the poem is written, the finality of the first line is subject to change; its ultimate absolute shape remains in doubt. It may be the most solid thing around, but still, like ice in spring, it is capable of melting. "On the way to the contagious hospital . . ." Is there any word that could take the place of "contagious"? Supposing (only for the sake of argument) Williams had written "On the way to the courageous hospital . . ." (A clinic in a leper colony hacked out of the jungle?) How wrong it would be, now that we know! How outrageous.

Is the first line — or even the whole poem — dreamwork? Or fancy footwork? Is it the agile cleverness of someone tuned up to receive what the receiver has taken in — and given out — before? It is hard to say. The freshness of certain poets gets lost, even as the skills increase. Yeats and Stevens and Williams got better as they got older. Other poets were not so lucky. Two things are equally boring in art: a lack of skill and too much of it.

Things deepen. Landscapes become engraved. Relationships become richer — or, sometimes, bitter. Either is grist, though I hate to say it, for the mill, because it is intensity that counts in certain poets, rather than the contemplative authority of the voice, its richness and depth.

I'd say there were three modes: the meditative (which includes the elegiac); the intense (which includes the narrative);

and the associative, which includes everything the first two do not cover but is particularly applicable, say, to Spanish and South American poets, who have had such an influence on United States poets. There, the image is central, the originality of the image and the ability to move on with a certain underground relevance from one image to another. Examples: the meditative — Stevens; the intense — Warren; the associative — Ashbery. None of these are pure distillations. I think, for instance, that part of Ashbery's current influence comes from the combination of two modes, the meditative *and* the associative, as if the deep image had found a philosopher.

The story counts for more and more. Openings of plays are clues, provide hints, because they are the precursors of action. In *The Seagull*, the first line is "Why are you wearing black?" The second, "I'm in mourning for my life." And though neither is the actual first line of the play, these are the first lines Shakespeare assigns Cleopatra and Antony — they are almost one-liners:

CLEOPATRA: If it be love indeed, tell me how much.
ANTONY: There's beggary in the love that can be reckon'd.

The whole extraordinary play is there in capsule. They have said, at the beginning, what they will eventually act out.

Think of the first shot in movies. *Casque d'Or* opens wonderfully. The world stays in motion. The long gliding of the canoes under the trees to the river bank followed almost immediately by the contained wildness of the dance — apache. In *Madame Rosa*, the three Hebrew letters on a street sign, casually planted in the opening shot. Who, in recent years, hasn't wanted the opening credits of movies to go on and on?

Often so much more alive, interesting, inventive than what follows.

Is it inevitability or familiarity that makes a first line sound right? To answer that honestly would be difficult. But take five lines with substituted words — words close to the meaning of the originals: "My heart hurts; and a drowsy numbness pains"; "Lay your sleeping head, my friend"; "The dresses go by me from the embassies"; "August is the cruellest month, breeding"; "He was in Venice writing letters home."

The Keats and the Stevens sound more plausible than the others, but in the first the level of discourse has changed. The alliteration lowers the temperature of the grand manner. And, in the Stevens, a canal is not a bay. A great deal hangs on that. "See Naples and die." Not Venice. The Auden switch changes a love poem into something innocuous and hesitant, something on the verge of the ludicrous. The Eliot loses its pathos and irony. August is very conceivably cruel: it's hot, it is the prelude to the end of things, the fall. The very notion that animated the line — spring, a time of joy; cruelty, a thing to fear — is gone. The paradoxical shock is missing. And the Jarrell is completely ruined. Everything magical in a magical poem has been flattened out at the beginning. And is there a better first line, by the way, in the use of sound and ideas working together than "The saris go by me from the embassies"? "Saris" and "embassies" rhyme. And carrying the same sound but, equidistantly isolated from the two- and three-syllabled plurals, is that wan, singular echo, "me." Also notable: with the exception of the repeated "the" and the rhyme words, every vowel sounded is different.

What sounds right may be what we have already heard.

Probably. But I doubt it in the case of poets, because a poet is the one to whom the new first line comes. Echoes, yes. Of what is read, what is lived, what is seen. But the echo is changed by the chamber in which it reverberates, and what brings new speech to birth are words and sounds that can be found anywhere: in books, popular songs, phrases, catch phrases, jazz, overheard speech, signs, menus, the talk of children, instructions in manuals, patent medicine throwaways, etc. And particularly the slightly out of kilter, the verbal connection shaded off. I can't think of a better example than "The Man-Moth," Elizabeth Bishop's poem based on a newspaper misprint of "mammoth."

The more transposable the better. Take a song from *Guys and Dolls*: "The Oldest Established Permanent Floating Crap Game in New York." Then isolate ". . . established permanent floating. . . ." The first line of a poem on the Taj Mahal? New York in certain lights? Monet's water lilies?

Or take song titles, particularly jazz: "Tuxedo Junction," "Avalon," "Big John's Special," "One O'Clock Jump," and those three spondee songs: "Blue Skies," "So Rare," and "Much More."

Poems that come from life come from characters: spokesmen, archetypes, legendary figures, the self. Does it matter whether they start in words or in experience? (And, for a writer, words are experiences.) Eliot saw the proper uses of drama, of dramatic tension, in lyric poetry. He went both ways: he started to write plays and ended up writing string quartets. Perhaps the most beautiful string quartets ever written in the English language. Song should never be downgraded, particularly in relation to first lines. Poetry is, essentially, the use of words to express the nonverbal. Because it uses words in a double way, its closest analogy is music, which uses no words at all, but equally expresses emotion, equally articulates form through sound.

Fantastically good prose can be a launching, like Cobbett in *Rural Rides*, or Sir Thomas Browne in "Urn Burial," or this, from Anthony Collett, which Auden reprints in his commonplace book:

> Far and wide through the moors of the northern countries run the dykes and sills of hard black basaltic rock called whinstone. Nature has forced it between softer layers of rock much as cement is driven between the crumbling stones of a cathedral wall. But this volcanic grouting is so much harder than sedimentary rock, and the operation was carried out so many hundreds of thousands of years ago, that the basaltic bonds have outlasted the layers which they compact, and now project beyond them. Dykes are vertical layers of whinstone, which out-top the moor's surface by 20 or 40 feet, like a wall.

Or good critical writing. Like Pritchett's. Or a more romantic version of scientific writing, from *The Ocean*, by F. O. Ommanney:

> The barnacle is a small shrimp-like creature which, when the tide covers it, stands upside down in its box made of plates of lime, feathering food towards itself with long curved legs. When the tide recedes it closes its box by means of four accurately fitting valves. In doing so it entraps a bubble of air and enough moisture to keep its gills damp. If you listen carefully just after the tide has left the rocks you may hear all around the whispering talk of the barnacles, a faint crepitation. It is caused by the tighter closing of the valves in millions of little houses whose

inmates are alarmed by the monstrous reverberation of your bare feet.

The half-seen, the barely glimpsed, if they make an impression, are more usable, usually, than the familiar. Though sometimes if the right connection is made, a place one has been steeped in comes alive. A similarity and a difference, like coming on a seacoast resort like St. Mawes in England having known Rockport, Massachusetts. A woman with a jar walking toward the water in Nicaragua. A lamp swinging in a doorway in Russia. A man settling in for the night at a pub in Wales. Are they not the old streets of childhood, under a streetlamp, while you skated at twilight? They are. And they are not. They are real and imagined. One doesn't have to read Freud to know how the imagined can become real, or Stevens to understand how the real can become imagined. Memory, the key to everything, brings with it nostalgia, which must be outgrown. Not to appreciate the world as objective means that the Nicaraguan woman, the Russian lamp, and the Welsh pub will never be more than children's paintings. Wonderful, for their age. And frightening ten years later.

All things noticed but never set down, or things never brought to consciousness — the conventional made fresh, the new brought into being — are the properties of poetry and the peculiar provinces of first lines. Whether they can be singled out, later, after one knows what comes after — again, one would have to be equivocal. "Each day with so much ceremony / Begins, with birds, with bells, / With whistles from a factory . . ." (How — in the first line — those commonplace monosyllables add weight to "ceremony"!) Eliza-

beth Bishop has a fine Italian hand at first lines. The undertow is felt at the water's edge. The matter-of-fact tone only
adds to the excitement.

It is true some poems escape this particularity of the first
line in a special way. Norman Dubie, say, where one enters
a *terrain*, and slowly, building up, in front of you, is the
detail of the story, the massing of the narrative in objects,
animals, discrete observations, as if one were crawling across
a painted canvas from one side, binoculars in hand, watching
the wonders, the grass, under one's feet, grow. That is different. Because there, the linear travel of the rail-line has become three-dimensional: the future of the poem is being built
in sections, sections of varying thicknesses. And it is different, too, in a Dave Smith poem, where the choral voice
sounds out of the bay, or out of the railway yard, that not-
quite-single-person's voice, which is the voice of the single
person speaking for many. I would say — using these two
poets as unwitting examples — that the more narrative the
poem the less dependent on the first line. But it would be a
mistake to make a hard and fast distinction between the lyric
and the narrative. It is precisely poets like Smith and Dubie
who have brought the excitements of the lyric — that is, of
language sounded for non-prose reasons — into the narrative, and precisely Elizabeth Bishop who has done the opposite. In narration, the onrushing power of the story may
seem to count for everything, but it only counts for half. It
is the voice of the narrator that is equally significant. That is
why detective stories seldom last. There is no voice behind
them.

The first line, then, is the kernel of the poem, however
pared down, embellished, or revised, whether it arrives,

originally, *as* the first line, ends up being the last ("The first shall be last and the last shall be first"), or becomes the nucleus around which the cells begin to construct an organism.

There are three characteristic "first" lines:

1) That line which is, in itself, a complete statement. The poem that follows extends or plays variations on the already-stated theme: "Do not go gentle into that good night"; "They flee from me that sometime did me seek"; "For Godsake hold your tongue, and let me love." There are subjects and predicates, nouns and verbs. And if we had to (we don't), we could accept short rations and make a very tiny poem out of the line itself. (Many people do: they know lines, not poems.)

"Great" first lines retain a relevancy outside the poem, being universal and local, immediate and abstract — the subjects above, being death, abandonment or betrayal, and sexual impatience — and are marked by incongruity, some hidden interest, either in the way the words are sounded, used, or positioned.

In the Thomas, there is the adjective "gentle" in place of the syntactically called-for adverb, the unusual use of the phrase "good night" — both blessed darkness and the familiar words of parting — the playing off of the soft "g" of "gentle" against the hard "g" of "good," and the strangeness of what the words convey: the notion that one can control one's own death. The line is both an admonishment and a declaration of love.

In the Wyatt, the same vowel sounded in "flee," "me," and "seek," the exaggerated drama of "flee," the special twist of "seek" — meaning "seek out"— and, for us, Wyatt's "sometime," a synonym for "once," with more than a slight ring of "once in a while." And though "sometime" is the one word

94

in the line that is not a monosyllable, it is, really, an amalgam of two monosyllabic words placed side by side. Oddest
of all is the very first word, the plural "They." Why not
"She flees from me who sometime did me seek"? This is
more than a lover's betrayal; this is a wholesale abandonment, which reverts, in the second line, to the singular —
"with naked foot stalking within my chamber." The plural
"They" tells us something about the narrator: is this "foot"
merely one of the many who have fled? So it would seem.
There is an elliptical "all" after "They" and an implied
past tense: "They all have fled who one time sought me
out. . . ."

In the Donne, the invoking of God for the most secular of
subjects, sex. The tongue is both an instrument of speech
and of love, and "hold" brings up two meanings at once — to
refrain and to embrace — as does "tongue," the organ of the
body and the word that stands for language. There's a further complication: The speaker — the poet — is forced into
speech. He cannot love while he is writing. The line is elec-
trified by contradictions.

2) Those first lines in which the second line already holds
sway, in which the thing to come is part of the originally
given words. You might say, these are the first *two* lines, or
three — whatever the case may be. For instance: "Remembering the Strait of Belle Isle or / Some northerly harbor of
Labrador, / Before he became a schoolteacher, / A great-
uncle painted a big picture." I would call the fourth line here
the "first" in the sense I mean it. Because the poem plays off
the central notion of "great *versus* big" in many subtle ways,
and ends with an affectionate, ironic contrast, one that tells
us all: "commerce [big] or contemplation [great]." (And how

nicely the conjunction that ends the first line works! It is secretly repeated three times in the following line.)

Or, for an example of a second line proper, "It is equal to living in a tragic land / To live in a tragic time."

3) The third example is not really a first line though it comes at the beginning of the poem. A syntactical diving board, and necessary, it has no particular interest in itself. Most contemporary poems begin this way, lower than low-keyed, with nothing particularly memorable either in the phrasing or the thought. In fact, it might be said that one of the habits of contemporary poetry is to be *against* the concept of the first line, its grandeur, its operative (and operatic) effect. As if to use words too well might be a sign of falsity, or excellence of phrasing a mark of inflation, of trying to win the reader over with fake enticements. It is a naïve view, but there is a lot to be said for it. Melodrama and sentimentality are the enemies. But sometimes feeling goes by the board as well. Whether the fear of rhetoric has led to the fear of feeling, or vice versa, would require a whole essay in itself. But the kind of line I refer to can begin wonderful poems without being wonderful: "There's a mystery" (David St. John's "Gin"); "A soft wind" (Philip Levine's "No One Remembers"); "With my eyes turned toward the sky" (David Ignatow's "Love Poem for the Forty-Second Street Library").

The writing of poetry seesaws, I think, between the desire to attain the first line and the desire to evade it. For in the first kind of first line there is the threat of the grandiloquent and of stopping — of there being nothing more to be said. In the second, the danger of getting lost in a muddle — too much has been given at once. And in the third, the problem of banality — of drifting into prose.

Once it has arrived, the first line should be revised in only one way: in terms of the ongoing.

Unlike the "foreword" to a literary work, first lines are introductions to worlds that never existed before and also parts of the worlds they introduce. We enter through them, but they are part of the structure, like doorways to houses. A good doorway doesn't exempt itself from architecture. A mystery whose solution falls into place only at the end, a first line is closer to an overture or a prelude, whose purpose is to say "This is a beginning" while being the very thing that has already begun.

From a Notebook

THE simultaneous desire for adventure and for safety, for a world in which the domestic and the wild are always within reach of each other, is a subject particularly meaningful to Frost. It is also one of peculiar American relevance, a comfortable form of pioneering in which the romantic has built-in guarantees: mobile homes with lavish living rooms, planes as big as movie houses (and showing the same films), campsites with hot and cold running water — frontiers upholstered in advance. In fact, the conquering of America by the TV screen may be part and parcel of this balanced disequilibrium, for with it, the wanderer stays securely at home in the partial dark, the world's possibilities flashing before him. The American dream: to be heroic and cozy at the same time.

The poet who comes off so badly in Thompson's biography as a mean-spirited megalomaniac is merely one of the worst examples of a common strain in American literary life. The spokesmen and spokeswomen for love, life, freedom, and so on, turn out, on closer inspection, to be figures struggling for power. The smaller the world the fiercer the battle. In the tiny world of poetry (tiny in its impact on the general public), these blemishes show up all the more baldly. More than one American poet has avoided the vulgarity of the marketplace only to meet it head-on in a literary Eden full of snakes. The egotism of writers can be more pathetic than most, and the poet's particularly so, for there is never enough adulation or cash to go round for an ever-increasing group of practitioners. (CODA lists the names and addresses of four thousand American poets in its current directory.) In a case like Frost's — one of the most famous and rewarded poets who ever lived — there couldn't be enough; adulation and power were compensations for one of the more hideous personal lives on record.

Frost is probably the only major American poet who felt that the formal tradition of English poetry flowed from natural sources and was not a collection of artificial forms imposed by civilization. No one, as far as I know, has discussed formal poetry on these grounds. Meter, "measure," accent, stress, tone, and phrasing are all terms that come from music. The connection between pulse beat and rhythm, heartbeat and dance, between the nature of the expected rhythmic resolution of a phrase to, say, the pattern formed by African drumbeats may be repeated, at variously refined distances, in the rhythms of formal poetry. It would be ironic if what look like arbitrary forms — the sonnet, the sestina, usually conceived of as complex designs originating in the courts of

France and Italy — conform to an instinctive need for rhythmic sensations as satisfactorily as clapping, marching bands, and disco music. The accurate transcription of rhythms in primitive poetry would be crucial in investigating this. Also: the satisfaction children take in rhyme; the development of a lingo like rhyming Cockney.

There is in Frost some unbending limitation that kept him, in my opinion, from being a great poet. Great poems, yes, but not the sweep of the work as a whole. If we take Shakespeare as the standard, in spite of Frost's surprising insights into the desperate isolation of women, there is little sense of the street side of life, little true humor: the clown, the buffoon, and the fool are missing. As a matter of fact, *childhood* is missing. Some great truths are uttered, there is a perfection of style, but one of the great subjects of the twentieth century makes itself felt simply by being absent: the city. Sometimes I think that for a poet of this century not to show any awareness of the city would be analogous to the absence of royalty in the work of an Elizabethan playwright.

Frost's lyrical and dramatic gifts are extraordinary; also the seeming simplicity with which a formal design is worked out. When politics enter, he is embarrassing. And he is embarrassing, too, sometimes when the natural world becomes an automatic resource, a way of getting something down. Too many poems about woods and streams seem like imitations of the great poems, as if they were reprinted from worn-down type, each copy getting fainter and fainter.

A commonplace book is a book in which someone keeps a record of whatever intrigues him — a passage found in a novel, a chance remark, a story snipped from a paper or a magazine. The entries can range from a recipe to an explanation of the universe. Being random and personal, a commonplace book has two major interests: the material itself, and the material as a revelation of the person who selects it.

Those readers who mistake a commonplace book for a diary will be disappointed in Auden's case. His views on the publication of personal letters and diaries have been made clear. He was repelled by the notion of a writer's nonprofessional work being offered to the reading public as a kind of immortal gossip column. We do not find in *A Certain World* intimate confidences, emotional confessions, or sexual revelations. Auden is even reluctant to assume the role of commentator: the quotations from other writers are generous; he speaks his mind only occasionally and briefly. The result reveals little about Auden, the man. What it does supply is a firmer foundation to already familiar inclinations. T. Sopwith's description of a visit to a lead mine makes Auden's childhood interest in geology and mining plausible, even intriguing. Sometimes an entry is surprising: the lyrics of a song from *Pal Joey* in a section on "Romantic Love." It's not odd that Auden should include it but that he should know it. (Conversely, it was equally surprising to find, in an interview in *Esquire*, that he didn't know who Ella Fitzgerald was.)

Topics are arranged alphabetically: Accidie to Writing. Besides literature and writing, two major interests become apparent: science — as language and vocabulary rather than scientific method or theory — and religion: its meaning, history, and ceremonies.

Auden prefers concrete to abstract ideas and likes things said plainly and clearly. Aside from being informative in a hundred diverse ways, *A Certain World* is a very good small anthology of prose style.

Auden was a curiously devout man. As early as the trip to China in 1939, he had abandoned whatever version of Marxism he had tentatively embraced. He is a good example of how reputations die hard; he was discussed as a political poet two decades after it had ceased to be true. No poet today has a like intellectual curiosity, a journalistic interest in the international event, or the compulsions of conscience that make a writer a commentator on his time. Because the range was wide, Auden's religious poetry seemed least characteristic. And then, there was an essential ambiguity in his attitude. A worldwide spokesman for the truth, who sounded off on many occasions, late and early, he was also the poet who said, "Poems do not make anything happen."

It is not so odd that because of a famous hat Marianne Moore should be likened to George Washington. She doesn't tell lies, either.

To be captured: the price of being beautiful. Tropical fish go on long journeys only to end up in a tank. The defense mechanisms of certain creatures in the animal and insect world are the very ones, in the human world, that turn safety into danger or doom: elephant tusks, the camouflage effects on butterfly wings, the tiger's fur, etc. Wonder how often the same thing happens with people.

Marianne Moore's last line in "Roses": "Your thorns are the best part of you."

What begins as a liberating force ends up as a constricting one when it becomes programmatic and theoretical and begins to ignore contradictory evidence. It is necessary to remember how narrow and snobbish Eliot's view of Lawrence was, that Auden thought Crane a bad influence on American poetry, how childish Williams could be in regard to Eliot. And then there are the great mistakes: Gide rejecting Proust (and then apologizing), Virginia Woolf being dense in regard to *Ulysses*.

Woolf's criticism, the four volumes of *The Common Reader*, are extraordinary in their historical sweep, as if someone very intelligent, completely open, and wonderfully alert were simply to sit down in a library, start reading, and then tell us what she thought as she went along.

Between the Acts takes up this historical thread and uses it as a fictional device. The pageant of English history in *Between the Acts* revisits the world of *The Common Reader*, as if Woolf had found a fictional outlet for all that information at last. And at the very end.

I once thought of writing a piece about punctuation to be called "Miss Harp, Meet Dr. Literal." Punctuation can never be truly definitive in poetry because it is a system of logic — an instrument of argument — devised to clarify syntax. Its main purpose is to get rid of ambiguity — hardly the main purpose of poetry, where ambiguity can be exploited to enrich meaning. Poets distort punctuation to indicate desired sound effects: pauses and stresses. The idea that a comma is a short stop, a semicolon a longer one, and a colon the longest has no basis in fact. Music has phrase marks, tempo indications, directions indicating whether to slow down, speed up, become louder or softer. The ideal form of punctuation for poetry would be a combination of musical phrase marks and syntactical symbols. No such system exists.

Something unpleasant rises from the pages of Reed Whittemore's biography of William Carlos Williams. Lack of recognition and reward is such an old complaint of American poets it is a surprise to find it cropping up in one of modern literature's giants. One forgets the long histories giants have, the years and years in which Williams had to fight to be taken seriously. Still, pettiness, the last thing one would associate with Williams the poet, was there in good measure in the man. Charming and warm with people he liked, he could be sulky and hotheaded when he thought he hadn't been given his due. He was incapable of seeing Eliot's virtues. To Williams, Eliot was, first, an academic traditionalist and later developed into the rival-monster. It becomes more difficult to understand when one considers that Pound was the mentor of both poets (though psychoanalysts might say that would be reason enough). The truth is Williams must have seen Eliot as a powerful threat not because he was an academic but because he was, in his own way, as revolutionary a poet as Williams, and though Eliot spoke for tradition, he spoke for it in a way completely at odds with the academic climate of his time. The attractiveness of the adolescent stays with Williams, but also the adolescent's defects: an aggressive shyness, a demand to be noticed, and the single-mindedness of a man with a theory who would allow for no exceptions — no *great* exceptions, that is, for he was willing to tolerate work very different from his own when it wasn't on a competitive level. The praise that greeted the first book of *Paterson* came from so-called enemies, critics as academic (in Williams's mind) as Jarrell and Lowell. And it was Auden who called "The Greeny Asphodel" "one of the most beautiful love poems in the English language." I doubt if Williams could have been that generous in reverse. Lowell publicly acknowledged the debt he owed Williams in the progression from the formal poems of *Lord Weary's Castle* to *Life Studies*. Yet one of the debilitating legacies of Williams's position is that in order to praise the first one needed to attack the second, or vice versa. The variable foot, Williams's metrical invention, was a way of characteristically justifying a freedom in poetry that required no justification. He was, alternately, rebelling against the big academic boys and at the same time playing their game. His talent so far outraced his gift for theory that one wishes he hadn't bothered to set it down, to philosophize and explain. Yet he must have felt isolated and embattled. His sheer hatred of Eliot is an enormous weakness, just as Eliot's inability to see Lawrence's virtues is *his* weakness.

Williams's generally overlooked Spanish middle name is important. The "Carlos" came from his English grandmother, who had married in Puerto Rico and spent many years on the islands. Oddly, his grandfather (from the opposite side of the family) knew the islands well, too. That Spanish middle name has taken its own revenge. For in place of the neatly manicured iambic-pentameter poems Williams detested, what we now have is a world-wide kind of lingua franca in which the translations of Swedish poems sound alarmingly like those of Chinese poems, and the similarities of diction, style, and overall dreariness stem from either conscious or unconscious imitation. Mark Strand and Charles Simic in *Another Republic* have isolated what they call an "international style," and I think there may be such a thing. But its coming through depends on the translator, and we are in the midst of a period characterized by brilliant translations and by hordes indistinguishable from each other. American poetry, in general, sounds like an imitation of the *translations* of Spanish and South American poetry that began to appear in the fifties. One set of stereotyped responses has been substituted for another.

The distinction between a light opera like *Die Fledermaus* and a grand opera like *Aïda* is easy to make. But what is one to do with *Cosi fan tutte*, where the libretto is obviously comic in intention but where the score has a profundity not to be found in either *Die Fledermaus or Aïda?* The disparity between apparently comic surfaces and their darker meanings has a long tradition: the Elizabethan fool speaking wise riddles in the guise of entertainment; the traditional clown, funny, mute, sad. Chaplin's *City Lights* is an example. Starting out as comic, his little tramp becomes a symbol for the isolated, the victim of society. We are amused but also moved. It is clear, everywhere but in America, that the comic and the profound are not antithetical. With the exception of Mark Twain, is there any other American comic writer who has been accepted into the pantheon?

Shakespeare, Mozart, and Chekhov are equally at home in tragedy and comedy; Dante, Beethoven, and Ibsen are not.

Poems don't lie. It is amazing to think how many people think they do — who categorize the "poetic" as a form of embroidery. It is such a profound error it hardly seems worth refuting.

The novelist controls viewpoint and can move inside the mind of a character with the same dexterity with which he describes the exterior of a house. The playwright cannot do this; he is stuck with representational actors who, no matter how elaborately disguised or symbolically profound, cannot transcend biological limitations. An actor must speak for himself, has arms that come into play as he speaks and legs that cannot be cut off at will. (Beckett worked precisely against these limitations in *Endgame*.) The actor is a presence in three dimensions resembling his total presence offstage.

The novelist, like the camera, can cut in anywhere, move through time and space, focusing here, underlining there. The consciousness of the novelist should rarely be felt; its main purpose — in the art of storytelling — is to pretend not to exist. Its secondary, and contradictory, purpose is to surprise us by its existence. This is not true of the camera, where we must be completely under its spell, except for special effects rarely used in the service of art — like divers being returned to a diving board, or when, self-consciously, the camera speeds up or slows down. The latter can be an important documentary technique: sports events, educational films (on surgery, for instance), and historical fact. What footage there is of the Kennedy assassination has been slowed down for examination to a sequence of stills.

The close-up must not seem to be either magical or a technical feat. But, of course, it is. We are watching a dinner party from a doorway. Suddenly we are hovering over a teacup so enlarged it might well be under a microscope. Somebody has put a poison pellet in somebody else's tea. The camera has zoomed in to let us know. Strangely, we never notice this change in distance, this speeding up of time. We have crossed the room in a split second, we have been given the superhuman ability to focus on what is usually invisible. It doesn't bother our sense of reality at all. Is that why movies have to be shown in the dark? Not only so they may be seen but to re-create the concentrated focus of dreams?

Architecture is in one way allied to the performing arts. Its façades are meant to be seen by a large public. The outside of a building is constantly showing off.

What attracts attention is what is noticed. What is noticed attracts more attention. As "public relations" increase, private relations suffer. More and more people are getting themselves across through (self-)advertising campaigns.

Time is important to people who waste it. It's the one thing that keeps on happening. As they rush between not doing anything and doing nothing, time becomes a series of events rather than a continuous process. They are the people who always ask, "What time is it?"

One has only to look at the folk heroes of "society" to notice that they share a quality in common — they enhance or decorate either the bodies or the houses of their clients. Once the hairdresser, the dress designer, and the interior decorator achieved status as social figures, fashion — once relegated to the *merely* decorative — became the touchstone of art, and art, the only discipline that produces works meant to be enduring, suffered the fate of the American car. "What's new?" became more important than "What's good?" Newness, sometimes a form of progress, is a form of vulgarity when it is isolated from any other value. The permanent is of interest only to a culture aware of individual mortality. It is ironic that the word "permanent" should have become a term in hairdressing. Ironic but just.

I have read several reviews in which the term "the New Criticism" was used as a phrase meant to evoke an automatic response, like "imperialist aggressor." It was meant to stand for everything sterile, impersonal, and academic, and particularly the last. Actually, the opposite was true. At the time Warren, Brooks, Tate, Ransome, and Winters began to publish, their work was a radical way of reading poetry and a way of saving poetry *from* the academics, who were teaching literature as if it were history. The New Criticism was an antidote to literature's being conceived as the amber in which the history of ideas was embedded. Ideas were being taught, not poems. The new critics said that whatever these may be, they are *poems* first, and anything else second; they are not merely history, philosophy, astronomy, etc. As usual, what began as an original critical approach *became* — in the hands of followers less intelligent — method without spirit, dry and reductive. But are there any good ideas that hasn't happened to — including those of Christ, Marx, and Freud?

The triangle is the quickest way to get at hidden human emotions: Chekhov, Proust, James. But not of real interest to Joyce, Mann, Kafka, Camus.

To a person interested in writing per se, Camus is a greater intelligence than Sartre. To a philosopher, the other way around.

People who love animals once loved people.

Essays that should have been written but never were: Tolstoy on *Madame Bovary*, Flaubert on *Anna Karenina*. James on Proust, Proust on James.

Lack of satisfaction in reading Maugham's stories, they are so obviously *stories*, so meant to engage the mind in a sequence of events that are somehow puzzling and then resolved. They are too patently meant to satisfy and astonish. In fact, they are something like polished O. Henry stories written by an infinitely more sophisticated intelligence. Something essential about life is missing and nothing important seems to occur. One longs in the face of so much that's professional for the ardor of the amateur. Paradoxically, the very satisfaction of the stories is a limitation, in the same way a detective story, no matter how good, is circumscribed by the choice of the genre. It is only when a subject becomes thematic and takes on human relevance *outside* the story that genre escapes its boundaries. For instance: the distinction between Agatha Christie and Dostoevsky, between le Carré and Kafka. One tends to underrate Christie and le Carré, but it is impossible to overrate Dostoevsky and Kafka. What is entertainment in Christie is transformed into something relevant to the contemporary world in le Carré; what is relevant in le Carré expands into what is universal in Dostoevsky; what is universal in Dostoevsky turns into something abstract — a permanent human fable rather than acts dependent on individuals and societies — in Kafka. Authority as an idea (even when not intended as such) goes up a thematic ladder: Scotland Yard (Christie), British Intelligence (le Carré), Justice (Dostoevsky), God (Kafka). The India of the British Empire is not thematic in Maugham, merely exotic background. It *becomes* thematic in Forster's *A Passage to India*.

Nothing is as boring as the avant-garde when it becomes a formula. In the Playwrights Unit, I saw a whole year's worth of "experimental" one-act plays in which animals talked, people hung on clotheslines, and lines were spoken to the visual counterpoint of two Ping-Pong balls moving up and down in space. How I longed for the curtain (there was one) to go up on a living room, in which a maid, answering a phone, said, "Lady Blah-Blah's residence."

The very work of art against which a new generation must revolt becomes — if you wait long enough — revolutionary. After one has read Burroughs, Sarraute, and Robbe-Grillet for six months, Jane Austen seems like a wild-eyed experimentalist who has just come up with an absolutely new kind of novel.

The truest changes in art are not changes of technique but of sensibility. And so the real pioneers are rarely recognized as such. They are too subtle to make good copy. Examples: Henry Green and Elizabeth Bishop.

Conscience and consciousness are the two great subjects of literature. That's why murder and love are so omnipresent.

But how much time is really spent in most people's lives either making love or committing murder?

If someone wrote a novel whose subject was *work*, it would be new. New and dull.

Auden said that he felt both Yeats and Rilke had lied. Example of first is the end of "Sailing to Byzantium" in the lines "Once out of nature I shall never take / My bodily form from any natural thing, / But such a form as Grecian goldsmiths make / Of hammered gold and gold enamelling. . . ." Auden said nobody wanted to be a mechanical, golden bird. But Yeats's statement is so obviously merely a way of conveying a conception that it doesn't seem like a lie to me. Someone who's going to die says he wishes he could be immortal, like a work of art. But Auden does have a point: would Yeats have wanted to be a golden bird *instead* of W. B. Yeats? The "once" in "Once out of nature" is the catch. Yeats wanted to be a work of art *after* he'd been W. B. Yeats. (Ironically, of course, that's what he is.) I think Auden meant Yeats wanted to be Yeats, alive, and Yeats, forever, and would have been furious to find himself a little golden bird on a golden bough, hammered Greek or otherwise.

The Poet's Story

IN Gorky's *Reminiscences*, he tells of having read some scenes from *The Lower Depths* to Tolstoy. Tolstoy wasn't pleased. He said, "Most of what you say comes out of yourself and therefore you have no characters." And that simple statement says more clearly than anything I know why poets attempt to write fiction. For the self — the *I* — is most typically the viewpoint from which a poem is conceived and written. With a few important exceptions — Homer, Chaucer, Browning — *they*, *you*, *he*, and *she* stand outside the poet — the net of reality, a huge temptation. And in time, I think, most poets fall into that net. It takes courage to enter one's own world with any degree of truth. It takes a different kind of courage to enter the worlds of other people — and, for a writer, a different kind of skill. Poets bring to the task one advantage and the defect of that advantage. Though they have learned to search for the truth, because that search has been directed toward themselves, their interest tends to be parochial or narcissistic or limited to the landscape and the psychology of the ego. That tendency must be overcome before a writer can produce poems of dramatic tension, a legitimate dramatic poem, or fiction. If writing could be conceived of as a religious matter, poets would be admired for being devout and scorned for having committed themselves to the wrong faith.

It would be difficult to make a list of fifty poems of this century that exhibit a true interest in character — character as I think Tolstoy meant it and demonstrated it. Psychology, yes — psychology is all over the place. But it is not the same as character. In fact, the very existence of the word "psychology" reinforces the fragmentation of character. Though we use the word so commonly, it was not always at the tip of everyone's tongue. Psyche was a character in a story before she became an attribute of everyone. Psychology can be dispersed: it can ring true in abstract statement, in insights and perceptions, strike home in a passing observation, and even be demonstrated in figures essentially hollow. And that is not only true of the figures in poetry, when they appear at all. A great deal of what passes for fiction consists of puppet plays; yet the puppets may ring true psychologically. The trouble is they don't necessarily ring true any other way. The shadings are off; if they're emotionally believable *and* interesting — almost anyone can be emotionally believable and dull — there's something wrong with their minds; or they don't walk properly; or they don't speak understandably; they can't swim; some of them can't even drive. I'm not speaking here of the mechanics of fiction, or true-to-life fiction, that low order, where the characters are merely accurate and live on streets that have real names and use the right golf clubs and eat the right entrails. No, I mean something like a mystery story where everything is obviously false with the exception of the motives of the characters (themselves false) in it.

Psychology, then, is the key to character but it is not character itself; after all, a key unlocks the door leading to something else. What is it, then, psychology unlocks? I think you might say that psychology is general and that character is specific. The door must be recognizable in order to be opened. But the room it opens on is capable of infinite variation. It is the credibility of each variation — the ability on the writer's part to describe precisely the individual room and to make it felt — that becomes his task and his difficulty. A chair's a chair . . . but *this* one? The wall is blue . . . but what *kind* of blue? The distinctions become increasingly difficult as one moves from psychological abstraction to characteristic experience. This is true not only of the so-called realistic novel but of any novel, for no matter how fantastic the variation or exquisite the conception, the novelist ultimately tangles with personality. The poet has already fought an analogous battle with imagery, having progressed from the general outburst to the specific metaphor. The struggle with character is similar. The amateur poet fails by making experience general. The amateur novelist universalizes character, and displays his not very fine Italian hand by allowing each character a dominant trait: Gloria is angry, Tom is sad, Helga is weatherbeaten.

Yet if psychology is general and character specific, something further needs to be said. General things are diffused; the specific usually has a direct impact. But in the case of psychology, because it is a medical discipline as well as a word that stands for human insight, the reverse is true. Psychology defines, character eludes — you'd think it would be the other way around. Though it categorizes, psychology tends to be increasingly cautious in its definitions. We now know that a word like "schizophrenia" covers more territory than language permits. Hardly meaningless, it nevertheless demands more and more qualification. And it is precisely in art that those qualifications already exist. Character cannot thrive in the abstract. What may be symptoms to a doctor are ways of behaving to a writer. Take Nicole in *Tender Is the Night*. Dr. Dohmler, at the Swiss clinic, makes a definite diagnosis: "Schizophrenia." But Nicole is more than a schizophrenic. Her charm, her anger, her sexuality, her selfishness, her terror are all made manifest despite the label. And in Chekhov's "Ward Six," Ivan Dmitrich is classically paranoid. Dmitrich would have no force or conviction if he were not subtle, penetrating, and masterful in argument.

Fitzgerald's novel and Chekhov's story are less concerned with mental illness than with its effects on other people — and they have certain resemblances. The leading characters in both are doctors dealing with psychotic behavior, and each of them reverses positions with the very character he is treating. Nicole drains Dick Diver. Dr. Ragin ends up in Ivan Dmitrich's place. But these likenesses are superficial. The overtones of the Fitzgerald novel are psychological, romantic, nostalgic, and, to a limited extent, social. The thrust of "Ward Six" is philosophical and political. It profoundly concerns itself with the difference between being a victim of evil and the luxury of rationalizations about it. It takes the enforced incarceration of Dr. Ragin in his own psychiatric ward to make him see what no amount of learning or training or observation or thought or imagination has been able to illuminate before. Evil is concrete and immediate; it is more than a philosophical abstraction. The sufferings of its victims are real, and those who do nothing in the face of it abet it. "Ward Six" opens up an abyss. An attack on the passivity of Tolstoy's moral theories, and a product of Chekhov's trip to the prison colonies on Sakhalin Island, it is a work of conscience — the most overtly political of all of Chekhov's stories.

"Ward Six" anticipates R. D. Laing by almost half a century. Both Chekhov and Laing test common assumptions, but Dr. Laing is shedding light on a problem Chekhov already understood. It would be false to confuse art, necessarily enigmatic and mysterious — it is always about to utter the unutterable — and science, which must describe, classify, and predict. Yet I would still go to Chekhov, who died in 1904, rather than to Dr. Laing, an expert in the field, to understand the human dimensions of the problem. The truth is, I learned more about the unconscious from reading Proust than from reading Freud.

People who are summed up in a word are people we are lying about. Art questions that lie constantly, by showing us how things really happen to people and, on a more profound level, by its shadings, by the intelligence that fuels its emotional force, and by its range.

Character is elusive not only by being truly reflected from life, where it is hopelessly enigmatic, but because character always has something left over, something not used by the author in the course of the story, novel, or poem. No pool is truly a pool once it has been drained. And so a character must exist outside of his framework — before and after the action. If he has no past or future in the reader's mind — no matter how unconsciously — he hasn't registered completely. Stories are read for thousands of reasons, but anyone who appears in a story has a pre- and a post-reality. An author has one limitation any mother transcends: he cannot give birth to a character; at best, he can catch the baby in swaddling clothes. He *can* kill a character off. In which case, he risks, like all of us, immortality or oblivion.

Immortality or oblivion — like ecstasy and glory — were once fairly common words in poetry, at least in romantic poetry. The poet progresses from lines without imagery meant to convey great feeling, like "the sky is full of joy," to something as specific, say, as Eliot's description of the sky as "a patient etherized upon a table." Vague exultation has become no exultation at all. A poet may reverse the process in the way Stravinsky, after *Le Sacre*, embraced neoclassicism — a very sophisticated embrace — but one might note that, for all its oddness, Eliot's image is supported by the most conventional of iambics. Simplifications of style, leanness of syntax, this or that new kind of poetry always point up the inescapable: after all is said and done, the poet is stuck with the image in the same way the novelist or storyteller is stuck with character. For both, memory is the great source; one doesn't set down, even in the present tense, at whatever level of consciousness, something that is not memorable. For a poet, memory connects — the very function of metaphor, where one thing reminds you of another, or rather, one thing *enlivens* another. For a fiction writer, memory accretes and sums up — the function of meaningful action. But because one term of a metaphor must precede the other, and because accretion involves process, memory is a function of time. That would seem obvious, but time is different for the novelist and the poet, for the fiction writer is dominated by the clock and the poet by the metronome. They are just dissimilar enough — metronomes can be sped up, slowed down, or stopped — to provide a fertile field of transaction.

From the beginning of this century, poetry and fiction have borrowed from each other, imitated each other, and in some cases become each other. Whitman and Rimbaud, an odd couple at first glance, are the godfathers of the prose poem. As prose moved into poetry — Ezra Pound and William Carlos Williams are crucial figures — so poetry moved into prose. Whenever poets escape from meter — Marianne Moore comes to mind — they approach the conditions of prose; the metronome becomes almost inaudible and one glances up at the clock. What is syllabic writing but a counting out? Counting out is not the same as measure, where duration and stress are more critical than number. Whenever prose writers depend heavily on cadence or the image, they move toward poetry.

In Cocteau's film *The Blood of a Poet*, the poet is spewed out of a mirror — Narcissus is being ejected by the pool. A mouth opens in the palm of the poet's hand and cries, "L'aire! L'aire!" That plea for oxygen implies a window. As I remember it, the poet breaks a windowpane and sticks his hand out into the air to let it breathe. But he never bothers to look out. His true adventures occur later when he is swallowed up by the mirror and enters "a hotel of follies." Nevertheless, the point has been made. The mirror is the totem of the poet, who looks *at* and *into* himself, who creates himself, as it were. And I would say the window belongs to the fiction writer, who looks *out* and *around*, and is a product of the world. In the love affair that has occurred in this century, the novelist has flirted with mirrors and the poet with windows. The increasing prominence of confessional writing in poetry and the numbers of fiction writers drawn to documentation suggest a new hardening of positions. Attempts to get at the truth, they may also, I suspect, be forms of camouflage. In telling all, the poet frees himself to deal with character — having been merciless toward himself, he is free to be merciless toward everyone. And the fiction writer, finding plot, character, and relevance preempted by clever mystery writers, excellent filmmakers, and exploiters of the topical, is increasingly drawn to the actual. Where is reality really to be found? In the blood and guts of one's own experience? In the external event examined with the same meticulous detail, the same concern for form, often, that one would bring to fiction?

The twentieth century is rich in great writers, but because Proust is as much an epic poet as a novelist, he is, to my mind, its key literary figure. He saw the significance of windows very clearly and the importance of mirrors by implication. Is there any other book that so strangely combines plunges into the interior of the self with so faultless a portrait of the external world — natural and social? It is obsessive in both directions. And it would be hard to explain away the fact that every crucial sexual scene in *A la Recherche* is seen through a window. I include in that grouping two scenes not ordinarily considered sexual: that one where Marcel looks out at the garden through his bedroom window and sees his parents dining with Swann, the first clue to the subject of voy-

eurism in the novel, and his playing with the magic lantern
in his bedroom, which shortly follows. The theme of the
voyeur — which is spun for us slowly — as well as the device of the magic lantern, tells us more or less the same thing:
for the voyeur, the distinction between windows and mirrors
is psychologically nebulous; the outward scene merely acti-
vates the inner compulsion of the viewer; what he sees is not
the reality of the act but a fantasy implicit in himself. The
disturbed psyche mirrors what is viewed through the window; the seeming observation is a narcissistic turning inward. The voyeur doesn't look at people in order to examine,
understand, or know them, but because they perform — like
marionettes of the unconscious — in a certain way. The *character* of the actors has no meaning, though their physical attributes may be of great significance. And the magic lantern,
projecting images of others, is manipulable. Not only can the
images be chosen but they can be projected at will, and in
Marcel's case, the characters he *thinks* he sees (he later finds
out more about them) do not conform to the fantasies they
first evoke. Moreover, he projects those images where he
pleases: on the door, the wall, the doorknob, and so forth.
Through the magic lantern, Marcel sees fragments of the history of France. That is its window side. It also has a mirror
side. In its repetition of chosen images that lead to fantasy,
its ability to frame a person, an image, or an act (the way a
window provides a frame for a voyeur), and by being physically manipulable, it is, by analogy, a masturbatory device.

In Proust, intelligence has emotional force, but the sexual
scenes often lack sensuality — Albertine and Marcel seem
strangely hermetic, as if the act of going to bed together, the
heart of their struggle, had somehow become metaphysical

before it was consummated. Swann and Odette exude a more gamey flavor. With Marcel and Albertine, we are analyzing feeling rather than experiencing it. We are being tortured, but tortured so intelligently that following the argument almost prevents us from feeling the pain. It soon becomes clear enough that that is what feeling is: pain. Proust was no fool; the window and the mirror, in the hands of the right magician, are interchangeable. That cup of tea out of which Combray is evoked is a mirror of the past but opens a window onto the future. What are mirrors and windows but the glassy fields of dissolution and envy? In the one we watch ourselves decay; through the other we see those things we long for and can never attain or become. What Marcel sees reflected through a window becomes his ultimate reflection — a word almost too luringly usable in Proust's case. In the end, the dirty pictures become focused: Marcel turns out to be as sexually compulsive as Mlle. Vinteuil, Swann, and Charlus.

Using the images that Cocteau and Proust provide as clues, I would say that the distinction between fiction writers and poets is becoming obsolete, that it might be more useful to think of authors as mirror-writers or window-writers. In the same way that liberal members of opposing political parties may be closer to each other in thought and spirit than to the conservative members of their own parties, so certain prose writers are closer to poets than to each other.

In America the two schools stem from two major figures, both poets, who may be viewed as their source: Emily Dickinson, the mirror, and Walt Whitman, the window. If it is confusing to have a poet — Whitman — stand for the generic prose writer, one can at least say that Whitman brought the devices of biblical prose into poetry: repetition, cataloguing, and cadence. It would be hard to find, in any case, another figure who so clearly illustrates what I mean.

Take two superb poems: Dickinson's "Because I could not stop for death," and Whitman's "When lilacs last in the dooryard bloom'd." They have in common the subject of death, but it would be inconceivable for Emily Dickinson to have written an elegy on the death of a public figure, an event external to her life, and a theme whose magnitude derives partly from the power and importance of the subject it mourns. The Dickinson poem, in spite of its intensity, reflects a smaller world. It is measured, literally and figuratively, it is compressed, whereas Whitman's poem is expansive and comes to include, finally, the entire United States. Both are poems of great feeling, perfectly true to themselves, and typical. Whitman's poem, for all its length, is organized around a few images: the star for Lincoln; the lilac for seasonal rebirth; the hermit thrush for Whitman himself. In the course of the poem, Lincoln's body is moved by train across the country. The Dickinson poem uses a similar idea, a carriage ride, sufficient to its scope, and the figure of Death is appropriately a courtier or suitor.

Who is a window? Who is a mirror? Proust may seem too much a mirror, but then one thinks of the party scenes, those gargantuan satires on middle-class and upper-class social life, and a window opens. Chekhov has a house full of windows. Strolling around, one becomes aware that two or three of the panes are mirrored. And in our time, Nabokov is a fine example of both. In spite of being the master depicter of motel life in America, he is essentially a mirror writer. He said: "Time is a fluid medium for the culture of metaphors." Norman Mailer, despite the obvious egotism, is a window writer. Can one imagine Nabokov — or Emily Dickinson — covering a moon launching, the conventions, or a prize-fight? It is not inconceivable, though, to think of Whitman in the role of the evangelical journalist. Good writers hover, like angels caught in a magnetic field, between the mirror and the window.

Some writers hover between, and some are caught between. The poet may decide that not everything can be got down in poetry. And he begins a story or a novel. It would be interesting to make an anthology of the beginnings of poet's novels, especially the unpublished ones. (Unpublished *novels*, not unpublished poets.) I would make a fairly safe bet that the first two pages consist of description in ninety percent of the cases.

We are at a railroad station in Malaya and the sky is turbulent and suffused. In fact, it is raining. It keeps on raining for a long time because the poet is afraid — with good reason — to begin the action, to introduce the inevitable character. Sooner or later, he has to, and Malaya pales before the all-too-recognizable instructor's wife, editor's lover, or professor's mistress. There she is, at the bar, in the hotel, at the counter, and little falsehoods begin to pile up. Some of them are merely the plague of fact. She says she has just had her hair done. Where would she get the hair rinse? The travel book informs us that there are no hairdressers in Malaya, and customs specifically forbids the importation of hair rinse. Or she has just finished a lemon ice. The latest issue of the *National Geographic* tells us that lemon ices have never been introduced into Malaya. But the real difficulty is that she is obviously not the person she is supposed to be. She is either too recognizable or not recognizable enough. Either she changes from minute to minute, or she is hopelessly consistent. Just as conversation is not automatically dialogue, people are not necessarily characters. Who *is* she? She is redheaded and envious. Then she is more envious. And her hair seems to get redder. Later, she is in an absolute rage of envy and completely rubescent. We find out, finally, that she is basically kind. We leave Malaya.

The Malayan novel has not been published — I hope. But poets' novels *are* published, and they stand a better chance than most of ending up at one end of the spectrum or the other. When they're bad, they couldn't be worse, and when they're good, they're superb. Fitfulness and experiment aside, the inner urgency that can lure a poet to prose can, paradoxically, produce work that closely resembles poetry itself. William Faulkner, Malcolm Lowry, Herman Melville, D. H. Lawrence, and James Joyce all started out as poets. Giving up poetry's official title, they continued on its secret missions. Are there really significant differences in the originality of conception, the play of language — the bolt of the imagination in general — between *Moby Dick* and *The Cantos*, between *Ulysses* and *The Waste Land*?

But Ernest Hemingway, Willa Cather, and Muriel Spark started out as poets, too, and in their work, the parting of the ways between fiction and poetry is clearer. The interest in words stays steady, but the language is stripped down, or at least grows sparer; a concern with dramatic structure develops and becomes individual. The metaphor ceases to be central, though the motif may take its place — that double-threading of language and concept that grows significant by repetition. (It is of interest to note how often motif is expressed in metaphor in the titles critics give to their works: *The Hovering Fly* [Tate]; *The Wound and the Bow* [Wilson]; *The Double Agent* [Blackmur]; *Stewards of Excellence* [Alvarez]; *Masks and Mirrors* [Bewley]; *A Sad Heart at the Supermarket* [Jarrell]; etc.) In Muriel Spark's *The Girls of Slender Means*, the words "slender means" take on a double meaning. During a fire, those characters slim enough to squeeze through a tiny bathroom window have the best chance of survival. The title *A Farewell to Arms* says goodbye to two things at once, love and war. But they crop up again in tandem in *For Whom the Bell Tolls*. What is unique in each of these writers, so different from each other, is the unmistakable sound of a voice. Words exhale temperament. We expect that individual voice — we demand it, in fact — in a poet. And though great fiction writers develop who are not poets to begin with — Proust, James, Tolstoy — they all have two qualities we assign to poets: a singularity and an authority of the imagination. Great novelists may be visionaries or enigmatic or focus on a social sewer; yet they must do two things at once: produce a recognizable world and create one of their own. The ability to make the official document personal is the true link between the novelist and the poet, for each stamps experience uniquely. A literary convention is a passport but, like the real thing, it can bear only one signature. When people say that something is Chekhovian or Proustian, it is odd, when you think about it, that they don't say, "That's pre-Revolutionary Russian" or "That's pre–World War I French," the stigma of long-windedness aside. They don't say it because that is not quite what they mean, though what they mean may certainly include the historical perspective and the period flavor. The social, political, economic, and military worlds of Russia and France are documented in many places. It is Chekhov's version and Proust's version that are so telling. What those worlds once were, the very sense of what it meant to be alive in them, has been re-created for us, yet belongs, in each case, to a single writer. It belongs to him because he has transcended it. We don't read Chekhov or Proust only for glimpses into worlds at a remove; we read them for glimpses into ourselves. No one is as egotistical as a reader.

There is the poetry *of* fiction, that quality of magic that comes from the demands of the medium itself, and there is poetry *in* fiction, two very different matters. The latter is an inferior brand if what is meant is merely "poetic prose." Hundreds of writers are labeled "poetic" for the wrong reason — a gift for description. It consists often of being partial to adjectives. At any rate, a gift is not an art. It is the mastery of a theme, a viewpoint, and a language that makes a superb writer. Poets may come to fiction for any number of reasons, but poets *of* fiction, as well as writers who come to it *through* poetry — window or mirror or both — invariably have one thing in common: they have style.

With the exception of those stories in which a poet deliberately turns his back on his usual subjects and methods, and consciously focuses on the classical ingredients of fiction — plot, character, and suspense — stories written by poets have a tendency to mythologize or to symbolize. They bear the mark of the fable.

In John Berryman's story "The Lovers," for instance, a passionate adolescent love affair is shadowed by an older ambiguous relationship, that of the narrator's mother and a stranger who mysteriously keeps turning up at the house. What becomes obvious to the reader is not obvious to the adolescent boy: the man is in love with his mother and she is not in love with him. We know practically nothing about the stranger, yet he achieves an extra dimension. His character is not to be one. His is the fate the narrator unwittingly suffers, the fate of the enchanted lover who, in order to save himself, must remove himself from enchantment. The stranger carries the knowledge the narrator is on the verge of learning, and, as such, he has something of the function, though none of the qualities, of the serpent in Eden. He is the unwelcome tarnisher, experience's bitter messenger. It is not *because* of him but *through* him that the narrator comes to the end of innocence. At the end, we realize that the story's title refers not to the two young lovers at its center but to the two hopeless men, who love and are not loved back.

The boy in the tree in Richard Wilbur's "A Game of Catch," who pretends to will and control each movement of two other boys playing ball, is an uneasy, painful Cain, striking out at others from a desperate isolation — the awful brother, the outsider whose only way of joining is to gain attention by being hateful. In Jean Garrigue's "The Snowfall," only the dead and the rejected finally embody the perfect realizations of love. Like the mother and the grandmother in Mona Van Duyn's "The Bell," the characters in poets' stories often seem larger than life — by their oddness, the glancing intelligence by which they are perceived, the undertow of metaphor that waits in the shallows. Transmutations of one kind or another extend their meanings. The two nameless lovers in James Schuyler's "Life, Death, and Other Dreams," for instance, seem less like characters than

archetypes. In the story's small coda, where the lovers lie
side by side in their graves, it is significant that the narrator
suddenly makes himself evident. Is he warning us — or himself — against the pretensions of art in an attempt to pre-
clude falsity? Is he simply admitting, through his "characters," that he hopes this story will be read? Self-
consciousness is subverted by being included, like the stage
manager's asides to the audience in a Chinese play — as
much a part of the convention as the action. Using awareness
of the medium in the medium itself can result in parody —
like bad movie music signaling the action ahead — but in
Schuyler's story, I take it to be a form of ironic honesty, like
saying "dear reader" to a reader one almost holds dear.

Objectifications can teeter between confession and mate-
rialization. In Elizabeth Bishop's "In Prison," the heroine's
one fantasy and desire is to be imprisoned. That fantasy tells
us not at all who the narrator is but very clearly the kind of
person she'd like to be, and allows the writer extraordinary
moments of landscape engraving, imaginative leaps — the
description of the walls and the courtyard — leaps that seem
more daring in a story so obsessed by confinement. And
there is that moment, too, in Kenneth Koch's "The Postcard
Collection," when the narrator suddenly breaks the thread
and says to an offstage character we don't know, "I love
you" — a break that both undercuts and highlights the speculation the postcards give birth to. In that switch of viewpoint, something about life and art is being said in the sim-
plest and yet most complicated of ways. For the utterance
itself is banal and direct, as if the author were saying,
"Enough of all this artifice and theory — the plain truth is
'I love you.'" Yet the postcards, created by artists of a

kind — there are little poems on the reverse sides — are sent by, and to, real people whose stories the writer is trying to reconstruct from the stained and defaced messages. The writings on the postcards are artful communications within an artful communication; they are at the heart of the story the writer is writing — a piece of artifice in itself. The postcards may be artifacts, the story may be a work of art, but the writer makes one thing clear: *he* is real. And there is that moment in James Merrill's story "Driver," when the protagonist, after a mystical revelation that reveals very little, reveals a *real* mystery to us: he is sixty years old.

There are other mysteries. The one that pervades the way of life of the mountain people in W. S. Merwin's "Return to the Mountains" — every detail is presented realistically, it seems, and yet with that shimmer, that discreet secrecy, which lets us know that what might seem obvious is not quite within our grasp. When the animals turn, like natural compasses, and point in one direction, and the narrator comes upon the strange balletlike action of old women sewing cauls — we are moved by . . . what? The venerableness of the symbols? The secret of life withheld from the narrator, as it may well be from us? The strange mixture of the exotic and the mundane that gives the story its flavor? Like Merwin's poems, "Return to the Mountains" is visionary in the most literal sense in that the use of the eye is the paradoxical key to what cannot be seen. It makes us aware that there is more than we can see, the revelation of which can never be final. The significant figures in Merwin's story are not characters but a chorus, and it appears with the force of a vision at the end.

Stories written by poets usually take place somewhere be-

tween the window and the mirror — stories of revelation ob-
jectified to a point, but not to the point of realism. They
bear the poet's particular badge: the mysterious and the real
held in suspension. You know more when you finish their
stories than you can say. If they could have been reduced to
statement, there would have been no point in writing them.

PART THREE

EUDORA WELTY

The Lonesomeness
and Hilarity of Survival

Losing Battles, Eudora Welty's novel, begins with a rooster crowing and the moon going down "one day short of the full." Although the day is specific — an August Sunday in the nineteen thirties, in the northeastern hill country of Mississippi, near the small town of Banner — the dawn we witness seems more like the first morning of the world. By the time the novel is over, the rich local speech of its characters has managed another note: the sound of a chorus telling its version of the story of the human race. One tale made up of many, layer on layer, the novel advances in a series of rural-comedy scenes that recall the head-on collisions and mock calamities of slapstick farce. But its real action winds downward and backward into the past through remembered incidents, each voice supplying another thread of the tangled story of the Vaughn, Renfro, and Beecham families as they gather to celebrate the ninetieth birthday of Elvira Jordan

Vaughn — Granny. Granny is eventually the center of a throng of people — her grandchildren, her great-grandchildren, babies, friends, neighbors, strangers — and dogs. Surrounding her, the crowd is itself surrounded by a natural world described in deliberately metaphorical terms; the long comedy is suffused by nature, not played against it, and it departs from the natural only through the machine and the homemade (the wreck of a truck, a banged-up school bus, a tin roof, a makeshift wedding dress) — the broken-down engines of poverty and the ingenious charms that ward it off.

Because *Losing Battles* is social rather than psychological, it is focused on the group. None of its characters occupies the stage for long; stage center belongs to the chorus. Its hero, therefore, is a *real* hero, in the theatrical sense, and his arrival is prepared for as carefully as the entrance of the lead in a romantic comedy. Nineteen-year-old Jack Renfro, who has served two years in the pen for trying to rescue Granny's gold ring while protecting his sister's honor, escapes from jail the day before he would have been paroled, in order to attend Granny's reunion. And when he appears, he is everything we expected: charming, undauntable, true-blue — the spunky teenager of the comic strip, the golden boy of legend. Yet in his seemingly competent hands the world continually flies apart. Waiting for him are his orphan-wife and former teacher, Gloria, and the baby he has never seen. As Jack, Gloria, and the baby — the tiny family inside the big one — wander away once or twice to undergo their adventures, a rival center of the story comes to light: an offstage character, Julia Mortimer, the teacher at the Banner school, whose career has spanned the generations. A disruptive force in the impoverished but exuberant lives of the Banner farmers, she is resisted, but her strength matches theirs, not so much in a losing battle as in a battle of equal powers — that is, until hers fail. The day of Granny's reunion turns out to be the day Julia Mortimer dies.

The coincidence is appropriate; Granny and Miss Mortimer, though never in conflict in the narrative, are opposed powers in the novel. Granny, the "source" of the more than fifty people present, hands on the torch of biological renewal. Miss Mortimer dreams of handing on a torch of a different kind; she has a vision of a stream of teachers and students following in her path, the bearers of a tradition of learning and knowledge. Gloria Renfro is the pivotal character between the two older women, the unwitting carrier of a double heritage, for she is both Miss Mortimer's chosen protégée and Jack Renfro's wife, both the mate and the educator of her husband. Lacking Miss Mortimer's sense of commitment and Jack's capacity for love in general, Gloria is endearing and life-size, a game fighter caught between larger forces — and, just possibly, a winner.

Granny's reunion is a day of revelations, each erasing a mystery, only to leave another in its place. When Judge Moody, the man who sentenced Jack, arrives, battle-scarred, after a scene that Harold Lloyd would have appreciated (the Judge abandons his Buick, its motor running, as it dangles precariously on top of a hill, the object of punishing attempts at rescue, including a charge of dynamite), he, too, it turns out, has secret information: a letter scrawled by Miss Mortimer before her death. He reads it as night falls over the reunion. In it Miss Mortimer sums up her life:

"I've had it driven in on me — the reason I never could win for good is that both sides were using the same tactics. . . . A teacher teaches and a pupil learns or fights against learning with

the same force behind him. It's the survival instinct. It's a
mighty power, it's an iron weapon while it lasts. It's the desperation of staying alive against all odds that keeps both sides encouraged. But the side that gets licked gets to the truth first.
When the battle's over, something may dawn there — with no
help from the teacher, no help from the pupil, no help from the
book. . . . Now that . . . I can survey the years, I can see it
all needs doing over, starting from the beginning. . . . I'm alive
as ever, on the brink of oblivion, and I caught myself once on
the verge of disgrace. Things like this are put in your path to
teach you. You can make use of them, they'll bring you one
stage, one milestone, further along your road. You can go crawling next along the edge of madness, if that's where you've come
to. There's a lesson in it. You can profit from knowing that you
needn't be ashamed to crawl — to keep on crawling, to be
proud to crawl to where you can't crawl any further. Then you
can find yourself lying flat on your back — look what's carried
you another mile. . . . And there's something I want to impart
to you. . . . It's a warning. There's been one thing I never did
take into account. Watch out for innocence."

Julia Mortimer's last and biggest lesson is that lessons
come from life, not from books, and she is buried not under
the doorstep of the Banner school, as she requested, but in
an ordinary grave. Banner takes her in, at last, all too literally.

The small-town values, the Baptist and Methodist sureties
that permeate *Losing Battles*, could easily seem remote — a
world under glass. Miss Welty transcends the narrow range
of its action without shifting focus or underlining a point.
From under the comic surface of the novel the vapors of the
dungeon rise. Brutality, senility, death, and murder make

their appearances, as ominous as the coffin in the back of the gravedigger's truck when he turns up, unbidden, at the reunion. And certain scenes have a startling, primitive intensity. When the mystery of Gloria's parents seems about to be solved, when it seems likely that she has always been a part of the family and is therefore a first cousin of Jack's, she cries out, "I don't want to be a Beecham! . . . I won't be a Beecham!" The gathered aunts, crying "Say Beecham!," throw her to the ground and force her to swallow chunks of watermelon, the juice covering her face and body like blood. The domestic, female world of food, child-rearing, and gossip suddenly takes on the shock of an initiation or a sacrifice. Granny gets up on a table to dance — a macabre bit of theater.

When violence crops up in *Losing Battles*, it is always in scale. The humor, on the other hand, is not; it is outsize, a humor of accordionlike expansion — the slow take, the double take, the take repeated. The long-windedness of Judge Moody's Buick scene is an integral part of what makes it funny: attempts to rise from the dust only fix the strivers more deeply in it. Losing battlers are dogged; they go on and on. The novel is not symbolic, an allegory or a parable, but as its characters stumble into a series of follies, which in turn lead to more, this effect of mistake piled upon mistake, this sense of endless wasted effort, reverberates largely in a book whose basic ingredients are the big ones: birth, love, and death — each leading to the others in endless repetition. In *Losing Battles*, it is effort and resistance that count. The title is ironic; there are no victories other than survival.

As comical and feeling as it is, *Losing Battles* is neither ingratiating nor sentimental. In its large design, human meanness and failure are given their just due. There are no false notes. Because nothing is shirked and nothing is whimsical, poverty never makes a sociological point. It isn't picturesque; it doesn't call for pity. No one in *Losing Battles* is a freak or a statistic. The ties that bind its people together are as necessary as water. Everyone (except Jack's young brother) is a prodigal talker, for the sound of the human voice is a major entertainment and a source of security; it has staying power. The people sing hymns, they listen to a sermon, they talk on through the day and into the night; the way a tale is told has as much value as the truth it tells. The idea that these characters are simpleminded or buffoons or hillbillies or crackers never comes up; Miss Welty is too good and too just a writer. And in the character of Granny she earns our complete confidence. Granny could, in other hands, have been maudlin or idiosyncratic. Here, perfectly poised and funny as hell, she eludes the obvious as well as the eccentric.

Losing Battles is the attempt of people in a history book they can't quite read to tell and reshape their story, to explain how it never was and never could be what it first appears to be. In one splendid passage Miss Welty makes her theme clear:

"And we're sitting here in the dark, ain't we?" said somebody.

"Turn on them lights, then, Vaughn!" Uncle Dolphus called. "Why did you let 'em snake in here and hook you up to current for? For mercy's sakes let's shine!"

Suddenly the moonlit world was doused; lights hard as pick-axe blows drove down from every ceiling and the roof of the passage, cutting the house and all in it away, leaving them an island now on black earth, afloat in night, and nowhere, with only each other. In that first moment, every face, white-lit but with its caves of mouth and eyes opened wide, black with the lonesomeness and hilarity of survival, showed its kinship to Uncle Nathan's, the face that floated over theirs. For the first time, all talk was cut off, and no baby offered to cry. Silence came travelling in on solid, man-made light.

Mostly talk (and what talk!), *Losing Battles* brings to life voices that are individually characteristic and yet archetypal. The folk tale, the metaphor, and the realistic novel have been welded into a single sound. For its author, a pastoral clearly needs farmers. The result is an epic of kin rather than a family chronicle, specifically American in its speech but universal in its poetry, as if Mark Twain and the Shakespeare of *A Midsummer Night's Dream* had collaborated in celebrating three basic human rituals: a birthday, a wedding, and a funeral.

EUDORA WELTY

A House Divided

Eᴜᴅᴏʀᴀ ᴡᴇʟᴛʏ's novel *The Optimist's Daughter*, which first
appeared in *The New Yorker* of March 15, 1969, is a miracle
of compression, the kind of book, small in scope but profound in its implications, that rewards a lifetime of work. Its
style is at the service of a story that follows its nose with the
instincts of a good hunting dog never losing the scent of its
quarry. And its story has all those qualities peculiar to the
finest short novels: a theme that vibrates with overtones, suspense, and classical inevitability.

Known as a "Southern regionalist," Miss Welty is too good
for pigeonholing labels. Though she has stayed close to
home, two interlocking notions have been demonstrated in
her fiction: how easily the ordinary turns into legend, and
how firmly the exotic is grounded in the banal. They are
subjects only partly dependent on locale. In *The Optimist's
Daughter* we are in the South once more, but a South where

real distinctions are made between Texas and Mississippi, and Mississippi and West Virginia. And if place has been Miss Welty's touchstone, the pun implicit in the word "place" comes alive in her new novel; its colloquial meaning — caste, class, position — is as important as its geographical one.

When Laurel Hand, a Mississippian living in Chicago, is summoned to a New Orleans hospital to join her father, a seventy-one-year-old judge who is about to undergo a critical eye operation, she clashes with his new, and second, wife, Fay. Laurel is a withdrawn widow still mourning for a husband killed in World War II, and Fay is a childish vulgarian embarked on the one secure relationship of her life. The conflict between these middle-aged women begins a war between worlds hopelessly at odds. Out of the discordant jumble of three lives trapped in a claustrophobic hospital room, a fourth figure emerges — Becky, the judge's first wife.

Because the struggle between Laurel and Fay is a battle of values, it takes place inside Laurel as well; she is forced for the first time in her life to examine what she believes in. The judge, hovering in some twilight zone of pain, immobilized by sandbags, is set upon by Fay, who breaks down under the tension. Though she is not the direct cause of his death, she is implicated in it. From Laurel's point of view, Fay scares him to death. Later, Fay claims that she was trying "to scare him into life." It is a tribute to Miss Welty's skill and fairness that we are able to entertain the notion seriously.

Still, there is a danger in *The Optimist's Daughter* of the case being stacked, of Laurel being too much the gentlewoman, and Fay too harshly the brash opportunist. In truth, Fay is a horror but eludes being evil. Barely two-dimensional, she is saved by being credibly stupid. Naïveté doesn't make her any less destructive but saves her from being malevolent. Laurel is too nice but escapes being a prig. If Fay were a monster and Laurel simply nostalgic, the arena of the action would shrink. What we would have would be case histories. Miss Welty redresses the balance in two ways.

She does something necessary by sketching in Laurel's background in a few delicate strokes. Her childhood days at Becky's mountaintop house in West Virginia, which recall Becky's childhood as well, are the most beautiful pages in the Welty canon, extraordinary passages in an extraordinary book. They yield more than the eye at first takes in. A rural world of innocence comes flying into the imagination as pure as a primary color; its arrival is real, not romantic, and gives genuine weight to a way of life Laurel must eventually abandon. As for Fay, the author does something audacious: she takes on Fay's family. The surprise appearance of the Chisoms — Fay's relatives — at the judge's funeral in Mississippi enlarges the frame of the novel, which is being widened, actually, from two directions: Laurel's past, and the future implicit in Fay.

The funeral itself is macabre and funny, like most funerals. Large emotions center the scene, but somewhere, not too far off in the distance, the edges begin to crinkle; life not being geared to deal with its big moments, comedy sneaks in the back door, a neutralizing antidote to the intensity of the book's strongly felt loyalties and losses.

Though they exist under the shadow of her domination and menace, Fay's relatives make solid claims on life — vitality and endurance — that have to be weighed against Lau-

rel's tradition and understanding. Fay is crude; her family is
common as dirt, but they make their point: it takes dirt to
make things grow. The difference between the crude Texan
and the genteel Mississippian is easy to know but hard to do,
and harder to do right. And more than Texas and Mississippi
are involved. An onrushing world of shoddy materialism but
of attractive energy is set against a vanishing world of civilized values but of special privilege.

Two kinds of people, two versions of life, two contending
forces in America collide in *The Optimist's Daughter*. Its small
dramatic battle sends reverberations in every direction.

Miss Welty is equally adept at redneck lingo, mountain
twang, and the evasions of middle-class speech, but it is her
inability to falsify feelings that gives the novel its particular
sense of truth. Fay doesn't only represent something; she *is*
something. And Laurel takes on flesh and blood as she is
slowly drawn back through time into the circumstances of
Becky's death. The judge's death is tragic, but there is something more tragic still, the separation of the sick and the
doomed from the people who love them. An unbreachable
wall, in Becky's case, turns the living into the enemies of the
dying and isolates them, on opposite sides, helpless.

An instructive scene that at first seems a digression underlines the moral subtlety of the novel. Four old-lady friends
of Laurel's are gossipping in the garden the day after the
funeral. Their malice toward Fay is well honed and well deserved, but an uncomfortable question formulates itself:
wouldn't any stranger intruding on the provincial bastion of
Mount Salus, lovable and loyal though it may be to its self-
elected members, get the same treatment? Fay is raked over
the coals, yet Laurel, the one person who has reason to hate

her, overhears rather than participates in the conversation. She can't stomach Fay, but she can't stomach this ganging up on Fay either. Because Laurel can see two things at once in a world where it's better to see only one, her position is complex but weakened. Her kind of moral strength has, inevitably, its corollary weakness. There's one truth she can't get around: Fay was her father's wife, and she didn't storm the gates of Mount Salus, she was invited in.

In a final confrontation scene, Laurel and Fay meet head-on. In the back of a cupboard, Laurel discovers an old breadboard — a beautifully carved and finished piece of wood made by her husband for her mother — now moldy, scratched, ragged, stained by cigarette butts. As if she still had something to protect, Laurel, in the face of Fay's insults and condescension, finds herself holding the board over her head, a symbol of everything, but now a potential weapon. When Fay tells Laurel that she doesn't know how to fight, Laurel suddenly realizes that Fay doesn't know what they're fighting for, that to win this particular battle, to *want* to win it, is already to have lost it. Fay's victory is to have inherited the house, but its human values, the meaning of the life that has been lived in it, escapes her, as it always has and always will. Laurel's victory is to have those values, finally, so firmly before her. But those values are all she has.

The scene is dramatically climactic but thematically inconclusive. When Laurel lets go of the breadboard, she isn't thinking of her dead father or her dead mother or her dead husband but, oddly, of *Fay's* nephew, Wendell, a little boy from Madrid, Texas, who attended the funeral without the faintest notion of what he was seeing or hearing. It is because of *him* that Laurel lays down her weapon, relinquishing the past to the dead at last. When she does, the question of whether there is to be a future assumes importance, for a fact that floated behind the scenes becomes apparent at the same moment: she and Fay share a common emptiness; both of them are widowed and childless. No matter who wins, that emptiness will echo across the rooms of what was once the most distinguished house in Mount Salus, or be replaced, ultimately, by new voices.

The best book Eudora Welty has ever written, *The Optimist's Daughter* is a long goodbye in a very short space not only to the dead but to delusion and to sentiment as well.

JEAN RHYS

Going to Pieces

In the current Jean Rhys revival, the last of her novels to be reprinted (though not to be written), *Voyage in the Dark* (1934), shares a theme with her other novels of the twenties and thirties — *Quartet* (1928), *After Leaving Mr. Mackenzie* (1930), and *Good Morning, Midnight* (1939) — and even with *Wide Sargasso Sea* (1966), a rather different affair from its predecessors. For most people, love and the act of love are the greatest accusations they ever make against the falsehoods of society; we are one thing as lovers and something totally different as working, social, and political creatures. The disparity is as old as Adam and Eve, but the truly innocent (as distinct from the merely chaste) cannot bear it, and that notion is either central or implicit in all the novels. Sins of the flesh, therefore, are often not sins at all but their opposite: innocence, unbelieving, trying to restore itself. What the world makes of this kind of virtue is something else again, and there is not one Rhys heroine (each a species of a generic one) who does not innocently, and somewhat lazily, come up against the Philistines. The latter are sometimes masked as bohemians but are not to be distinguished from the chief enemies — the bourgeoisie and the authorities. Respectability is the great antagonist. It is also the despised haven.

The pattern of the Rhys heroine is set by Marya Zelli in *Quartet* — an unsuccessful actress–chorus girl turned artist's model or mannequin, who slowly drifts toward the vaguer forms of prostitution and is picked up variously by younger men equally wounded — middle-class Englishmen trying to revive themselves — or aging gentlemen fending off, or cynically making the most of, their last illusions — all unable to say what they feel, all afraid of being used, of giving in to emotions damaging to self-esteem. And the truth of the matter is that the men are spoilers, searching out the weak case, just as the women — most superbly realized in *After Leaving Mr. Mackenzie* — can be formidable. One grows formidable by having nothing to lose, by being free of hope. This involuntary process doesn't necessarily work to one's advantage. Meanness here derives from the need to defend that scrap of self-respect each person carries inside him like a furled flag. Even Mr. Mackenzie, even Heidler, a monster of selfishness in *Quartet* — modeled after Ford Madox Ford, an early sponsor of Miss Rhys's work — have a certain pathos, a kind of sinking familiarity, as if the women they help do in were also a denied part of themselves. The awful thing is to come up against someone who won't play by the rules, someone who knows and is willing to say the rules are lies. But one can stay innocent too long. Truthsayers are also threats — to themselves as well as the men they involve. Stupidity and cru-

elty are parceled out on both sides. Relationships are barters
and chillingly ambivalent — the trading of a moment of affection or sex for a dinner or two, a hotel room, some ready
cash.

The connection between love and money may be Miss
Rhys's most original contribution to the history of emotional
exploitation. For everything in society is geared to revealing
power as masculine and to hiding the thousand subtle ways
by which power uses money to enslave. And hers are novels
of subjugation: the fat cat and the underdog tied together by
invisible threads; subjugation either by addiction — sex or
drink — or by the manipulation of passivity. Sensuality is at
war with will and can be worked on, from varying distances,
to escape the worst of human conditions — isolation. The
aging gamine whom Miss Rhys pursues through these books
with a relentlessness as cool as it is remarkable, considering
the unmistakable autobiographical flavor, slowly goes to
pieces. Living day to day, mostly in Paris, at one hotel a
little seedier than the one before, she is a girl (later a woman)
to whom an encounter, a drink, a sunset, a bar of music have
the enchantments they have in life, but who comes to see
them, finally, as ends in themselves. Sensuousness in these
books is comforting — perhaps their only comfort. And their
chief psychological state is uneasiness. Miss Rhys writes of
this with an acuteness other writers reserve for madness, and
she sees the strong connection between these states of mind.
To hate the respectable world and to be dependent on it, to
be rebellious and helpless at the same time, produces resig-
nation and rage; there are no more uncomfortable bedfellows. This psychological state is mirrored in a social one: if
Marya Zelli, Anna Morgan, Julia Martin, and Sasha Jansen

are on the market, ready to be martyred, the male middle class knows a victim when it sees one, being so easily victimized itself. In this case, the predators and the prey are warily conscious of how quickly one step down leads to humiliation and one step up to anonymity and safety. Julia, in *After Leaving Mr. Mackenzie*, and Sasha, in *Good Morning, Midnight*, are on to the game, but they have no more idea of how to change the rules than they have the power to do so. To be a sort of aristocrat of the emotions and a penniless pretty girl, unable to *do* anything, is to be vulnerable. Money is never there when it is needed, affection is elusive when it might be most healing. The girls are too bright and, most of the time, too feeling to use weapons in return. They are slowly driven out of their wits by the harshness and unnaturalness of the world, by its lack of affection and warmth. They come into the world unarmed, and the world smashes them —"smash" is a particularly meaningful word for Miss Rhys — in an unequal war. The battles take place at a restaurant table, a hotel desk, a bar, or an interview — any of the small vectors of power where the victim and the victimizer juggle the balances.

But mainly these beauties are victims of themselves and of time, which has its own sliding scale — the necessary, the bearable, the desperate. They have the blindfold quality of stutterers walking in darkness, unable to speak when speech is required, unable to move, except from room to room, from hotel to hotel, from lover to lover. And when the lovers run out, the one-night stand takes their place. To get to the *tabac*, the beauty parlor, sometimes even downstairs is to walk the prison round. These are novels of dispossession written by someone with a strong sense of place. If all this sounds like "privileged despair" (to use Kenneth Tynan's phrase), it doesn't read like it. Every centimeter of torture is carefully measured out, and with an exactness and a lack of sentimentality all the more painful for being temperamentally unavoidable. To be wretched to the very roots of existence yet to be coolheaded, watching the wretchedness, is the fate of these women, and particularly of Sasha, in *Good Morning, Midnight*, for that book is the culmination of the story, the last sounding of the theme, and the most abstract of the novels, ending with Sasha's ghostly seduction by a man in a white dressing gown who, like a fateful moth, has flittered, seemingly unimportant, through the corridors of her hotel. When he moves from the corridor into the bedroom, he sums up Sasha's fate as he sums up all the strangers, charming and dreadful, who wander in and out of the first four novels. A dead child haunts two of them, the husbands and lovers have different names, but it is the same story we are reading, over and over, in various degrees of intensity, at different stages of the same career — the story of an exile from life, sometimes dressed in an expensive fur coat, a relic of former affluence, who is broke, aging, and alone.

Voyage in the Dark is the most harrowing of the novels because it is the most realistic, a love story that takes place in the present, where no marriage, no broken framework is to be taken for granted from the start. The girl is Anna Morgan, and to counteract the gray drabness of the London skies she keeps remembering scenes from her childhood on the island of Dominica — Miss Rhys's birthplace, where she spent her first sixteen years. But it is only in *Wide Sargasso Sea* that she is able to put together her two landscapes — the West Indies and England. Its ending leads us to the attic in *Jane*

Eyre where the first Mrs. Rochester is confined. In capitaliz-
ing on the fact that the first Mrs. Rochester was born in the
West Indies, and by working backward, Miss Rhys has
opened up a seam in the Brontë novel and then resewn it
with her own peculiar needle. It is a spellbinding book, labeled in its present hideous paperback edition a "Gothic,"
but it bears about as much resemblance to the genre as *The
Turn of the Screw* does to the ordinary ghost story. Good as it
is, something too theatrical attaches to it. For the first time,
Miss Rhys uses the landscape of her childhood as more than
a contrasting backdrop; its tropical color and languor are released as if they had been held under pressure for a long
time. But she has fused it with something bookish, and what
might have been the most personal of the novels is the most
literary. In spite of its staginess, it is marvelously adroit tech-
nically — each of its three sections is told from a different
viewpoint — but, more important, a world is at last revealed
to us that we can transpose backward, with some hesitation,
but with some meaning, to the books as a whole.

And that is the world of magic — the West Indian staples
of voodoo, witchcraft, and possession. It throws a shadow
rather than a glimmer on the psychology of the earlier novels, for the idea that one is being forced to behave rather than
willing one's behavior is a notion as common to the mentally
disturbed as to those who believe in magical forces. One's
fate is held in someone else's hands; and, as we watch An-
toinette turn into the crazed Mrs. Rochester, the passivity
of the earlier heroines takes on a different cast. Not only is
there an exaggerated notion of the male's powers to complete, but magic accrues to certain acts that will soothe and
heal. Clothes are very important in this respect, and so are

makeup and mirrors — strange little throwbacks, once they are looked at this way, to a world far more primitive than Paris or London. It makes us realize, perhaps for the first time, how dominant the idea of fear is in Miss Rhys's work. It is as if behind the scenes in the first four books a world had been withheld that doesn't explain action or motivation but colors them in a new and revealing way. To be down on one's luck is to overvalue the chance rescue, to give it a significance it doesn't quite have. Once that significance is granted, the way is clear for seeing significance in everything. And that, in turn, opens the door for the arrival of the gods.

Though *Wide Sargasso Sea* is the most dramatic of the novels, it is the least telling in the Rhys canon precisely because the heroine *does* go mad, and because she commits a final demonic *act* — the burning of Thornfield Hall. Miss Rhys's specialty is neither action nor madness but the precipitants that precede them. The suicide at the coastline, not the floating corpse, is her real subject. *Wide Sargasso Sea* is an ingenious tour de force, but it is not the genuine Rhys article. For the earlier novels — and particularly *After Leaving Mr. Mackenzie* and *Good Morning, Midnight* — are unlike anything else in English. They bear a close allegiance to the tight French short novel expanded to its limits, rather than the cumulative drama of build-up and crisis. Colette comes to mind, but briefly. The music-hall flavor suggests a connection, but there is a finer sense of social institutions in the English writer and a far less developed concern for the natural and the familial. The relationship between Colette and Sido would, I think, have been outside Miss Rhys's range (one never thinks of her as having parents), though the relationships between Hester and her stepdaughter, Anna, in *Voyage in the Dark*, and between the two sisters, Julia and Norah, in *After Leaving Mr. Mackenzie*, are poisonous and true but somehow exceptions, and rather surprising in the work as a whole. Yet Miss Rhys knows something about bureaucratic humiliation, the cold machinery of prisons and hotels, which either escaped Colette or escaped her interest, for Colette is basically a joyous writer and Miss Rhys a despairing one.

The difficulty of saying how or why her books seem so original may be a sign of their authenticity. They seem peculiarly timeless for works focused on such particular times and places as the twenties and thirties in London and Paris. A casualness of style, a natural sense of form suggest either the consummate letter writer or an arduousness belied by their surfaces. They are novels of streets and rooms as unforgettable as maps if one had to navigate by them, yet they manage inside their small frames to be significant. They have the quality of the best books by seeming to have written themselves, and, reading them, one flinches at truth after truth. *Tigers Are Better-Looking* (1974), a collection of short stories, has been brought out by Harper & Row. Miss Rhys is being resurrected in bits. The best story is the first one, "Till September Petronella," in which the now-familiar central figure goes off to join an artist and a music critic, and the girl friend of one of them, in the country. It is a perfect Rhys novel in miniature, a bonsai of compression. It, and a story about a West Indian woman in London, "Let them Call it Jazz," funny and pathetic by turns, are the high points. Selections from her very first book, *The Left Bank* (1927), are included, with its original introduction by Ford Madox Ford.

The right word for these is "sketches," and most of them *are* dated and trifling. They have some historical interest, they fill in a gap. The story is not as congenial to Miss Rhys as — I was about to say the novel. But it is her *version* of the novel I mean — which reads as if a piece of French literature had happened to be written in English — and it is hers alone.

ELIZABETH BOWEN

Interior Children

FOR a writer, the wrong reputation can be as deadly as none. Elizabeth Bowen was always noted, but not always for the right reasons. Although she died as recently as 1973, her reputation had begun petering out in the sixties, when to mention love seemed frivolous, and the word "civilization" began to give off a slight stench. Elizabeth Bowen was a civilized writer preoccupied with human relationships. Since her death, the social setting against which the novels are played out has vanished more quickly than anyone could have predicted, and the novels have not had time to slip into the permanent shelters of the more constrained worlds of, say, Trollope and Jane Austen. Although she was alive at the beginning of the last decade, Elizabeth Bowen may be an unknown writer to the present generation. With the exception of *Pictures and Conversations*, a collection of autobiographical writings and other fragments, which was published in

1975, and a paperback edition of *The Death of the Heart* (1938), her books have been hard to find for years. In a recent biography, Victoria Glendinning stated the case for her subject in a few sentences: "She is a major writer; her name should appear in any responsible list of the ten most important fiction writers in English on [the British] side of the Atlantic in this century. . . . She is what happened after Bloomsbury . . . the link that connects Virginia Woolf with Iris Murdoch and Muriel Spark." Now, happily, Avon Books is reprinting all the novels, in paperback — starting backward, with *Eva Trout* (1968).

When she hit on the phrase "the death of the heart," Elizabeth Bowen hit on the key to all her fiction. Her characters, cut off from natural growth, either achieve a worldliness that catches them up short or remain interior children — dissemblers to the world. Thwarted feeling runs through the novels, and landscape plays a special role: nature is not only descriptive but thematic, and sets in bold relief the submerged emotions and sexual detours typical of Bowen's characters, who are plunged into atmospheres recognizable but timeless, as if the owner of a travel agency in the thirties (Emmeline in *To the North*, of 1932) or the head of an international conglomerate (Constantine in *Eva Trout*) were to be found in the Forest of Arden. I can think of no other writer capable of creating Arcadias so oddly sulfurous, in which schoolmistresses, shop owners, moonstruck juveniles, and retired army majors wander; yet the backgrounds never seem incongruous. Because Bowen's command of social comedy is authoritative, her dialogue demanding, and the psychological tension subtle, I don't think it has been noticed that the settings, which pass for versions of reality, are heightened — a unique blend of precise description and landscapes that could exist only in the imagination. Natural or urban, they transform themselves quickly into a series of dissolving and reforming paintings. Here is Karen arriving by boat from England at Cork in *The House in Paris* (1935):

On the left shore, a steeple pricked up out of a knoll of trees, above a snuggle of gothic villas; then there was the sad stare of what looked like an orphanage. A holy bell rang and a girl at a corner mounted her bicycle and rode out of sight. The river kept washing salt off the ship's prow. Then, to the right, the tree-dark hill of Tivoli began to go up, steep, with pallid stucco houses appearing to balance on the tops of trees. Palladian columns, gazebos, glass-houses, terraces showed on the background misted with spring green, at the tops of shafts or on toppling brackets of rock, all stuck to the hill, all slipping past the ship. . . .

The river still narrowing, townish terraces of tall pink houses under a cliff drew in. In one fanlight stood a white plaster horse; clothes were spread out to dry on a briar bush. Someone watching the ship twitched back a curtain; a woman leaned out signalling with a mirror: several travellers must be expected home. A car with handkerchiefs fluttering drove alongside the ship. On the city side, a tree-planted promenade gave place to boxy warehouses; a smoky built-over hill appeared beyond Tivoli. But Cork consumes its own sound: the haze remained quite silent.

Because of the prevailing notion of being cut off from the natural, of being expelled from a garden, an oblique view of the Creation shapes Bowen's fiction. In her version of the Fall, the gifts of sexuality and knowledge provide the temptation to be human, not evil. Compared to being human, being evil is an easy achievement — it lacks shading. The story of the Creation is moral and possibly funny — never have two people been given such lavish gifts and made to pay for them so quickly and so drastically. To be moral and to be funny are qualities inimical to our age when taken together, but they are the very stuff and weather of Austen and Wilde. All the essential stories (with the exception of the miraculous conjuring of Eve out of a rib) are embedded in the original triangle of man, woman, and tempter. What Bowen saw was how the qualities that save us in one way destroy us in another, and she dealt always in doubles, not only in having major characters underlined by minor counterparts — Lois and Livvy in *The Last September* (1929), Portia and Lilian in *The Death of the Heart* — but in the very depiction of character itself. Portia, the center of the reader's compassion, is at the same time a terrible bore. Stella, in *The Heat of the Day* (1949), is intelligent and yet a pawn. Karen, in *The House in Paris*, is sensitive in regard to her aunt's doom yet evasive and cowardly when it comes to Leopold, her illegitimate child. Leopold is rescued, but not by her, and, as always in a Bowen novel, a larger problem looms: without her, can it be considered a rescue? The heart died hard and is capable of a unique extinction: it tends to expire over and over.

After *The Death of the Heart*, Elizabeth Bowen was tagged as a writer for whom adolescence provides special insights, but her true subject is manipulation — emotional, social, sexual — and particularly the compelling power of the past to direct, compromise, and destroy the living. The late-blooming passion of Irene and Mr. Quayne provides *The Death of the Heart* with the heart in question, but it also adds just the right historical flavor of disheveled romance to the foreground. The letters that Jane finds in the attic in *A World of Love* (1955) — letters written to her mother by a soldier killed in the First World War — become a source of fantasy more meaningful than any reality she has yet known. And Mme. Fisher, an ancient witch, flat on her sickbed in an upstairs room in *The House in Paris*, having destroyed one generation with her neurotic need to dominate, is still busily maneuvering for the control of a second. Throughout Bowen's fiction, convention and habit are not as lethal an enemy of feeling as is doubt. Ambiguity is most brutal to the young, who fight for a single-edged interpretation of the world, only to come up against larger and more baffling uncertainties. The battleground is usually a house, itself double-edged — its architecture and history suggesting the solidity of structure, but a structure whose walls are always shaken by the pressure of the lives lived within them, leading either to decompression or to explosion. In Bowen novels, the two sides of the coin clash, and nowhere more sharply than in the unfinished "The Move-In," the last fiction of hers that we have, in *Pictures and Conversations*, where a carful of young people arrive at night demanding to be let into an establishment (a house) that refuses to admit them.

The battlers are mainly women. The enigmatic men — Markie (*To the North*), Eddie (*The Death of the Heart*), even Henry (*Eva Trout*) — are charming, demanding, and undependable: quicksand into which the female characters stumble. Deeply uneasy, hopeless when not provided with roles, the men often bring an irrelevant and unwanted integrity to bear on situations no longer responsive to it — Edward in *Friends and Relations* (1931), Major Brutt in *The Death of the*

Heart. And there are the malevolent males, each with a beneficent side — Julian in *To the North*, and St. Quentin in *The Death of the Heart*. Compassionate irony is reserved for young males, a touch of gleeful malice for divorcées and obstreperous adolescent girls. The social comedy, even in *Friends and Relations*, is never pure — the psychological insights are too penetrating. *A World of Love* is something else again: pastoral romance edging a ghost story out of the way. Underground eroticism and erratic insecurity leading to violence count for more and more over the years. Three suicides, two murders, one plane crash, and one car crash are strewn among four novels.

Upper-crust middle-class life is the usual milieu, but the family is more crucial than has been acknowledged — and particularly the missing mother in *The House in Paris*, *The Death of the Heart*, *To the North*, and *Eva Trout*. That is where the Bowen preoccupation (but not obsession) with love begins. It is seen as the one important choice people not very free still think they are free to make, and they make it, usually, under a disastrous cloud: they have never known or have lost their mothers.

The disasters continue and proliferate. Overall, the novels are pessimistic and present the reader with an insoluble dilemma: innocence (or the lasting memory of it) and civilization are equally unavoidable. We bring the first condition with us into the world, which provides us, mercilessly, with the second. Between the two, some rite of passage must take place. The Garden of Eden can become rustic, suburban, a jungle, or otherwise hellish — the desert is no more than a stone's throw away. As the story of the Creation makes quite clear, you cannot have it both ways. But there is in the story a dissembler, and it is he — inexplicable, perhaps even help-lessly acting out injunctions he would prefer to avoid — on whom the Bowen instinct for drama focuses. In her version, he assumes his usual role of the manipulator, but he has an unusual aspect. He is doomed throughout eternity not for being evil but for being ambiguous: from one point of view unleashing demonic appetites and murderous intelligence, and from another providing the sources of the greatest hu-man achievements — love and knowledge. In the Bowen canon, the snakes — if you can label them at all — are not only equivocal but reluctant.

Yet to pretend that the snake and tree do not exist is to be a simpleton. Whichever way Portia turns in *The Death of the Heart* is the wrong turn. The world has no use for innocence, and with good reason: everyone has once been some version of Portia, and no one wants to be reminded again of that large, uncurable wound. The innocent are not quite the un-equal contestants one might imagine. They go through their paces in the novels giving tit for tat:

> Innocence so constantly finds itself in a false position that in-wardly innocent people learn to be disingenuous. Finding no language in which to speak in their own terms, they resign themselves to being translated imperfectly. They exist alone; when they try to enter into relations they compromise falsify-ingly — through anxiety, through desire to impart and to feel warmth. The system of our affections is too corrupt for them. They are bound to blunder, then to be told they cheat. In love, the sweetness and violence they have to offer involves a thou-sand betrayals for the less innocent. Incurable strangers to the world, they never cease to exact a heroic happiness. Their sin-gleness, their ruthlessness, their one continuous wish makes

them bound to be cruel, and to suffer cruelty. The innocent are so few that two of them seldom meet — when they do meet, their victims lie strewn all round.

The profundity of this and the cleverness are inextricably mixed. Its author was herself aware that "cleverness" could be damaging. A certain aphoristic tendency (especially in the early novels) to "smartness" is delightful in itself but suspicious in its virtuosity. This is from *To the North*:

> Lady Waters was quick to detect situations that did not exist. Living comfortably in Rutland Gate with her second husband, Sir Robert, she enlarged her own life into ripples of apprehension on everybody's behalf. Upon meeting, her very remarkable eyes sought one's own for those first intimations of crisis she was all tuned up to receive; she entered one's house on a current that set the furniture bobbing; at Rutland Gate destiny shadowed her tea-table. Her smallest clock struck portentously, her telephone trilled from the heart, her dinner-gong boomed a warning. When she performed introductions, drama's whole precedent made the encounter momentous.

But Miss Bowen was so much more than a merely clever writer that the charge deserves merely passing notice. More to the point, she seems to have been born with a genius command of English prose style, and the problem of her kind of gift was what to do with it. Words are the drunken part of her otherwise sober books, and there is a question whether any subject, theme, character, or scene ever became important enough — ever held a match to the style per se. Still, she was able to feel what she had originally felt before the world became transparent, and her ability to recover the past, both in her intellectual grasp of the locally historic — *Bowen's Court* (1942), *The Shelbourne Hotel* (1951), *A Time in Rome* (1960), all works of nonfiction — and in her magic transformation of landscape into its verbal equivalents, is reflected in the mature style. Here are the opening paragraphs of her unfinished autobiography in *Pictures and Conversations*:

The day this book was begun I went for a walk. The part of Kent I am living in has wide views, though also mysterious interstices. It can be considered to have two coastlines: a past, a present — the former looks from below like a ridge of hills, but in fact is the edge of an upland plateau: originally the sea reached to the foot of this. Afterwards, the withdrawal of the sea laid bare salty stretches, formerly its bed; two of the Cinque Ports, Hythe, New Romney, consequently found themselves high-and-dry, as did what was left of the Roman harbour under the heights of Lympne. . . . The existing coast-line, a long shallow inward curve westward from Folkestone to the far-out shingly projection of Dungeness, is fortified for the greater part of its way by a massive wall, lest the sea change its mind again. Inside the sea-wall, the protected lands keep an illusory look of marine emptiness — widening, west of Hythe, into the spaces of Romney Marsh, known for its sheep, its dykes, its sunsets and its solitary churches. On a clear day, the whole of this area meets the eye: there are no secrets.

Not so uphill, inland. The plateau, exposed to gales on its Channel front, has a clement hinterland, undulating and wooded. It is cleft by valleys, down which streams make their way to the sea; and there are also hollows, creases and dips, which, sunk between open-airy pastures and cornfields, are not to be guessed at till you stumble upon them: then, they are enticing, breathless and lush, with their wandering dogpaths and choked thickets.

A true wit, in the Restoration sense, Elizabeth Bowen had a flair for comedy that eluded Virginia Woolf. Bowen suffered the madness of her father, Woolf her own madness; each was in touch with secret springs of irrationality. But Elizabeth Bowen was born in Dublin, not London, and Irishness is not Englishness. She belongs to an Anglo-Irish tradition that includes Sheridan, Goldsmith, and Shaw. Comedy was not only in the genes but in the air. The odd mixture of the truly felt and the devastating is her forte. The view is bifocal. Sentiment and irony, operating in tandem, make one more set of contradictions added to others, beginning with the doubleness that the hyphen between "Anglo" and "Irish" implies: to be extraordinarily verbal and yet to stammer; to inherit a great house and yet to have a strong emotional sense of dispossession; to have a temperamental affinity with the bohemian while being basically conservative; to savor solitude and social life with equal relish. An accident of birth was compounded by circumstance: when Elizabeth Bowen was seven, her father had the first of several mental breakdowns and she and her mother were forced to leave Ireland for England. The scenery of Kent was forever after associated with her mother, while there could hardly be any mistaking the paternal associations attached to Dublin and Bowen's Court. Her mother died when Elizabeth was thirteen, and so, in a sense, she was doubly abandoned. The Gates of the Garden closed behind her twice.

The strategies of Bowen plots re-create analogies of the Garden's story, the action often centering on a triangle, because there one party, at least, is temporarily without knowledge. As the light dawns, the wrecking crew arrives. In the attempt to protect, to save face, to inflict damage — or all three at once — further harm is perpetrated, and the by-stander (a character or society at large) is always happy to rub salt into the wounds. Two of the members of the triangle are often rationally solicitous of one another, like Karen and Naomi in *The House in Paris*, and two hopelessly caught in a magnetic field of attraction, the sensuality of which they never allow themselves particularly to enjoy, like Karen and Max in the same novel. Impulse is converted not into guilt but into something worse: a philosophical awareness of plea-sure. In Bowen novels, the cells of the flesh know one thing, the mind another. Equally powerful, they undermine each other's ability to focus a clear-cut view of reality, just as a highly developed sense of the absurd interferes with passion and commitment. Emmeline's nearsighted unworldliness, Dicey's attempts to dig up the past in *The Little Girls* (1964), and even Eva Trout's blundering stabs at becoming real are all credible pieces of worlds, but the view is always partial, because some key factor is unavailable to the viewer.

The most complex example may be Harrison in *The Heat of the Day*. One of those unsuccessful hangers-on in peacetime who find their true vocation in the confusion of a war, he works for a counterintelligence outfit. Spying upon Stella, whose lover, Robert, turns out to be a genuine spy infiltrat-ing British Intelligence at its highest levels, Harrison hopes to extort Stella's compliance, even her gratitude and love, through blackmail by keeping his knowledge of Robert's trea-son from the authorities. At the beginning, Stella doesn't know Robert is a spy; she becomes aware of it through Har-rison's spying on her. Robert doesn't know about Harrison, and the last thing Stella can do is to let him know. Harrison is a menace but pathetic — he has learned that without power he is unlovable; he's bargaining for *his* life, it becomes clear, as well as Robert's. And certainly Stella is gambling for hers, caught between betrayal on the one side and threat on the other. Whether the bargain will be kept, whether it should be kept, whether it even exists forms the equivocal matter of the novel. Set against the background of wartime London, the novel's moral implications are more than emotional. Like *The Last September*, *The Heat of the Day* reflects a world of national turmoil, in which human relationships become another form of intelligence, of espionage. If there is a death of the heart, there is a little secret service, too.

The strange obscuring of Bowen's achievement stems in part from a misunderstanding: her novels are testaments not to romantic love but to its power, and no two things could be more different. But it also comes in part from life. Because she was Anglo-Irish (the last of the breed, according to Mrs. Glendinning's book), Bowen's views of England and of Ireland were the exact opposite of those of most Americans and Englishmen. For her, Ireland, with its "repetitive eighteenth-century interiors [and] their rational proportions and faultless mouldings . . . without shadow, curiousness, or cranny," was civilized and sane, and England insubstantial and stormy: "Everything, including the geological formation, struck me as having been recently put together. . . . *Would* it last? The edifices lining the tilted streets . . . seemed engaged in just not sliding about. . . . My thoughts dallied with landslides, subsidences and tidal waves." Bowen is essentially the product of a divided culture, a divided family, and a divided nation, and no one is better on the demon relationships of opposing — but mutual — interests that tie servants and masters, the innocent and the worldly, the loving and the unlovable together. Irish in England and English in Ireland, she grasped early the colonial mentality from both sides, and saw how, in the end, it was a mirror image of the most exploitative relationship of all: that of the adult and the child.

Elizabeth Bowen, 1899-1973

SHE was rare. A large-boned, red-haired beauty with a face of such distinction that the only comparable one in recent history is Virginia Woolf's. What they said when they met remains unknown. Their few meetings in *A Writer's Diary* are unilluminating. Perhaps they never discussed writing. Perhaps Mr. Woolf was a judicious editor — one wonders why "Bowen, Elizabeth" doesn't appear in the index. Possibly Mrs. Woolf's "malicious streak" came into play. If Elizabeth Bowen had a streak at all, it wasn't "malicious" — "mischievous" would be closer to home. In fact, it would be hard to imagine anyone kinder. But kindness, these days, suggests some sort of namby-pamby person, soft and easily swayed. Nothing could be farther from the truth. She could be acerbic, was one of the wits of her time, and could detect, from a great distance, the faintest whiff of the false. With the pretentious, she could be devastating.

170

The combination of a wit so accurate and a warmth so pervasive led to mistaken impressions. It was hard to believe that these usually incompatible forces were held in such arresting suspension. She was wrongly thought of — as recently as 1971 in London — as "a woman's writer," all heartthrob and fuzz. If they'd read her, Congreve would have been shocked at the opinion and so would Henry James. She belongs to the great tradition of English moral comedy going back to Jane Austen, stopping off at Henry James, with some of the aromas of Proust, a writer she greatly admired. She was incapable of dishonesty, though she may have written too many blurbs for unknown writers. She was more generous than can be imagined and had no sense of the "strategy" of literary careers or the dark scrimmage of "reputations." She had so much intrinsic power that I don't think the idea of acquiring any ever crossed her mind. In all, the matter of semblances never came up, so strikingly positive was her impression, so absolutely steady the aura around her, and so precise what she thought and what she had to say.

Yet there were always fascinating undercurrents, overtones that struck original notes. She was one of those very rare people who create more life around them than is actually there and who heighten the momentousness of everything simply by appearing. She was intensely private but enormously enjoyed sociability. In fact, many of her qualities would have been paradoxical in a lesser person, and what was original in her work stems from that very doubleness: a true understanding of the most subtle undertows in human relationships and an absolute sense of social comedy. Not side by side but simultaneously. She gave every leverage to the individual, to friends, to anyone she loved, and she was a great friend of the young, which many famous writers are not. At least four of her students — at Wisconsin, Princeton, and Vassar — became close personal friends. She was tough on bores by ignoring them, disliked diamonds in the rough, and was the least snobbish person I knew.

Independent to an extraordinary degree, she loved company (after a certain hour of the day), and gave of herself so easily that you always had the dazzling, and dangerous, impression that you were the particular center of her interest. It took some time to learn that a lot of other people felt exactly the same way. Great demands were made on her attention because her uniqueness hardly went unnoticed and because she was never a bore. In her presence you felt warmed by her warmth, flattered by her distinction, stimulated by what she had to say, and amused by the way she said it; she made you feel that you were absolutely at the top of your form.

It was fun to be with her, and if that sounds childish, there was something wonderfully childish about her. It showed itself in her smile, which was immediate and crooked, and a laugh that hid her teeth so that she often looked like a little girl trying to conceal braces. When you secretly looked at her teeth, just to make sure, they were adult and intact. She chain-smoked constantly, which probably killed her, because the second before the last time I saw her (which was the summer of 1971), she had a cough so monstrous that I did what I would never think of doing: I asked if she had thought of giving up smoking. She had, but she wouldn't; it might keep her from writing; she might gain weight.

Her amazing vocabulary was partly the result, I think, of her conquering her stutter. She seemed to know synonyms for every word in English. Her celebrated command of language may have begun as an effort to circumvent it, and her wit, in part, derived from the successes and the failures thereof. Example: She and I and a mutual friend were driving to dinner. She was supposed to have gone to the country the previous weekend. It turned out she hadn't. The friend asked why. She said, "I didn't go because my hostess was suffering from . . . from . . ." We waited patiently for the disease to be named. Finally, she said, "from . . . from . . . personal mistrust."

The wit didn't depend on peculiarities of speech alone. Hardly. On the hottest New York summer night I remember, she gave a dinner party. She had been detained and had to shop at the last minute. When I arrived, the drinks were impeccable, everything went swimmingly. After drinks, you went into another room for a stand-up dinner. And that was rather unbelievable. Elizabeth was notoriously near-sighted and she must have gone into some delicatessen and ordered a buffet. There was a salad that looked as if it had been briefly shampooed. The lettuce leaves had suspicious ruffles. I was standing next to her, and she tasted the salad first. She turned to me and said, "You know, this just doesn't have that *je ne sais quoi*."

In the summer of 1952, John Brinnin and I spent four days at Bowen's Court, and those four days remain one of the high points of my life. The house was severely beautiful stone, untainted by the touch of ivy; the lush Irish summer was at its height; the countryside was literally breathtaking. And Elizabeth at the center gave it a special charm by seeming just as delighted to be there as we did. There was a library — silhouettes on the mantelpiece, shining glass cases of books, a brown velvet sofa in front of the fireplace — a room that was Elizabeth Bowen's, the writer's room. I remember one day looking through the bookcases and finding the typed manuscript of *The Death of the Heart*. *My* heart turned over.

She read omnivorously. In 1971, she was reading Pushkin, all the poems, in translation. Before that, she'd been in the hospital for a month and had reread all of Iris Murdoch's novels. She loved books the way few people do. Poetry and painting meant more to her, I think, than music. And architecture meant most of all. There is hardly a more telling evocation of Rome than *A Time in Rome*, that neglected book, which starts, so innocently, as a travel book, and ends, so brilliantly, with the mortal uncertainties of Saint Paul.

But all of this is mainly anecdotal and nostalgic. The real thing, the important thing, is the work. Just how important remains to be seen. I think she was one of the natural masters of English prose. I hope *Collected Impressions* will be reprinted, and in paperback. Anyone interested in writing should have it close by — the essay on Flaubert is worth the price of admission. Her *Collected Stories* was long overdue — "Her Table Spread" could be used in every short-story class to advantage. It does in twelve pages what a lot of writers never get around to doing at all. An early novel, *Friends and Relations*, since it's practically unknown, should be made available, and I think *To the North*, a small marvel, is still strangely unappreciated. That's true, too, of *A World of Love*, the fifth chapter of which I would recommend to anyone writing a novel. There will be a reassessment, naturally. It's high time. Meanwhile, in regard to the mastery of English prose, I offer as evidence the end of this last paragraph of introduction to *Ivy Gripped the Steps*, a book of short stories, all of which take place during the London blitz:

This discontinuous writing, nominally "inventive," is the only diary I have kept. Transformed into images in the stories, there *may* be important psychological facts: if so, I did not realise their importance. Walking in the darkness of the nights of six years (darkness which transformed a capital city into a network of inscrutable canyons) one developed new bare alert senses, with their own savage warnings and notations. And by day one was always making one's own new maps of a landscape always convulsed by some new change. Through it all, one probably picked up more than can be answered for. I cannot answer for much that is in these stories, except to say that I know they are all true — true to the general life that was in me at the time. Taken singly, they are disjected snapshots — snapshots taken from close up, too close up, in the middle of the *mêlée* of a battle. You cannot *render*, you can only embrace — if it means embracing to suffocation point — something vast that is happening right on top of you. Painters have painted, and photographers have photographed, the tottering lacelike architecture of ruins, dark mass-movements of people, and the untimely brilliance of flaming skies. I cannot paint or photograph like this — I have isolated; I have made for the particular, spot-lighting faces or cutting out gestures that are not even the faces or gestures of great sufferers. This is how I am, how I feel, whether in war or peace time; and only as I am and feel can I write. As I said at the start, though I criticise these stories now, afterwards, intellectually, I cannot criticise their content. They are the particular. But through the particular, in wartime, I felt the high-voltage current of the general pass.

SYLVIA PLATH

Dying: An Introduction

THE story of a poet who tries to end her life written by a poet who did, Sylvia Plath's *The Bell Jar* was first published under a pseudonym in England in 1963, one month before she committed suicide. We had to wait almost a decade for its publication in the United States, but it was reissued in England in 1966 under its author's real name. A biographical note in the present edition makes it plain that the events in the novel closely parallel Sylvia Plath's twentieth year. For reasons for which we are not wholly to blame, our approach to the novel is impure; *The Bell Jar* is fiction that cannot escape being read in part as autobiography. It begins in New York with an ominous lightness, grows darker as it moves to Massachusetts, then slips slowly into madness. Esther Greenwood, one of a dozen girls in and on the town for a month as "guest editors" of a teenage fashion magazine, is the product of a German immigrant family and a New England suburb. With "fifteen years of straight A's" behind her, a depressing attachment to a dreary but handsome medical student, Buddy Willard, still unresolved, and a yearning to be a poet, she is the kind of girl who doesn't know what drink to order or how much to tip a taxi driver but is doing her thesis on the "twin images" in *Finnegans Wake*, a book she has never managed to finish. Her imagination is at war with the small-town tenets of New England and the big-time sham of New York. She finds it impossible to be one of the army of college girls whose education is a forced stop on the short march to marriage. The crises of identity, sexuality, and survival are grim, and often funny. Wit, irony, and intelligence, as well as an inexplicable, withdrawn sadness, separate Esther from her companions. Being an involuntary truth-seeker, she uses irony as a weapon of judgment, and she is its chief victim. Unable to experience or mime emotions, she feels defective as a person. The gap between her and the world widens: "I couldn't get myself to react. I felt very still and very empty. . . ." "The silence depressed me. It wasn't the silence of silence. It was my own silence. . . ." "That morning I had tried to hang myself."

Camouflage and illness go together in *The Bell Jar*; moreover, illness is often used to lift or tear down a façade. Doreen, a golden girl of certainty admired by Esther, begins the process by getting drunk. The glimpse of her lying with her head in a pool of her own vomit in a hotel hallway is repellant but crucial. Her illness is followed by a mass ptomaine poisoning at a "fashion" lunch. Buddy gets tuberculosis and goes off to a sanatorium. Esther, visiting him, breaks her leg skiing. When she has her first sexual experience, with a young math professor she has picked up, she hemorrhages.

Taken in by a lesbian friend, she winds up in a hospital. Later, she learns that the friend has hanged herself. A plain recital of the events in *The Bell Jar* would be ludicrous if they were not balanced by genuine desperation at one side of the scale and a sure sense of black comedy at the other. Sickness and disclosure are the keys to *The Bell Jar*. On her last night in New York, Esther climbs to the roof of her hotel and throws her city wardrobe over the parapet, piece by piece. By the end of the novel, she has tried to get rid of her very life, which is given back to her by another process of divestment — psychiatry. Pain and gore are endemic to *The Bell Jar*, and they are described objectively, self-mockingly, almost humorously to begin with. Taken in by the tone (the first third of *The Bell Jar* might be a mordant, sick-joke version of *Breakfast at Tiffany's*), the reader is being lured into the lion's den — that sterile cement room in the basement of a mental hospital where the electric-shock-therapy machine waits for its frightened clients.

The casualness with which physical suffering is treated suggests that Esther is cut off from the instinct for sympathy right from the beginning — for herself as well as for others. Though she is enormously aware of the impingements of sensation, her sensations remain impingements. She lives close to the nerve, but the nerve has become detached from the general network. A thin layer of glass separates her from everyone, and the novel's title, itself made of glass, is evolved from her notion of disconnection: the head of each mentally ill person is enclosed in a bell jar, choking on its own foul air.

Torn between conflicting roles — the sweetheart–*Hausfrau*–mother and "the life of the poet," neither very real to her — Esther finds life itself inimical. Afraid of distorting the person she is yet to become, she becomes the ultimate distortion — nothing. As she descends into the pit of depression, the world is a series of wrong reverberations: her mother's face is a perpetual accusation; the wheeling of a baby carriage underneath her window, a grinding irritation. She becomes obsessed by the idea of suicide, and one of the great achievements of *The Bell Jar* is that it makes real the subtle distinctions between a distorted viewpoint and the distortions inherent in what it sees. Convention may contribute to Esther's insanity, but she never loses her awareness of the irrationality of convention. Moved to Belsize, a part of the mental hospital reserved for patients about to go back to the world, she makes the connection explicit:

> What was there about us, in Belsize, so different from the girls playing bridge and gossiping and studying in the college to which I would return? Those girls, too, sat under bell jars of a sort.

Terms like "mad" and "sane" grow increasingly inadequate as the action develops. Esther is "psychotic" by definition, but the definition is merely a descriptive tag: by the time we learn how she got to be "psychotic" the word has ceased to be relevant. (As a work of fiction, *The Bell Jar* seems to complement the clinical theories of the Scottish analyst R. D. Laing.) Because it is written from the distraught observer's point of view rather than from the viewpoint of someone observing her, there is continuity to her madness; it is not one state suddenly supplanting another but the most gradual of processes.

Suicide, a grimly compulsive game of fear and guilt, as addictive as alcohol or drugs, is experimental at first — a little blood here, a bit of choking there, just to see what it will be like. It quickly grows into an overwhelming desire for annihilation. By the time Esther climbs into the crawl space of a cellar and swallows a bottle of sleeping pills — by the time we are faced by the real thing — the event, instead of seeming grotesque, seems like a natural consequence. When she is about to leave the hospital, after a long series of treatments, her psychiatrist tells her to consider her breakdown "a bad dream." Esther, "patched, retreaded, and approved for the road," thinks, "To the person in the bell jar, blank and stopped as a dead baby, the world itself is the bad dream."

That baby is only one of many in *The Bell Jar*. They smile up from the pages of magazines, they sit like little freaks pickled in glass jars on display in the pediatric ward of Buddy's hospital. A "sweet baby cradled in its mother's belly" seems to wait for Esther at the end of the ski run when she has her accident. And in the course of the novel she witnesses a birth. In place of her never-to-be-finished thesis on the "twin images" in *Finnegans Wake*, one might be written on the number and kinds of babies that crop up in *The Bell Jar*. In a gynecologist's office, watching a mother fondling her baby, Esther wonders why she is so separated from this easy happiness, this carrying out of the prescribed biological and social roles. She does not want a baby; she is a baby herself. But she is also a potential writer. She wants to fulfill herself, not to *be* fulfilled. To her, babies are The Trap, and sex is the bait. But she is too intelligent not to realize that babies don't represent life — they *are* life, though not necessarily the kind Esther wants to live; that is, if she wants to live at all. She is caught between the monstrous fetuses on display in Buddy's ward and the monstrous slavery of the seemingly permanent pregnancy of her neighbor Dodo Conway, who constantly wheels a baby carriage under Esther's window, like a demented figure in a Greek chorus. Babies lure Esther toward suicide by luring her toward a life she cannot — literally — bear. There seem to be only two solutions, and both involve the invisible: to pledge faith to the unborn or fealty to the dead. Life, so painfully visible and present, defeats her, and she takes it, finally, into her own hands. With the exception of the psychiatrist's disinterested affection for her, love is either missing or unrecognized in *The Bell Jar*. Its overwhelming emotion is disgust — disgust that has not yet become contempt and is therefore more damaging.

Between the original and the second publications of *The Bell Jar* in England, Sylvia Plath's second, and posthumous, volume of poems, *Ariel*, was printed. Some of the poems had appeared in magazines, but no one was prepared for their cumulative effect. Murderous experiences of the mind and the body, stripped of all protection, they were total exposures, and chilling. They made clear almost instantly that someone who had been taken for a gifted writer might well be one of genius, whose work — intense, luxurious, barbarous, and worldly — was unlike anything ever seen before. Although the extraordinary quality of the poems made her death the more lamentable, that death gave her work certain immediate values it might not otherwise have had. Death cannot change a single word written down on paper, but in this case who the poet was and what had been lost became apparent almost at the same time, as if the poems had been given and the poet taken away in one breath. An instantaneous immortality followed. Sylvia Plath also became an extra-literary figure to many people, a heroine of contradictions — someone who had faced horror and made something of it as well as someone who had been destroyed by it. I don't think morbid fascination accounts for her special position. The energy and violence of the late poems were acted out. What their author threatened she performed, and her work gained an extra status of truth. The connection between art and life, so often merely rhetorical, became all too visible. The tragic irony is that in a world of public-relations liars Sylvia Plath seemed a truth-dealer in life by the very act of taking it.

The Bell Jar lacks the coruscating magnificence of the late poems. Something girlish in its manner betrays the hand of the amateur novelist. Its material, after all, is what has been transcended. It is a frightening book, and if it ends on too optimistic a note as both fiction and postdated fact, its real terror lies elsewhere. Though we share every shade of feeling that leads to Esther's attempts at suicide, there is not the slightest insight in *The Bell Jar* into suicide itself. That may be why it bears the stamp of authority. Reading it, we are up against the raw experience of nightmare, not the analysis or understanding of it.

A Pinched Existence

A GOOD case could be made for the short story being the most flexible of all forms and, as such, the key to "modernism": it can accommodate everything from the prose poem to the well-made plot; allows for the undercurrents that emanated from Vienna in the 1920s, the seemingly formless but beautifully condensed character studies that began arriving from Russia with the advent of Chekhov. It can be analytic or lyrical, dramatic or rhapsodic. No other English practitioner of the form — English by way of the Commonwealth — was as influential in the decades that spanned the period between World War I and the 1950s than Katherine Mansfield. Her work is temporarily in eclipse in America, but there is hope of a reassessment.

It is clear from reading two new biographies — *The Life of Katherine Mansfield* by Anthony Alpers and *Katherine Mansfield* by Jeffrey Meyers — that their subject would have understood what Proust meant when he wrote that "the true paradises are the paradises we have lost." Being an expatriate, she was divorced from her childhood in a special way: the distance between the realm of the adult and that of the child took on a physical dimension; her lost paradise could be located on a map. It had not always seemed a paradise, and it took her a long time to realize it was lost. By the time she did, the peripatetic wanderings of the outsider had become the enforced regime of the tubercular: Mediterranean winters, English summers. Dislocation had become chronic.

When Mansfield returned to her birthplace, Wellington, New Zealand, in 1906, at the age of eighteen, after four years of schooling at Queen's College in England, she was unhappy, moody, rebellious; London glittered across the ocean, Wellington was a backwater. And she was haunted by a series of strange or tragic incidents. On the day her mother gave a garden party, a poor neighbor died in a traffic accident (the situation of one of her most famous stories). Though a summer cottage was now available for the use of the children — four girls, of which Katherine was the third, and Leslie, her young brother — it became the scene of an unhappy lesbian affair, her second in the three years that marked her return to Wellington. Saddest of all, her beloved grandmother died, the person she was closest to in the family.

Incriminating papers were found, having to do either with the two love affairs or with an obscure incident involving a sailor, and Mansfield was sent to "King County" on a caravan expedition that left on November 15, 1907, and returned the week before Christmas. The country was rough, the party of eight traveled by horse and carriage, pitching tents when they made camp. They ventured into exotic territory: Maori country, thermal regions, pumice hills. It was a coun-

try of white dust and velvety mineral-spring baths, and
Mansfield's account of it, *The Urewera Notebook*, is interesting
as the writing of a gifted adolescent describing a short journey through a strange culture at a remote time. Though the
trip provided Mansfield with the background of a famous
story, "The Woman at the Store," she remained restless and
obviously determined to get back to London; her father finally relented. She was nineteen when she left Wellington
for the second and last time, in 1908. Though she couldn't
have known it, more than half her life was over.

That the rest of it could have taken place in a mere fifteen
years is amazing, so crowded are the canvases of both biographies, so rapid the changes of address and fortune. On the
way back to London, she must have felt relieved; she was
going back to a world she thought she loved, the world of
the theater, of intellectual exchange, of poetry, of music —
everything she felt nourishing and vital. Yet, seven years
later, in 1915, when her brother, Leslie, was blown to bits
in World War I, that world fell apart, and her childhood in
New Zealand took on its true value: like Proust's Combray
springing out of a cup of tea, it came back freshly revealed.
The New Zealand stories — "Prelude," "At the Bay," "The
Doll's House," "The Woman at the Store" — were a far cry
from the sophisticated tales-with-a-twist she had been turning out for the English magazines, Orage's *New Age* in particular. The New Zealand stories, her finest work, are com-
memorations, garlands for Leslie, and there is a touching
journal entry in regard to them and to him:

Now, as I write these words and talk of getting down to the
New Zealand atmosphere, I see you opposite to me. . . . Ah,
my darling, how have I kept away from this tremendous joy?

If "Prelude" and "At the Bay" tend to make the London and Mediterranean stories seem thin by comparison, it must be remembered that Mansfield was a stranger among strangers, that she moved in a world of artists, intellectuals, and writers; they were not, in the end, to be her cup of tea. Something of the ventriloquist's effect clings to most of the European stories, as of voices overheard and reprojected; they lack the allure of subterranean interest. She was dealing with people basically alien to her — people who tended to hide behind masks (as she learned to do). Reality and fantasy had been replaced by gossip. A rich stream of family life — natural-animal-physical — was nowhere to be found. Thin soil produced thin work.

The equivocal nature of the world in which she found herself in 1908 can be suggested by two incidents that occurred much later, in 1917. Virginia and Leonard Woolf set the type for *Prelude* at the Hogarth Press — an act of devotion, though endlessly delayed. But here is the entry in Virginia Woolf's diary on the night Mansfield came for dinner to see the pulled proof of the first page:

> We could both wish that ones first impression of K.M. was not that she stinks like a — well civet cat that had taken to street walking. In truth, I'm a little shocked by her commonness at first sight; lines so hard & cheap. However, when this diminishes, she is so intelligent & inscrutable that she repays friendship.

The relationship between Virginia and Katherine was a wary one. They teetered always on the edge of something more — both were capable of loving women — but drew back out of uncertainty and mistrust. They shared, too intensely, in Mr. Meyers's words, "a painful creative conjunction of imagination, isolation, and illness."

In both their cases, much of the charm is masked pain; yet they envied different things in each other: Woolf wrote in her diary a few days after Mansfield died, in January 1923:

> When I began to write, it seemed to me there was no point in writing. Katherine won't read it. Katherine's my rival no longer. . . . I was jealous of her writing — the only writing I have ever been jealous of. . . . and I saw in it, perhaps from jealousy, all the qualities I dislike in her.

And again, with greater sympathy and perception:

> I never gave her credit for all the physical suffering and the effect it must have had in embittering her.

What Katherine Mansfield envied in Virginia Woolf was something quite other. Here, in a letter of complaint, she is writing from Italy in 1919:

> You know it's madness to love and live apart. That's what we do. . . . It isn't a married life at all — not what I mean by a married life. How I envy Virginia; no wonder she can write. There is always in her writing a calm freedom of expression as though she were at peace — her roof over her, her possessions round her, and her man somewhere within call.

The person addressed is John Middleton Murry. Katherine and he met in London when she was twenty-three, he twenty-two and the editor of *Rhythm*, a literary magazine of the day. He became her lover and then her husband; thirteen of the thirty-five years she lived were spent in and out of his company. As her literary executor, he carefully selected passages, and censored or deleted others, in the journals, notebooks, letters, and scrapbooks he edited after her death. The process was self-serving on the one hand, and a genuine attempt to create a literary monument on the other. Running a small Mansfield industry, Murry managed to create an image of Katherine as a limp, sentimental person. He described her as "a flower." Worse, in a series of books, lectures, and statements of his own, he distorted her gifts and her person, characterizing her as "the most wonderful writer and the most beautiful spirit of our time."

This kind of thing does not lack long for a backlash. Murry's aggressively projected posthumous image of Mansfield was the largest single reason for the decline of her reputation. It focused attention on the person at the expense of the work; it made unjustifiable claims and was so patently false to anyone who knew her (the very people who would be writing about her) that falseness became associated with the work itself — a delicate business, since some of it *is* marred by girlishness and obviousness. Mr. Meyers sees Murry as an ass and an enemy — someone who made a reputation for himself out of Mansfield's life and work he never could have achieved on his own:

> Murry was a kind of rancid Rousseau: his thought was equivocal and confused, he had an endless capacity for self-deception, he disguised a total egocentricity behind his mock-saintliness and was always eager to display his stigmata before the public. Katherine, who loathed his self-pity, accused him of being "just like a little dog whining outside a door," and impatiently ex-

claimed: "When you know you are a voice crying in the wilderness, *cry*, but don't say 'I am a voice crying in the wilderness.' "

Mr. Alpers is more lenient. Murry, after all, was poor, remarkably passive, and lacked talent. Whatever may be said against him, he was the single most important person in Mansfield's life. In any case, some of the best English short stories of this century got tarred by the same adolescent brush with which Murry had redrawn the life.

The information supplied by Mr. Meyers and (sometimes in too generous detail) by Mr. Alpers redoes that portrait in more realistic colors. Atypical as the life was, it still had archetypal figures in it: if there is a generic artist's-father, Harold Beauchamp might well be he. "A settler type, a self-made tycoon, and a friend of politicians," he was domineering, not unkind, valued money, and had a remarkably close, perhaps obsessive, relationship with his wife, "an aristocratic-looking beauty," who was delicate, brave, and, to her children, seemingly aloof. The parents' closeness tended to shut the children out, especially Katherine, who was the ugly duckling — fat, homely, wearing steel-rimmed spectacles, and hobbled by a stutter — an ugly duckling who later turned into a beauty. Harold Beauchamp eventually became the head of the Bank of New Zealand, and the Beauchamp children, moving from one more expensive house to another, grew up in an atmosphere that was an odd mixture of frontier democracy and unusual affluence. When the family sailed for England in 1903 to install three of the girls at Queen's College, the Beauchamps thought nothing of reserving the entire passenger accommodations of the ship for themselves.

Katherine had a special reason for wanting to get to England. At thirteen, she had fallen violently in love with a young cellist, Arnold Trowell, fifteen. He was to follow shortly to study music on the Continent.

Her letters to Arnold are the first examples of a too easily proffered affection, a tendency exhibited again almost immediately with Ida Baker, whom she met on her first day at Queen's. Ida responded beyond anyone's wildest dreams. Referred to as L.M. in the journals (standing for Lesley Moore, an invented name), she became a slave, on call at all times, dropping everything to join Mansfield whenever she was needed. The case was so odd, so intense, right from the beginning, that it seems, as Mr. Meyers says, more like one of imprinting than of human affection.

On Mansfield's side, there were the increasing demands illness brings, and in the long years of enforced exile abroad, L.M. was her frequent companion. Mansfield felt love and hatred in equal proportion, and contempt, even revulsion; L.M. was indispensable but a surrogate. To be dependent on someone not quite loved but loyal exacerbates the roles of server and served, caretaker and invalid. Mansfield and L.M. acted out this small range of unequal roles time after time. It wasn't a question of being the wrong sex; the person in need was in danger of being suffocated by the comforter. But for all of Mansfield's complaining, L.M. provided for her what Leonard Woolf had supplied for Virginia: a reliable pillar of strength. In fact, in her relationship with L.M., Mansfield had unwittingly handed Murry a sop for his guilt: no matter how distant, lonely, cold, and in debt Katherine might be, she wasn't *really* alone: L.M. was there, taking care of her.

Mansfield's father, the richest man in New Zealand, kept

her on a small allowance that was "worse than nothing," according to one observer, forcing her to lead "a pinched existence." And her first year in London on her own was a disaster. The romance with Arnold cooled; she switched her affection to his twin brother, Garnet; became pregnant; impulsively married George Bowden, a musician she'd known for only three weeks; left *him* on their wedding night; rejoined Garnet, who was playing in the orchestra of an opera company in the provinces (shades of Colette and Jean Rhys!); and ended up bereft, ill, pregnant, with no one at her side but the ever-faithful L.M. Mansfield's mother was coming to England. When she arrived, Mrs. Beauchamp whisked her daughter off to a German pension to have the baby, and departed. When Mrs. Beauchamp returned to Wellington, she cut Katherine out of her will.

In Germany, Katherine had a miscarriage, but managed to produce the sketches that make up *In a German Pension*, her first book. The strokes are broad, the Germans drawn with exaggerated vulgarity. Later on, even though she was very badly off, she refused to allow it to be reprinted. And, back in England, she began that peculiar searching for a place to live that was to characterize the rest of her life. Even after she and Murry had decided to live together, there were frequent moves, endless flats, more little houses. Poverty was the immediate cause, but one suspects the compulsions of dislocation were at work. Mansfield often seems like a soul searching for a place to rest. The trips to Switzerland and France begin with high hopes and end in terror: the cases of medical bungling are hair-raising; the pleas to Murry to join her abroad, increasingly urgent. The one time they were happy — at the Villa Pauline in Bandol from January through April 1916 — ended with their yielding to the blandishments of the Lawrences, who had a place in Cornwall. The Murrys and the Lawrences met when D. H. Lawrence walked into the offices of *The Blue Review*, formerly *Rhythm*, in June 1913. The two couples took to each other at once, and there were visits to the Lawrence place in the country. After an interval in Paris and several tries at Chelsea flats, the Murrys decided to live on the cheap in the country. They moved into a cottage three miles from the Lawrences. Now, four years later, they joined once more in an effort to realize Lawrence's dream of an ideal little community and Katherine Mansfield's fantasy of a permanent abode — a dream house, referred to as The Heron, after Leslie's middle name. But the Lawrences were violent, Lawrence had a crush on Murry, Katherine disliked Frieda — though she wore the wedding ring of Frieda's first marriage to her grave — and, in the end, it was impossible to work, impossible to live. Lawrence was magnetic, but he and Mansfield were too much alike under the skin, their partners too different. They kept meeting and parting, like two pairs of birds going through their ritual dances. But the joinings were more territorial than nuptial, and Lawrence — to whom Mansfield was deeply attached — was, in the end, unspeakably cruel to her at one of the gravest moments of her life. She was at Menton in February 1920, ill almost to the point of death, and could have used whatever warmth a letter from an old friend might bring. Lawrence wrote: "I loathe you. You revolt me stewing in your consumption. You are a loathesome reptile — I hope you will die." The letter, almost ludicrously vile, has never been found; but Mansfield quoted it in one of her letters to Murry, and L.M. remembered it.

What Lawrence hated most in Mansfield, according to Mr. Alpers, was the mirrored fear of the disease of which he was already a victim and of which he would eventually die.

The death of Leslie had been the first great spiritual upheaval in Mansfield's life. When the world seemed worthless, her work had saved her. As she became more ill, the pleasures of life *and* the satisfactions of her work deserted her. This emptiness in the face of death led to her final decision to join Gurdjieff's community of mystics at Fontainebleau, where body and soul were one; if there was to be a cure, it would be, once and for all, out of the hands of doctors. Although the decision was not an easy one and was a long time in coming, it had been in the air. Orage, Gurdjieff's disciple in London, had taken Mansfield to meetings in which Gurdjieff and Ouspensky were discussed, and she was to some extent familiar with their teachings. She had reached a point of illness where nothing seemed worth trying save a miracle. She had been relinquishing a certain kind of reality and fear for a long time. Tragically, just as she achieved a kind of spiritual inner peace, her confidence in her work slipped away. What should have been a great meshing of inner and outer forces eluded her, though it is clear to a reader — it may not have been to her — that the work got better as the life got worse. She wrote to Murry from Menton on October 18, 1920:

You know, I have felt very often lately as though the silence had some meaning beyond these signs, these intimations. Isn't it possible that if one yielded there is a whole world into which one is received? It is so near and yet I am conscious that I hold back from giving myself up to it. What is this something mysterious that waits — that beckons?

And then suffering, bodily suffering such as I've known for three years. It has changed for ever everything — even the *appearance* of the world is not the same — there is something added. *Everything has its shadow.* Is it right to resist such suffering? Do you know I feel it has been an immense privilege. . . . It has taken me three years to understand this — to come to see this. We resist, we are terribly frightened. The little boat enters the dark fearful gulf and our only cry is to escape —"put me on land again." But it's useless. Nobody listens. The shadowy figure rows on. One ought to sit still and uncover one's eyes.

She arrived at Fontainebleau on October 16, 1922. L.M. had helped her, but left on October 20 to take a job on a farm. Murry appeared, by invitation, on the afternoon of January 9, 1923. That evening Katherine died of a hemorrhage.

Mansfield's reputation remains uncertain; she suffered the fate of the cult figure: the interest in her life has overtaken the work itself. Rereading her, one is struck by the variety of characters; she deals equally well with shopkeepers, prostitutes, neurotic young women, married men, children (remarkably). She was no mere lyrical twang, no fine piece of iridescent shell endlessly turned to the same light. Her reputation for "purity," her forced martyrdom as an exponent of mere sensibility, has obscured her toughness, the ruthlessness of her judgment, her fine eye and ear. The work varies; the ups and downs are inexplicable, cropping up at all stages of her career. A masterpiece like "The Stranger" is followed by something as meretricious as "Taking the Veil"; the glories of "Je Ne Parle Pas Français," with its controlled masculine point of view, its queer but deadly pace, its frissons slowly building into a chilling portrait — the uncanny effect of its drama as a whole — all this is suddenly deflated, it seems to me, by a story such as "The Life of Ma Parker," a rewrite, with a slight twisting of circumstances and character, of Chekhov's "Grief." "Bliss," though detested by Virginia Woolf and found artificial by Elizabeth Bowen, remains a fine story — until the last scene. Facile but not fake, it bobs on a real current. The slick denouement is one of Mansfield's problems — as if O. Henry and Virginia Woolf had somehow been forced to share the same skin. But there are stories that rival Chekhov, as well they might: he was the one writer above all she adored. Mansfield was the only writer of this century who was devoted exclusively to the short story. Her ability to transform herself into someone else on one long, sustained lyrical note — the true mark of the good storywriter — was a matter of impulse as well as skill.

These two new biographies rest much of their authority on the subject as witness. In a sense, they feed on, and compete with, the journals, notebooks, and letters. Though the Meyers volume is two-thirds the size of the Alpers, Mr. Meyers covers the essential ground and is clear-eyed and straightforward. Mr. Alpers, whose book is a revision and expansion of an earlier work, places the writer in a larger picture and provides a valuable chronology; but he can be intrusive and often fails to distinguish the important from the unimportant detail. Both books rescue a complex and heroic woman from the dullness of sanctity.

JEAN STAFFORD

Jean: Some Fragments

I MET her by subletting an apartment in New York, hers and
Robert Lowell's, in the early forties. The war was on; I had
been hired by the Office of War Information on 57th Street
and was looking for a place to stay. Cal was still in jail, serv-
ing out his term as a conscientious objector; Jean had finished
Boston Adventure and was waiting for it to be published. She
was going away somewhere for a few months — England, I
think — but maybe it was Boston. I don't remember. The
apartment, in a brownstone on 17th Street overlooking Stuy-
vesant Park, was graceful and old-fashioned and full of things
Jean loved: Victorian sofas, lamps with pleated shades, deep
engulfing chairs, small objects on tables, and books, books,
books. Those in the bedroom bookcase were mainly religious; she was a Catholic convert at the time, or at least re-
ceiving instruction. She had a weakness for mechanical toys:
a bear that turned the pages of a book (named after a well-

known critic), a fire truck that turned at sharp right angles and raced across the floor at great speed. When Jean returned from England (or Boston), she would visit me occasionally, always bringing a pint of whiskey in a brown paper bag — either as a matter of scrupulous courtesy or because she felt she couldn't count on my supply — and we would drink and talk. And laugh. A demure quality about her alternated with a kind of Western no-nonsense toughness, and she shed years every time she laughed, showing her gums like a child or an ancient. Funny and sharp about people, she loved gossip. We became friends.

We developed, over the years, a tendency to make elaborate plans that were never carried out. This was particularly true of travel, which we both dreaded. Europe eluded us at least six times. We *did* get to Boston once for a Thanksgiving weekend, but even then something went wrong. We were to meet on the train but never did. We found each other, finally, in South Station, exhausted and bewildered.

I remember seeing a life mask of Jean — Jean the way she looked before the car accident that changed her face forever. (I had known her only since the accident, which occurred while she was married to Lowell.) A handsome woman, she had once been beautiful in a more conventional way, or so the mask suggested. "The Interior Castle" describes the surgical procedure with chilling exactitude; its central conceit is of the brain as a castle probed and assaulted by alien forces. I often forgot that Jean had been through this traumatic ordeal, and the long adjustment that must have been necessary afterwards. That fact, when I remembered it, always made the killing of the girl (rather than the boy) in *The Mountain Lion* more poignant. It also cast a light on Jean's predilection for masks and disguises. She liked to dress up — but in the manner of a child at a Halloween party. Once she came to my house for drinks and emerged from the kitchen wearing a joke mask with a big red nose. Another time I visited her in East Hampton and she answered the door dressed as a cocktail waitress, or something very close.

On her back door, there was a warning sign forbidding entrance to anyone who used the word "hopefully" incorrectly.

A noted hypochondriac, she outdid everyone in real and imagined illnesses. I was waiting for her outside Longchamps at 48th and Madison (bygone days!) when I noticed her suddenly across the street on crutches. It was snowing, I think, a nice, light New York snow. Astonished, I walked over to help her — she was already in the middle of the street by the time I got to her. She was wearing a red plaid cape, very stylish, peculiarly suited to crutches — no sleeves got in the way. When we were safely back on the sidewalk, she said, "Look! Look at these!" and showed me her wrist. Little white blotches were appearing, a sort of albino rash. "What is it?" I asked. "I don't know." She hobbled into lunch. I hadn't even had time to ask about the crutches before she'd been stricken by something new. I never did get the story about the crutches straight. A hypochondriac myself, I was outclassed.

Jean enjoyed medical discussions, symptoms, diagnoses, horror stories, freak accidents, diseases, cures. She owned a

Merck's Manual and a gruesome textbook we would sometimes pore over, looking at the more hideous skin diseases in
color. She was an amateur authority on ailments, including
her own.

Although she was easily influenced, she was the least imi-
tative person I knew. Older women of distinction became
her friends — at least twice — and she would bank her originality in a deference of a peculiar kind, as if a mother with
standards — a woman of impeccable authority — had been
in the back of her mind all the while. But in dress, manner,
and ideas she was independent and crotchety, and about
writers her opinions were her own and unshakable. She
adored cats, old furniture — Biedermeier especially —
books, bourbon, odd clothes. Like the dress she used to
wear that looked like a man's tuxedo and seemed to have a
watch pinned to the lapel. The plaid cape. Fawn slacks and
sweaters. She was a special mixture of the outlandish and the
decorous. She paid great respect to the civilized, but something ingrained and Western in her mocked it at the same
time. Think of Henry James being brought up in
Colorado. . . .

Her favorite cat, George Eliot, used to sit under a lamp,
eyes closed, basking in the warmth. Jean was proud of that,
as if it were some extraordinary feline accomplishment.

In Westport, before she married for the second time, she
had her own apartment for a while. I noticed two typewrit-
ers, one big, one small. I asked her about them. "The big
one's for the novel and the little one's for short stories."

We were going to a cocktail party for St. Jean-Perse. I called for her. We had a drink and then another. Then — and how many times this happened between us! — one of us asked the fatal question: "Do you *really* want to go?" We never got there.

The Met. An opera box. Jean and I turned to each other after the first act of *Andrea Chénier*. This time, the fatal question remained unspoken. We got up and left.

Guilty dawdling became a kind of game between us, as well as a safety valve. If I secretly didn't want to go somewhere, I knew I could always stop off at Jean's and that would be a guarantee of never arriving at my original destination. In any case — or every — Jean was more interesting than anywhere I might be going.

A stitched sampler with the words "God Bless America" hung over her television screen.

She had a dream, a dream in which Arran Island (the one off Scotland, where her forebears came from, not the Aran Islands off Ireland) and the Greek island of Samothrace were historically connected. She paid a visit to Arran Island, and, eventually, she and A. J. Liebling, her third and last husband, went to Samothrace. She began to read seriously in anthropology and archaeology, particularly Lehman on the digs in Samothrace. But I think the broad view of ancient history and mythology required to complete a project mainly intuitive and then oddly confirmed by fact became too complicated and technical for her. What she had started to write with so much enthusiasm couldn't be finished. I stopped asking her about it the way I later stopped asking her about the novel in which her father was the chief character. But one day she let me read what she had of the Samothrace piece — about forty pages — and it was some of the most extraordinary prose I'd ever read. After I'd finished it, I looked at her and said something like, "My God, Jean, if you don't go on with it, at least publish *this*. . . ." I don't know what happened to it. Although Joe Liebling did everything to encourage Jean to write, she was intimidated by his swiftness, versatility, and excellence as a reporter. She shot off in journalistic directions of her own — the book on Oswald's mother, for instance. One day, Joe and I were riding up together in the elevator at *The New Yorker*. I told Joe I'd read the Samothrace piece and how good I thought it was. "I know," he said, "I wish you'd tell her." "I *have*," I said. And added, "I wish I could write prose like *that*. . . ." Joe, about to get off at his floor, turned to me and said, "I wish *I* could. . . ."

She was a born writer, and if certain mannerisms entered her prose later on, there was no question, in my mind at least, that she was one of the most naturally gifted writers I'd ever known. She simply couldn't write a bad sentence, excellence was a matter of personal integrity, the style was the woman. She couldn't stand the half-baked, the almost-good, the so-so. She made her views clear in a series of brilliant book reviews, still uncollected. They are all of a piece throughout, united by a single sensibility and an unwavering intelligence. And the annual round-up reviews of children's books she did for *The New Yorker* were scalpel-like attacks on mediocrity, commercial greed, stupidity, and cant.

One of her qualities hardest to get down on paper was the young girl always present in the civilized and cultivated woman. The balance was delicate and impossible to pin down. Like her conversation, it vanished into smoke. But what smoke!

A strangely momentous occasion: when she and Joe Liebling took an apartment on Fifth Avenue and 11th Street — an elegant, rambling apartment in a house built by Stanford White — before they moved in, Jean and Elizabeth Bowen and I walked about the rooms, talking about rugs, draperies, and so on. One of the rare times in New York City when people were dwarfed by space. Steve Goodyear gave Jean two plants. One, a rubber plant, had leaves that scraped the ceiling — eighteen, maybe twenty feet high.

Jean and I (at Fifth and 11th) sometimes would take out her Ouija board when I came over early for a drink. (This must have been in the late fifties.) The person always summoned up by Jean was her brother Dick, killed in the Second World War. The board would begin to shake, she would become excited by the message she read. . . . But these sessions never lasted long. Joe Liebling didn't like Jean using the Ouija board, and when we heard his key in the door, the board was hastily put away.

The farmhouse Joe Liebling bought in the thirties was first his, then theirs, then hers. It brought her enormous pleasure. She embarked on a long series of renovations, mostly of the interior; each change was a great source of satisfaction, perhaps too much so, for a writer discovers — especially a writer who lives alone — that a house can become a formidable enemy of work. Creative energy is drained off in redecorated guest rooms, expanded gardens, kitchens designed and redesigned to be more practical, new wallpaper, decking, house plants — the list is endless. In Jean's case, off the downstairs dining room she built a new bathroom in one direction and a new study–*cum*–guest room in another; a second new study appeared upstairs. The kitchen was revamped. The thirty or so acres surrounding the farmhouse boasted a particularly beautiful meadow some distance behind her house, a greensward worthy of a château. The shingled farmhouse was ample but modest. Its small living room had a fireplace set at an angle so that no one could ever quite face it. There was a larger dining room and a kitchen and pantry. Farmers didn't waste their money on unnecessary fuel, and, originally, the living room had been a concession to formality rather than a social center. The Liebling-Stafford house had been built for practicality (close to the road in case of a snowstorm), snugness, and warmth. It was a comfortable house and Jean fell in love with it — slowly, I think. It became —in the end — her refuge and her garrison, the place she holed up in and from which she viewed the world. The literal view was pretty enough because, from the front window, across Fire Place Road, you could see the water of an inlet, often intensely blue. There was an apple tree in the backyard, seemingly dead. It developed a new twisted limb and became grotesquely lovely. Behind it, there were many yucca plants with their white desert flowers, and in front of the house a mimosa tree that bloomed each spring.

In spite of a certain reputation for waspishness, the result of a sharply honed and witty tongue, Jean was generous and courageous. When she was accused of being the leader of the supposedly quixotic NBA jury that chose Walker Percy's *The Moviegoer* as the best novel of the year (no one had ever heard of Walker Percy before), she stood up for herself, and for him. And the same thing was true when John Williams's Prix de Rome was withdrawn. She spoke up for anyone she admired. Her nervous but good-natured allure derived from a special combination of the tart and the sweet. She was a surprisingly fine cook, liked entertaining and being entertained (at least for the better part of her life), and, above all, enjoyed good conversation.

She could resist a good writer if she disliked his person, but she was far more open to affection and the giving of it than seems generally known. She put herself out for people she liked and did nothing at all for people she didn't.

Youthfulness of manner was belied by the satiric thrust of her language, the slightly breathless drawl of her speech, the odd sense that she was searching for the next installment of words, another piece of the story, some phrase that would precisely focus what she had in mind — habits of speech cruelly underlined by her stroke, when she became unsure — she, of all people! — of her words. It was unfair and particularly cruel to be stricken at the very center of her being: talk, words, speech. It was not unlike — in the meanness of the affliction undercutting the essential person — Beethoven's going deaf.

She was anecdotal in the extreme, turning everything into a story. This became, later on, and long before the stroke, somewhat edgy. A certain amount of complaining, of being the great-lady-offended had become habitual. Something on the order of "And do you know who had the *nerve* to invite me to dinner last Wednesday?" And so on. But then it would turn out that she had *gone* to dinner, so that the point of the complaint seemed muddled. Once she had taken a real distaste to someone, she refused any invitation, any offer of friendship. And she made enemies easily by being outspoken, opinionated, strict in her standards. Once she took a real scunner to someone, she rarely changed her mind.

She felt abandoned by her friends, sometimes, and they, sometimes, by her. She would forget you for a time and then be hurt and surprised that she had been temporarily forgotten. People I think she liked without qualification: Mrs. Rattray, Saul Steinberg, John Stonehill, Peter Taylor, Elizabeth Bowen, Peter De Vries.

We had dinner together for the last time on July 13, 1978, in East Hampton, at a restaurant called Michael's. I called for Jean. Not being able to drive had once united us; now I had a driver's license. Convenient as it was, I'm not sure Jean approved of it. We arrived — down dark paths to a restaurant on the water. Jean, who had been drinking at home, ordered another bourbon. The question of what to order loomed. No menu came to hand; a young waitress reeled off the available fish of the day. Jean deferring, I ordered striped bass. Then Jean said, "I cannot do striped bass." But she didn't seem to be able to do anything else, either, and, after some confusion, I asked the waitress to give us a few minutes. I went over again what fish were available. The waitress came back. Jean said, "Striped bass." I asked her if she was *sure*, considering that she'd said she couldn't do striped bass, and she said she was *absolutely* sure. But when her dish came, she said, "This isn't what I wanted." I wanted to send it back; Jean said not to. Then she added, "What I really wanted was the finnan haddie." There hadn't been any finnan haddie; it had never been mentioned. And I realized we were in some kind of trouble, though most of the conversation was rational, pleasant, at times funny. Suddenly she said, "What do you think of friends?" I was surprised, but babbled on about how they might be the most important people in one's life, not the same as lovers, of course, but desperately needed, a second family, essential. . . . Jean said, lighting a cigarette, "Yes, I must give them up. I'm going to give up smoking." And it became clear she had meant the word "cigarettes" or "smokes" when she said "friends." And I suddenly remembered something: years ago, way back, a mutual friend had described cigarettes as "twenty little friends in a pack — twenty friends always available. . . ." I thought: Could there be a memory behind the choice of every mistaken word?

We talked on the phone twice while she was in New York Hospital. I called again on the afternoon of March 26 because I was going up to see my doctor on East 68th Street and thought I'd stop by and see her. The voice on the phone told me she was no longer there. They had no forwarding address, no information. I called East Hampton. No answer — odd, because there had always been a phone machine where you could leave a message. I couldn't figure out where she'd gone. To the Rusk Rehabilitation Center, it turned out later, a special outpost of the hospital. I found out the next day she had died that afternoon.

PART FOUR

ANTON CHEKHOV

Hingley's Biography

READING the biographies of great writers, one gets the impression that literature is mainly the occupation of mistreated children — those preoccupied with being unloved or being unable to return love. These deficiencies branch out into all sorts of tributaries: anger, shyness, aggression, despair. We admire and analyze the products of these disorders as if unhappiness were an oyster exuding pearl after pearl. And we should feel guilty — we probably do — once we know this secret of art. For aren't we in the uncomfortable position of welcoming bad news? Where would we be if Proust's mother had kissed him good night? If Beethoven's nephew had been a little nicer? If Chekhov — in this case — had been treated with the affection he claims he missed during a childhood of enforced churchgoing, shopkeeping (his father was a grocer), and schoolwork? We are given enigmas — the artist's way of handling the impossible — and the biographer, confronted with enigmas, becomes obsessed by fact. *This* explains *that*, he keeps telling us, with a certain amount of rueful hope.

But sometimes it is in the nature of the artist to accomplish the opposite, to give us work that takes on the illusion of fact — photographs snapped without filters, perfectly clear, without affectation — and to save the real enigma for the life itself. And Chekhov would seem to be a case in point, for literary criticism has never been able to make him one of its martyrs — about a certain kind of excellence there is little to say — and, of all writers, he strikes us as the least neurotic, the one least having us on, the man who has nothing to hide.

Yet reading Ronald Hingley's *A New Life of Anton Chekhov* (1976) — "new" because he wrote an earlier biography in 1950 — one realizes that the more we know of Chekhov the less apt any of the standard portraits seem: the gray patriarch of twilight Russia, black coat buttoned to the neck, pince-nez and cane, gloomily tracing the decline of an attractive but listless gentry; its counterimage — the lively and witty host, always surrounded by people, teaser of women, doctor, builder of schoolhouses, planter of trees; the elegant Chekhov, staring with just a bit of world-weariness straight into the camera, perhaps recalling the gambling tables of Monte Carlo, the palm-lined boulevards of Nice; the adventuresome loner, crossing the five thousand miles of Siberian wasteland (before the construction of the Trans-Siberian Railroad) by horse and buggy, flatboat and steamer, to take a census of the exiled prisoners on remote Sakhalin Island; and the official Soviet version, hand to dedicated breast, gazing off into a revolutionary future.

The blurred outlines of all these pictures must have some

truth, for we are dealing, after all, with the same man, and one who lived only to the age of forty-four. Mr. Hingley goes to great lengths to take down these well-worn icons. What he puts in their place is a rational metamorphosis, the transformation of the grandson of a freed serf into the most admired short-story writer and playwright of his day — and of this century.

A spirited and humorous child, Chekhov was filled with contradictions from the beginning. Like Keats, he studied medicine, became a writer, contracted tuberculosis, died young, and became celebrated for a posthumous body of work, the letters. Hingley doesn't tell us anything new, really — that is, about the life itself — but he manages to add enough detail to make the truth more believable. Chekhov was that paradoxical creature in whom subtlety and honesty were mixed in equal parts — uncomfortable bedfellows. He saw more than anyone around him and what he saw was either ludicrous or painful. But the pain was not only outside. An ironic man, he seems to have known everything about love but how to feel it, or — if that seems an unfair description of someone who has taught us so much about it — at least how to express it. For what amazes one reading any Chekhov biography, including this one, are two basic facts: everyone adored him; no one felt close to him. He was a moral man and a free one, and, though he eventually married — very late — marriage, perhaps intimacy of any kind, were not freedom's noteworthy ingredients. Story after story, play after play make the same point: if life is a disappointment, love is the biggest disappointment in it. Behind every social failure — of class, illusion, accomplishment — there lies an unconnected couple.

And that may be why Hingley spends a bit too much time on Chekhov's "loves," a subject he feels he neglected in the earlier biography. Chekhov's attitude toward sex was surprisingly prudish; on the other hand, many examples are quoted from his correspondence with Alexander and Nicholas, his older brothers, and, in their cases, prudishness may have been the other side of caution. Both brothers were charming, alcoholic, and self-destructive. Hingley's insistence on delving into Chekhov's love life makes the biographer seem sometimes like a high-wire artist balancing on a wire that isn't quite there. Gossip is never teased into fact; still, Hingley overdoes it, for in a biography, any conjecture is easily confused with history, and very little in the area of passion can be pinned down. Even if it were, with someone as elusive as Chekhov, its significance would remain in doubt. The man who invented a way of revealing everything about character through the seeming miracle of making character inarticulate surely was on to the trick himself, and it was a technique that could easily be reversed.

If there were no great loves, there were flirtations and romances, and we know most about the one with Lika Mizinova because Chekhov made the most use of it. Lika, in love with Chekhov for many years, was tolerated, indulged, but not wildly encouraged, and she finally ran off with Potapenko, a Ukrainian writer. Potapenko and his amour were trailed across Europe by his ferocious wife, Mariya Andreyevna, who was good at making scenes. Potapenko, a tower of Jell-O, abandoned the pregnant Lika in Paris and the Potapenkos departed for Italy. Lika appealed to Chekhov for help; he was polite but not cooperative, and, as Hingley points out, if she had read "A Dreary Story," published five years earlier, where a similar appeal goes unanswered, she might have saved herself the trouble. Chekhov had once before exploited the lives of his friends in the story "The Butterfly," but Lika and the Potapenkos turned up, all too visibly, as Nina, Trigorin, and Arkadina in *The Seagull*.

Chekhov was not quite the traditional angel of legend; he could be two-faced and insensitive, and manipulated people for his own ends. Not many occasions present themselves to support these assertions, but Hingley is fair in pointing them out, and he does so almost gratefully, as if thankful for the few shreds of evidence that might rescue Chekhov from the danger of becoming a plaster saint.

Illness and impotency — a frequent complaint — must have had their psychological effects. But circumstances may have been crucial in Chekhov's reluctance to form any sort of permanent relationship. He was the third child in a family of six children; his father left Taganrog — Chekhov's provincial birthplace — bankrupt, stealing off into the night to avoid his creditors; and by the time Chekhov arrived in Moscow to study medicine, he was not only the center of a family struggling for survival but its openly acknowledged head.

From the age of twenty, Chekhov was in varying degrees, and at various times, responsible for a family of from four to eight people. It was not the kind of situation, even if he were the kind of man, to make marriage attractive. His younger sister, Masha, remained a spinster, and it is clear from Hingley's account that every time she made a bid for freedom, Chekhov, through the simple expedient of withholding emotional support, made a difficult decision impossible. Until Chekhov married the Moscow Art Theater actress Olga Knipper, Masha was his housekeeper, hostess, companion, and nurse.

If Hingley doesn't quite solve the ambiguities of Chekhov's

emotional life, he does something more important. He provides a coherent structure for a body of work that has floundered in confusion from the beginning. American readers, in particular, are bedeviled by edition after edition in which the stories appear haphazardly, where no attempt is made to arrange the contents chronologically (Robert Payne's *The Image of Chekhov* is an exception), and we are given, willy-nilly, early and late work thrown together, no corresponding Russian titles, and no dates of composition or publication. Something called "Grief," about a horse, in one paperback, turns up as "Misery" in another, but then, there is "Grief" again, which turns out to be another story entirely, about a bishop, something we had formerly known under the title of "Anguish."

Hingley redresses all these wrongs: first, in his admirably translated and edited Oxford *Chekhov*, a nine-volume chronological edition of the plays and stories, and in this biography, where, dividing Chekhov's work into two main categories, he allows the second to be the period of the major stories and plays, dating from 1888 with the publication of "The Steppes."

The first category, the more or less immature work — there are early masterpieces, genius not fitting easily into grooves — is subdivided into four distinct periods, the earliest being that of the skits, jokes, one-liners, puns, and sketches Chekhov turned out for the humor magazines of the day under the pseudonym of Antosha Chekonte to help support himself while studying medicine. The three remaining periods simply correspond to whichever magazine Chekhov happened to be publishing in most frequently at the time: *Splinters*, *The Petersburg Gazette*, or *New Time*.

There are overlappings and problems — one-act plays were hammered out of stories, early work was revised to surface again, the most notable being the transformation of the middling *The Wood Demon* into *Uncle Vanya* — but in the main the method works, and, for the first time, all of Chekhov's writing falls into place as if, at last, an extraordinarily complex series of facts were reduced to basic propositions. Even tables in an appendix, forbiddingly academic and scientific elsewhere, are helpful and illuminating here. Hingley has created order out of a mess, and the whole hodgepodge of Chekhov's fiction is put into clear relief, the Russian compositions matched with their English equivalents.

Certain Chekhovian stereotypes are abandoned or corrected. Chekhov and Stanislavsky had a running battle in regard to the production of the plays. But though Stanislavsky may have been heavy-handed, and given to a naturalism the plays made obsolete, in one way he was right. Chekhov claimed Stanislavsky's interpretations had made "cry-babies" out of his plays, but to call *The Cherry Orchard* a comedy is to be disingenuous. Hingley thinks Chekhov, trying to assure a certain "lightness" of tone, used the word "comedy" as a signpost, a guarantee against heaviness. Perhaps so. But the result has been a series of productions of the plays veering sharply toward melancholy — or, as an antidote, the bucolic. In any case, who but a madman would leave a performance of *The Seagull* laughing?

Gorky called Chekhov the only free man he knew. Immune to cant at a time when the air was practically solid with it, Chekhov was able to resist the deadliness of prescribed truths, whether of the left or of the right. Even his admiration and love of Tolstoy didn't blind him to the inan-

ities of Tolstoy's theories. Chekhov made his position — or
non-position — unequivocal: "I am not a liberal. I am not a
conservative. I am not an advocate of moderate reform. I am
not a monk. Nor am I committed to non-commitment. I
should like to be a free artist, that's all."

Chekhov had — still has — a way of surprising his readers
by not raising his voice to denounce the lazy, the sexually
loose, the ne'er-do-well, or to praise the philanthropist, the
samaritan, and the morally correct. The moral complexity of
the stories and plays stems from this undercurrent of ambiguous sympathy, this withholding of judgment. In "The
Duel," Layevsky, the sloppy adulterer, is more congenial
than Von Koren, the enlightened Darwinian. Motive counts
more than action because motive ultimately reveals itself.
What Chekhov hated most was rigidity, authoritarianism,
and hypocrisy. He saw little difference between the dead
hand of the imperial censor and the pernicious overseers of
the liberal press; he was hounded equally from both sides.
Chekhov once said, "Morals do not purify plays any more
than flies purify the air," and felt that fanaticism of any
stripe was the ultimate danger. And in denouncing the editors of *Russkaya mysl*, a liberal paper (one he later published
in), he made a prediction:

Just you wait. . . . Under the banner of learning, art and per-
secuted freedom of thought Russia will one day be ruled by
such toads and crocodiles as were unknown even in Spain under
the Inquisition. . . . Narrow-mindedness, enormous pretensions, excessive self-importance, a total absence of literary or
social conscience: these things will do their work [and] will
spawn an atmosphere so stifling that every healthy person will

be . . . nauseated by literature, while every charlatan and wolf
in sheep's clothing will have a stage on which to parade his
lies. . . .

And Chekhov was right to distrust the mind devoted to
one idea. Governments are more easily changed than cultural
climates; the imperial censors of Czarist Russia have their
Soviet counterparts. And Soviet editors (not necessarily will-
ingly) have bowdlerized Chekhov's correspondence. An in-
correct political opinion or a sexual reference — prudery and
repression going hand in hand — is expunged from the text
or given the usual three-dot treatment. In the present and
forthcoming Soviet edition of *Works and Letters*, 1974–1982,
replacing the earlier edition of 1944–1951, some progress
has been made (in the few early volumes Hingley has been
able to examine). But it is progress of a dubious kind. The
word "Yid," for instance, is now printable. But whether this
is a relaxation of censorship or a footnote to unofficial anti-
Semitism remains moot. According to Hingley, the word
was less pejorative in Chekhov's time than it is now. But it
was always condescending, if not worse, and disheartening
coming from Chekhov. He was hardly an anti-Semite, having been engaged to a Jewish girl, come to the defense of a
Jewish student denied entrance to his school under the quota
system, and taken up the cause of Dreyfus. Still, there it is.

Where Hingley is most original is in tracing the growth of
Chekhov's fiction. He distinguishes the finest work — "Ward
Number Six," "A Dreary Story," "The Kiss," and so on —
from the very good work, separating the cream from the
cream. And he deplores the botched ending of "The Duel,"
a flawed masterpiece, which resolves itself in an atypically

sentimental manner in its last pages. One goes back to that story, and others, with a new eye. They are mentioned by Hingley in passing, for he insists this book, unlike the earlier one, is purely biographical. The panorama of the whole is laid before us, the ups and downs, the hills and the valleys; and if Hingley's perspective somehow manages to go flat on heights and to skim some depths, we understand the relation of the stories to the life and the times, to each other, and, to a lesser degree, to the plays. Hingley also points out what may be either a repetitive subject or merely a technical device in the more structured stories and the plays: the opposition of two male characters in basic philosophical or emotional conflict: Treplev and Trigorin, Von Koren and Layevsky, Serabryakov and Vanya.

Many Chekhovs appear in Hingley's biography: the natural mimic, got up in dark glasses and fur coat, sneaking into the balcony of Taganrog's theater; the writer at one summer dacha or another, fishing, hunting, mushroom-gathering; the estate owner at Melikhova, planting his orchards, running a small medical clinic; the famous playwright uncomfortably taking his bows after the premiere of *The Cherry Orchard;* the friend of Bunin, Gorky, Tolstoy; and finally the celebrated exile dying in Yalta of tuberculosis, a disease he couldn't or wouldn't diagnose for over ten years, in spite of his medical training.

Confronted with all this documentation, the most complete ever assembled in an examination of Chekhov's life, why is it that the man who so convincingly coalesces into a single portrait in the letters eludes a biographer as knowledgeable as Hingley? It is partly, I think, Chekhov's ability to hold two things at once in suspension: the sensitivity and the candor, the "poetry" of the plays and their clear-headed-ness, the scientific discipline of the doctor and the imaginative freedom of the writer. We have in Chekhov someone contradictory but completely trustworthy, someone devoted to truth by temperament rather than by doctrine.

It takes a superb writer to make discordant notes sound like a single tone. And Hingley is not a superb writer; in fact, he is often a dull one, given to odd grammatical quirks, an occasionally highfalutin vocabulary ("subvention," "swived," "equipollent"), and a style sometimes too sprightly, as if to counteract the drugs of academe. And he makes one brave but classic misjudgment, in my opinion, in preferring *Ivanov* to *The Seagull*. Hingley has written the most informative biography of Chekhov we have, the one based on the most recent evidence, the most advanced scholarship. But somehow the right tone is never struck, the man we get to know so much about dips under the net and, with a little smile, a wave of the hand, disappears. We are indebted to Hingley in a thousand ways: for rescuing us from inflated translations, for putting work in its proper sequence, for correcting the record where Soviet censorship has intervened. But for the live Chekhov, flesh and blood, the letters are still the richest source.

ANTON CHEKHOV

Three Sisters

"Loneliness is a terrible thing, Andrei."

In *Three Sisters*, the inability to act becomes the action of the play. How to make stasis dramatic is its problem, and Chekhov solves it by a gradual deepening of insight rather than by the play of event. The grandeur of great gestures and magnificent speeches remains a Shakespearean possibility — a diminishing one. Most often, we get to know people through the accretion of small details — minute responses, tiny actions, little gauze screens being lifted in the day-to-day pressure of relationships. In most plays, action builds toward a major crisis. In *Three Sisters*, it might be compared to the drip of a faucet in a water basin; a continuous process wears away the enamel of the façade.

Many stories are being told simultaneously: the stories of the four Prozorov orphans — three girls, one boy, grown up in varying degrees — living in one of those Chekhovian provincial towns that have the literal detail of a newspaper story but keep drifting off into song. There is the old drunken doctor, Chebutykin, once in love with the Prozorovs' mother. There is a slew of battery officers stationed in the town — one of them, Vershinin, a married man, falls in love with the already-married middle-sister, Masha; another proposes to the youngest, Irena; and still a third, Soliony, also declares his love for her. There is Olga, the oldest sister, and Kulighin, Masha's awkward schoolteacher husband. And there is Natasha, the small-town girl who sets her heart on Andrei, the brother. It is Natasha's and Andrei's marriage that provides the catalyst of change. Each of these characters might be conceived as a voice entering the score at intervals to announce or to develop its subject, to join and part in various combinations: duets, trios, and so on. *Three Sisters* is the most musical in construction of all of Chekhov's plays, the one that depends most heavily on the repetition of motifs. And it uses music throughout: marching bands, hummed tunes, "the faint sound of an accordion coming from the street," a guitar, a piano, the human voice raised in song.

Yet too much can be made of the "music" of the play at the expense of its command of narrative style. Private confrontation and social conflict are handled with equal authority, and a symbolism still amateur in *The Seagull*, written five years earlier, has matured and gone underground to permeate the texture of the work. No dead bird is brought onstage weighted with meaning. No ideas are embalmed in objects. What we have instead is a kind of geometric structure, one angle of each story fitting into the triangular figure of another, and, overlaying that, a subtle web of connected images and words. Seemingly artless, it is made of steel. In a letter to his sister, Chekhov complained, "I find it very difficult to write *Three Sisters*, much more difficult than any of my other plays." One can well believe it.

Because immobility is the subject — no other play catches hold of the notion so definitively, with the exception of *Hamlet* — secondary characters carry the burden of narration forward. Natasha and Andrei establish the main line of construction; their marriage is the network to which everything else attaches. Yet Andrei never spins the wheels of action. That task is left to Natasha, a character originally outside the immediate family, and to another stranger to the domestic circle, Soliony. One a provincial social climber, the other a neurotic captain, each takes on, in time, an ultimate coloration: Natasha, the devouring wife; Soliony, the lethal friend.

Natasha's motives are obvious enough to be disarming — disarming in its literal sense: to deprive one of weapons. No one need *suspect* her of the worst; her lies are so transparent that every civilized resource is called upon to deal with the transparency rather than the lie.

Soliony lacks accessible motivation but is easily recognizable as a true creature from life. Panicky and literal, he is repellent — one of the few repellent characters Chekhov ever created. If Soliony is shy, shyness is dangerous. Instinct, not insight, leads him to the weak spot in other people. A deeply wounded man who has turned into a weapon, he is a member of a species: the seducer-duelist, a nineteenth-century stock character Chekhov manages to twist into a perverse original.

When Irena rejects him, he says he will kill anyone who wins her; and in the name of affection, he makes good his threat. Ironically, Irena's halfhearted relationship to Tuzenbach becomes the fatal rivalry of the play; Tuzenbach has won Irena's hand but not her heart. Moreover, Soliony is introduced into the Prozorov circle by Tuzenbach, who therefore begins the chain of events leading to his own death.

Nothing redeems Soliony except the barbarity of his manner, a symptom of an alienation deep enough, perhaps, to evoke pity. A person who cannot feel pleasure and destroys everyone else's, his touchy uneasiness is irrational, the punishment it exacts inexhaustible. Unwilling to be mollified by life's niceties or won over by its distractions, he is a definite negative force in a play in which a lack of energy is crucial. Natasha turned inside-out, a killer without her affectations and pieties, he is, if never likable, at least not a liar. He tells us several times that, even to him, the scent he uses fails to disguise the smell of a dead man. That stench rises from a whole gallery of literary soldiers. No matter how heroic a military man may be, he is, functionally, a murderer. Soliony reminds us of that easily forgotten fact; he is the gunman of the play.

And the gunshot in *Three Sisters* is fired offstage — a shot heard before in *Ivanov*, *The Seagull*, and *The Wood Demon*. In *Uncle Vanya*, the shots occur *on*stage; half-farcical, they are not without psychological danger. Vanya shoots out of humiliation; his failure to hit anything only deepens it. The offstage gunshot in *Three Sisters* does more than end Tuzenbach's life and destroy Irena's marriage. A final fact, it leaves in its wake a slowly emerging revelation, the dark edge of an outline: the black side of Irena.

In the scene just preceding the shot, Tuzenbach makes a crucial request. Irena has described herself earlier as a locked piano to which she has lost the key.

TUZENBACH: I was awake all night. Not that there's anything to be afraid of in my life, nothing's threatening. . . . Only the thought of that lost key torments me and keeps me awake. Say something to me. . . . (*A pause.*) Say something!
IRENA: What? What am I to say? What?
TUZENBACH: Anything.

Tuzenbach, about to fight a duel with Soliony, needs Irena's reassurance. Forced to obscure a fact while trying to express an emotion, he says ". . . nothing's threatening." He is telling a lie, and, unaware of his true situation, Irena can hardly be blamed for not understanding its desperateness. There is something odd about Tuzenbach's request in the first place: he already knows Irena doesn't love him and is hoping against hope for a last reprieve. The inability to bare or face emotional realities — a favorite Chekhovian notion — is only partly in question here; here there is something worse: to feel the demand but not the attraction. For even if Irena understood Tuzenbach's request, her response, if honest, would have to be equivocal. They are both guilty; he for demanding love where he knows it doesn't exist, she for not loving. He is asking too much; she is offering too little.

Tuzenbach's request echoes almost exactly the one Katya makes to the Professor at the end of "A Dreary Story," where it is met with the same failure:

"Help me, help me!" she begs. "I can't stand anymore . . ."
"There's nothing I can say, Katya . . ."
I am at a loss, embarrassed, moved by her sobbing, and I can hardly stand.
"Let's have lunch, Katya," I say with a forced smile. "And stop that crying. I shall soon be dead, Katya." I at once add in a low voice.

"Just say one word, just one word!" she cries, holding out her hands.

Katya seems as impervious to the Professor's death sentence as he is to her despair. Each is too full of his own suffering. The characters in *Three Sisters*, like Katya and the Professor, do not hear each other's pleas, partly out of selfishness — other people's troubles are boring — partly out of self-protection. If they *did* hear them, what could they do?

Needs, revealed but never satisfied, drive Chekhov's characters toward two kinds of action: the deranged — Vanya's hysterical outbursts, Treplev's suicide — or flight. They desert each other — as Katya deserts the Professor half a page after the dialogue above, and as Trigorin abandons Nina in *The Seagull*. Nothing could be more Chekhovian than the last sentence of "A Dreary Story." The Professor, watching Katya go, wonders if she'll turn around and look back at him for the last time. She doesn't. Then he says to himself "Goodbye, my treasure" — end of story. But those three words are endlessly and ambiguously illuminating. Does he love Katya? Is she his treasure because this is the last feeling he will ever have? Is this final desertion the one symptom of his being human? Is there a tiny sarcastic twinge to "treasure"? In regard to people, every credible truth is only partial.

The inability to respond evokes responses: coldness, hatred, contempt. Loneliness can be viewed as humiliation and misfortune as insult. What cannot be given is interpreted as being withheld. The wrong people always love each other — bad luck or the telltale sign of a fundamental incapacity to love. The typical Chekhovian character longs for what he can neither express nor have, and each unrequited wish is one more dream in a universal nightmare. If the great treachery lies in the disparity between what we feel and what we say, between what we want and what we get, do we have — through an unconscious perversity — a vested interest in disparity itself? Proust, the ultimate dissector of jealousy, thought so, and it is odd to think that Chekhov, working with such different material and in such a different way, may have come to a similar conclusion. The truth is that what is interesting about love is how it doesn't work out, and Proust and Chekhov saw that truth and that interest from different angles. Surprisingly, like Proust in *Remembrance of Things Past*, who provides us with not one example of a happy marriage in over four thousand pages, Chekhov offers us none either.

And both Proust and Chekhov concern themselves with a social class that is about to be overwhelmed by forces rising from below. In Proust, the class distinctions are clear; we know exactly who is noble, and who is middle-class. We have to, because the impingement of one upon the other is one of the themes of the novel. That certainty eludes us in Chekhov's case. Olga, Masha, and Irena belong to a social class that has no counterpart in America. We see them as a kind of provincial nobility (partly because we have got to them so often through English accents), whereas they represent the lowest rung of a rural aristocracy, a sort of down-at-the-heels upper middle class living in the country: squires going to seed, a gentry saddled with land that no longer interests them, fitful leftovers unable to cope with the unfamiliar and the new. Chekhov's plays suffer from classlessness in translation, and more than classlessness in certain productions: maids become heroines and stable boys stars. The main difficulty is: one can hardly imagine Irena in Kansas, say, stretching her hands toward an imaginary New York. She would have already been there, traveling by jet. And, in *The Seagull*, would anyone have the faintest notion of just what *kind* of bank Madame Arkadina kept her much-discussed securities in?

But power, as a source, is general no matter the specific version, and both Natasha and Soliony are interested in it. Each is allowed to inherit a particular world: domestic tyranny in Natasha's case, the completed fantasy of the romantic egoist in Soliony's: the destruction of the rival lover. The passivity of the others gives them permission, it invites them in.

An embittered fact-monger, Soliony is unable to respond to any shade of irony. And though Irena is too young to know it, to be literal and humorless — qualities equally at home in the romantic and the dullard — can be as poisonous as deception or ingrained meanness. Worldliness is never an issue in *Three Sisters*, though it might well be. Vershinin brings a breath of it in the door with him, but it is the weary urbanity of a disappointed middle-aged man. A lack of worldliness in people forced to live in the world is always a potential source of suffering. Those people doomed to love late and to be ultimately denied love, like Masha and Vershinin, arrive at knowledge by way of lost opportunities and through a web of feeling. In *Three Sisters*, we get two warped versions of worldliness: Natasha's grasping selfishness and the doctor's cynicism. They are the merest echoes of the real thing. What we have in its place is calculation on the one hand and frustration on the other. There is no wise man in the play for the others to turn to; there is no mother and father for children who remain children, though they walk about as if they were adults, to run to for comfort and advice. In Chekhov's view, even worldliness, we suspect, would be another inadequate means of dealing with life, as powerless as innocence to fend off its evils, and, because it comes in the guise of wisdom, perhaps the most deceptive of all.

It is not always clear in various editions of the play that these revelations occur over a period of five years. We watch Irena, in fact, change from a young girl into a woman. The time scheme is relatively long, the roles are enigmatically written and need to be played with the finest gradations in order to develop their true flavors and poisons. If Natasha is immediately recognizable as evil, or Soliony as the threat of the play, a great deal is lost in characterization and suspense. Irena's cry of "Moscow! . . . Moscow!" at the end of the second act should be a note in a scale, not a final sounding. She has not realized, she is *beginning* to realize that what she hopes for will remain a dream.

Compared to *The Seagull* and *Uncle Vanya*, a technical advance occurs in *Three Sisters* that may account for a greater sounding of the depths. Chekhov's mastery of the techniques of playwriting may be measured by his use of the gun; it is farther offstage here than before — not in the next room but at the edge of town, which suggests that it might, finally, be dispensed with, as it is in *The Cherry Orchard*, where the only sound we hear, ultimately, is an ax cutting down trees. As he went on, Chekhov let go of the trigger, his one concession to the merciless demands of the stage. The gunshot in *Three Sisters*, unlike the shot in *Vanya*, is terminal. But Tuzenbach's death has further implications; it is partly the result of, and the price paid for, Irena's lack of love. Something suicidal colors Tuzenbach's death, and we pick it up in his last big speech:

TUZENBACH: . . . Really, I feel quite elated. I feel as if I were seeing those fir-trees and maples and birches for the first time in my life. They all seem to be looking at me with a sort of inquisitive look and waiting for something. What beautiful trees — and how beautiful, when you think of it, life ought to be with trees like these!
(*Shouts of 'Ah-oo! Heigh–ho!' are heard.*)
I must go, it's time . . . Look at that dead tree, it's all dried-up, but it's still swaying in the wind along with the others. And in the same way, it seems to me that, if I die, I shall still have a share in life somehow or other. Goodbye, my dear . . . (*Kisses her hands.*) Your papers, the ones you gave me, are on my desk, under the calendar.

Tuzenbach never had much of "a share in life"; he has always been a "dried-up [tree] . . . swaying in the wind." If Irena had been able to love him, would he have tried to talk to Soliony or to Dr. Chebutykin and in some way mediated the pointlessness of this ending? A pointlessness equally vivid, one suspects, whether he had married Irena or not.

The key to Irena's heart, that locked piano, is lost. Neither Tuzenbach nor Soliony ever had it. So their duel, though in deadly earnest, turns out to be an ironic, even a ludicrous footnote. Who holds the key to Irena's heart? Someone off-stage — like the gun — whom she hopes to meet in Moscow. "The right one" is how she describes him, the unmeetable ideal who dominates the fantasies of schoolgirls. The doctor may comfort himself with bogus philosophy and claim that nothing matters, but the others tend to confirm not his thesis but its perverse corollary. By the indecisiveness of their actions, by their inability to deal head-on with what is central to their lives, they make, in the end, what matters futile. They unwittingly prove Dr. Chebutykin's false notion: what *does* Tuzenbach's death matter? Would Irena be any more lonely with him than without him? Would he have been content living with someone who doesn't love him, he who needs love to make himself feel lovable? Would Irena have joined him in "work" — her idealized version of it — and now be working alone? At what? Reality intrudes upon a pipe dream, but even the reality is dreamlike. The Baron's sacrifice does little for the cause of either work or love.

Of the three sisters, Olga is the least interesting: nothing romantic attaches to her. She is neither unhappily married nor unhappily *un*married. A person of feeling who has suppressed or never felt the pull of the irrational, she is the substitute mother or the spinster-mother — a recognizable type for whom the traditional role is the aunt, boringly earnest but secretly admirable. She represents a standard of behavior unwillingly, almost painfully, for her nerves are not equal to the moral battles in which she must take part, yet those very nerves are the barometric instruments that register ethical weather. Two sets of values are in conflict in *Three Sisters* as well as two social classes, and nothing makes those values clearer than Olga's and Natasha's confrontation over Anfisa, the eighty-year-old nurse. To Olga, Anfisa deserves the respect accorded the old and the faithful. Natasha uses Anfisa as another means of enforcing a pecking order whose main function is to make her status visible. She demands that Anfisa stand up in her presence like a soldier at attention. In this clash of feelings and wills, Olga doesn't defend Anfisa as she should: in true opposition, in attack. She is too stunned, too hurt. She says, ". . . everything went black." Natasha, out to win, wins in spite of what would ordinarily be a great drawback — her affair with Protopopov. Even her open-faced adultery, commented upon by the doctor in the third act, doesn't undercut her position. People prefer to ignore her rather than precipitate a series of crises whose logical end could only be an attack on Andrei. And Andrei cannot be attacked. Affection, pity, and, most of all, necessity are his three shields. Natasha has found the perfect nest to despoil. Andrei was always too weak, too self-centered, in spite of his shyness, to guard his sisters' interests. Now he is not only weak; he is torn.

But Olga is too morally good to let Natasha's rudeness to Anfisa pass without protest — as so many other instances have passed: Natasha's request for Irena's room, made both to Irena and Andrei, for instance, which is met with a kind of cowed acquiescence. It is a demand so basically impossible that no immediate way of dealing with it comes to hand. Natasha apologizes to Olga, but it is an apology without understanding, without heart. Actually, it is motivated by Natasha's fear that she has revealed too much, gone too far. Finally, Olga removes Anfisa from the household. There is a tiny suite for her at the school where Olga becomes headmistress, a place where Anfisa may stay for the rest of her life. It is easier — and wiser, too — to get out than to go on fighting a battle already lost. But whether the existence of that suite sways Olga in her decision to *become* a headmistress is left hanging.

Though Natasha and Soliony are the movers and shakers of the play, another neurotic character, invisible throughout, is a spur to its conflicts: Vershinin's suicidal fishwife of a mate, whom he fears, comes to detest, and yet who controls his life. He is weak, too, unable to make a clean break with his own misery. Chekhov points up one of the strangest true facts of emotional life; nothing binds people closer together than mutual unhappiness. And that is why Chekhov is sometimes so funny. The very horrors of people's lives — short of poverty and disease — are also the most ludicrous things about them. Vanya with a gun! How sad! Yet everyone laughs. The absurd and the tragic are uncomfortably close. Like the figure of the clown, and the wit in black humor, Chekhov teeters on a seesaw. Even a suggestion of the excessive would be ruinous. One gunshot too many, one sob prolonged a second longer than necessary and we have crossed over to the other side. Chekhov, to be played properly, has to be played on a hairline.

Vershinin's mirror-image is Masha, the most interesting of the three sisters, an interest dramatically mysterious because we know so little about her. But we know she is a woman of temperament, a woman capable of passion — and that in itself distinguishes her from Olga, to whom something of the old maid clings, just as something of the ingenue mars Irena. Masha wears black throughout the play, reminding us of her namesake, Masha Shamrayev, in *The Seagull*, who also always wears black because she is "in mourning for [her] life." (It may be of some interest to note that, in the same play, Madame Arkadina's first name is Irena.)

Masha is the onlooker who comments or withholds comment, often to devastating effect. She is the one free-speaker of the play. She tells us the truth about Natasha from the beginning, if only by implication; as a matter of fact, she tells us the truth about everything, even herself, blurting out the facts to her unwilling listeners, Olga and Irena, who don't want to hear of her love for Vershinin, don't want to be involved in a family betrayal. If adultery is a black mark against the detested Natasha, what must one make of it with the beloved Masha? The categories begin to blur, the certainties become uncertain. Like a lot of truth-tellers, Masha is morally impeccable in regard to honesty but something of a menace; she puts people in impossible positions. She is the romantic heart of the play just as Irena is the romantic lead. Unlike Irena, Masha is a lover disillusioned by life, not deluded by it. She married her schoolmaster when she was a young student and bitterly learns that the man who struck her as superior is at heart a fool. The reigning intelligence of the play is Masha's. It might have been the doctor's if intelligence were not so dangerous a gift for a man who has taught himself to be disingenuous.

Masha is still something of an impulsive child, a far different thing from being an adolescent like Irena, or living a self-imposed second childhood like the doctor, whose drunken dream is to make second childhood permanent. Masha isn't interested in intelligence *per se* and the doctor can't afford to be. If he ever let himself know what he knows, it would destroy him. And so he protects himself by a kind of slow-motion destruction, infinitely easier to handle. He keeps telling us how impossible it is to bear reality in a play in which everyone else keeps saying how impossible it is to know what reality is.

In spite of a loveless marriage (from *her* point of view),

Masha has Kulighin who, for all his absurdity, has something everyone else lacks: a true position. Too emasculated to oppose Masha's affair with Vershinin, he nevertheless loves her, sticks by her, and would be desperate without her. A stuffed shirt, a mollycoddle, a bower and a scraper, his ridiculousness masks the genuine feelings of a boy — he loves out of dependency, but who else is able to love in *Three Sisters*? Masha, yes, but her love is romantic; Irena, no, *because* her love is romantic. Kulighin ends up with something: he may wander about the stage calling for Masha, who never seems to be there, but he has the *right* to call her and knows she will go home with him in the end. She has nowhere else to go.

The three marriages in the play — Masha-Kulighin, Vershinin and his offstage wife, and Natasha-Andrei — are all unhappy. Strangely, Masha and Kulighin do not have children, and no mention is ever made of their childlessness. A matter of no significance, it seems, yet it becomes important in regard to Natasha, for it is through the cardinal bourgeois virtue of motherhood that she manipulates the household. Masha provides no counterweight. A subterranean notion percolates at the lowest level of *Three Sisters* — moral righteousness as the chief disguise of self-interest. Power is consolidated under the smoke screen of moral urgency. The Dreyfus Affair, the Reichstag fire, and Watergate are extensions of the same basic principle. Natasha's emotions are as false as her values. Under the camouflage of maternal love, she gains possession of Irena's room and has the maskers dismissed. Whatever *she* may think, it is clear to us that what motivates her action is not her love for her children but her love for herself.

And something similar may be said of Soliony. The duel,
though illegal, was a process by which men of Soliony's day
still settled matters of honor too refined or too personal for
the courts. But it was also a vehicle for macho pride hidden
in the trappings of a gentleman's code. Emotional illness has
never found a better front than ethical smugness.

In contrast to the Prozorovs as we first see them, and in
spite of her malevolence, Natasha is creating a true family,
one with a real mother, father, and children, where only
a semblance of family life had existed before. The ghosts of
family attachments haunt the wanderers crossing the thresh-
olds of rooms, as if they were searching for a phrase impossible to recall, or had fixed their eyes on an invisible figure.
The word "orphan" rings its bell. And Natasha, carrying the
energetic serum of the new, has only one goal: to possess a
material world. Starting out as a girl who doesn't even know
how to dress, she ends up as an unwitting domestic servant
of change, dusting a corner here, tearing down a cobweb
there. Not one of these acts has a generous motive. She is
only a force for progress by being lower class and on the
move. She thinks of herself as the mistress of a house that
had for too long been in disorder without her. And in a certain sense, that view is not irrational. Two questions that can
never be answered are asked *sotto voce* in the play: What
would have happened to everyone if Andrei hadn't married
Natasha? and, What will Andrei's and Natasha's children be
like?

But even Natasha is up against something too subtle to
control. Conquerors have their opposites — losers. But Natasha is working not in a house of losers but of survivors.
Something too lively makes Chekhov's characters, even the

desperate ones, convincing candidates for yet another day of hopes and dreams. One feels their mortality less than their indestructability. Everyone casts the shadow of age ahead; it is hard to think of anyone dying in a Chekhov play who isn't actually killed during the action. Some predisposition to live, some strain of the *type* transfixes the individual into permanent amber, so that, unheroic as they may be, we think of them somewhat in the way we think of Shakespearean heroes. They may languish in life but they refuse to die in art, and with a peculiar insistence — an irony only good plays manage to achieve because it is only on the stage that the human figure is always wholly represented and representative. When we speak of "Masha" or "Vanya," we are already talking about the future. One of the side effects of masterpieces is to make their characters as immortal as the works in which they appear. And so Natasha is stuck among her gallery-mates forever, always *about* to take over the house.

And she is about to do so by exploiting bourgeois morality for ugly ends — an old story. But the subject is the key to Chekhov's method here: the business of unmasking. The soldiers' uniforms hide the same boring civilians underneath. It is important for Tuzenbach literally to take off his clothes and become a civilian "so plain" that Olga cries when she first sees him. Natasha's sash is a tiny repetition of this motif when she reverses roles and comments on Irena's belt in the last act, a bit of signaling uncharacteristic of Chekhov, who rarely stoops to a device so crude. It is already clear that the outsider of Act I has become the dominating power of the household.

Unfulfilled wishes allow for seemingly random duets that enrich the texture of the play by showing us major characters

in minor relationships — psychological side pockets of a sort
that cast desperate or ironic lights. Olga and Kulighin, for
instance, in their discussion of marriage, defend it as an in-
stitution and as a source of happiness. Yet Olga is a spinster
and Kulighin a cuckold. Both schoolteachers, they are drawn
together by their profession and by a kind of innocent ideal-
ism that overrides fact and disappointment. Theirs might
have been the only happy marriage in the play, and Kulighin
says he often thinks if he hadn't married Masha, he would
have married Olga. In the face of adultery, alcoholism, compulsive gambling, irrational rage, and attempted suicide,
Olga still believes in the "finer things," in the vision of human goodness.

Similarly, Irena and Dr. Chebutykin are connected by a
thread of sympathy and habit — the oldest and the youngest
in one another's arms, each equally deluded, alcohol fuzzing
the facts for the doctor, and the determined unawareness of
youth providing Irena with a temporary protective barrier.
These uneasy alliances are touching because they rise out of
needs that bear little relation to their satisfactions. It is precisely Kulighin's marriage to Masha that makes Olga more
deeply aware she is a spinster; it is Chebutykin's drinking
and his smashing of her mother's clock that will finally curdle
Irena's affection for him. And this kind of delicate interplay
between the loving and the hateful aspects of relationships is
reinforced often by the action of the play itself. It is Chebutykin, for example, who is the Baron's second at the duel in
which Irena is deprived of her husband-to-be, her one chance
of making a bid for another life. Trusted by the Baron, Chebutykin has some reason for hoping the Baron is killed —
namely, to protect the continuation of his relationship to

Irena. If that is true, there is a further irony: the doctor doesn't realize that he has already put that relationship in serious jeopardy. And then there are relationships by omission: Andrei's outpourings to the deaf servant Ferapont, Masha never addressing a single word to Natasha throughout the entire course of the play. Masha — like her creator — makes the inarticulate eloquent.

The random duets are complemented by a series of trios. Two are obvious: Masha-Kulighin-Vershinin and Irena-Tuzenbach-Soliony. But a third is not: Chebutykin's ambiguous relationship to Irena provides her with an underground suitor; his is one of those fatherly-grandfatherly roles whose sexual, affectionate, and narcissistic aspects are impossible to unravel, and he places himself in position as a member of a male trio: Tuzenbach-Soliony-Chebutykin. The doctor has a claim on Irena; he was her protector in the past; she is his lifeline now. It is through the subtle shifts of Irena's relationship to Chebutykin that we watch Irena grow from an unknowing girl into a woman who is beginning to see the truth. Chebutykin is onstage, but by being a kind of subliminal lover, he brings to mind, or to the back of the mind, three *off*stage characters essential to the conflicts of the play: Vershinin's wife; Natasha's lover, Protopopov; and the sisters' mother, each an invisible figure in a triangle. If Chebutykin was once in love with the Prozorovs' mother, he was part of an unacknowledged trio: the mother of the sisters, their father, and himself. The mother's image is kept alive in Irena, who resembles her. These offstage-onstage love affairs — one of which we see, one of which we watch being covered up, and one of which we merely hear about — complicate the action and reinforce the play's design of interlocking triangles.

Irena is part of two other triangles, one onstage, one off. A study in ingenuousness, an ingenuousness that will become educated before our eyes, she is joined to Second Lieutenant Fedotik and Rode by the enthusiasms and innocence of youth. If the play were a ballet, at some point they would have a divertissement to themselves. They isolate Chebutykin in a particular way: the contrast between their trio and the doctor makes time physically visible. And then Irena might be considered part of yet another triangle; her dreamed-of "someone" whom she hopes to meet in Moscow is as much of a threat to her happiness with Tuzenbach as Soliony is. It is he, in her mind, who holds the key to the locked piano. Overall, we have our fixed image of a trio, our superimposed stereotype: the three sisters themselves.

The themes of *Three Sisters*, the gulf between dream and action, between hope and disappointment, have finer variations. Even accepting the "real" is thwarted. Irena's compromise in marrying the Baron proves to be impossible. Having given up Moscow, Irena is not even allowed, so to speak, its drearier suburbs. She has met the fate that awaited her all along. Her cry of "work, work," echoed by Tuzenbach, is a hopeless cry. The issue is real, the solution false: What could a dreamy schoolgirl and a philosophical Baron contribute to a brickworks?

But something more than simple evasiveness frustrates the actors in *Three Sisters*. There is a grand plan working out its design, moving the players beyond their ability to act. And the military here perform a special function. When the battery is moved to Poland — its rumored destination was Siberia — the soldiers and officers reverse positions with the sisters, who can never get to Moscow, the dreamland of easy solutions. The sisters are psychologically "stationed" in the

house by a force as ineluctable as that which sends the soldiers on their way. The dispatchment of soldiers is an event
inevitable in time. And illusion gathers strength in ratio to
time: the longer an idea is believed the more powerful it becomes. "If we only knew," the sisters say at the end. "If we
could only know. . . ." Know what? Something already
known — time moves people without their moving: the soldiers are forced to go, the sisters to stay. The object the doctor breaks in his drunkenness is a clock, and for good reason.
Time's pervasiveness — its importance — is stressed many
times in the play: the announcement of what time the maskers are to arrive; the hour set for the duel (at one point, the
doctor takes out his hunting watch to verify it); the fifteen
minutes Natasha allows herself on the sleigh ride with her
lover; the no longer avoidable date on which Andrei's papers
have to be signed; the very first scene, in fact, which is both
an anniversary and a name day. As the minutes tick themselves off, action is always being performed, even by omission. Deluded into thinking time is eternal, events infinitely
postponable, the sisters keep hoping problems will solve
themselves, somehow, in time. They do, but not as a re-
quital to hope. Birth and death, introduced in the anniversary–name day occasion of the first scene, are more sharply
contrasted and connected in the last. Natasha's newest baby
is wheeled back and forth in a carriage, a bit of counterpoint
to Tuzenbach's death. In between, we have, simply, age —
the eighty years of Anfisa's life.

Time sounds a recurrent note in *Three Sisters*; place is more
subtly emphasized. The idea of a journey hovers in the air
and charges the atmosphere — the journey never taken, the
journey never to *be* taken. The repeated sounding of "Mos-

cow!" is more than the never-to-be-reached Eldorado of the work or its lost Eden; it is a symbol of distance itself, that past or future in space from which the characters are forever barred. On this score, the play peculiarly divides itself on sexual grounds: the men want to stay, the women to go. Memory lures them in opposite directions, and Masha's halting bit of verse clues us in. What cannot be remembered takes on importance; it begins to have the force of a prediction in the same way that the unconscious, unable to bring significant material to the surface, determines future behavior. What does her verse mean? Where has she heard it? She says nothing for the first fifteen minutes of the play, she hums a little tune, remembers a line of verse she can't quite place. She has given up the piano. Enraged beyond speech, she feels — when we first see her — that any communication would be a betrayal. What Masha remembers most vividly, and whose betrayal she cannot forgive, is herself. Even music and poetry, because they evoke memory, are forms of conspiracy: they reveal the sensibility she has forfeited for the stupidity of the world she lives in.

The women want to go; more than that, they want to go *back*. Back to a life they once lived (they think), certainly not the one they are living. As for a brave new world, there are no explorers in *Three Sisters*, no wanderers ready to set forth for the unknown. The word "Siberia" runs its little chill through the kitchen. The play is nostalgic, for one set of people would do anything *not* to be removed from where they are (a form of self-miring in the present as if it *were* the past), and one set would do anything, short of what is necessary, to *be* removed. The setting is . . . where? A country town. But it is the least realistic of Chekhov's plays, or at least what is realistic about it always suggests the allusive, one image connecting with or piling up on a similar one. Masha gives up the piano; Irena is a locked piano; Andrei plays the violin. Vershinin receives letters; Kulighin has his notebooks; Andrei is translating an English novel. A whistled phrase is a signal from Vershinin to Masha or vice versa; the doctor bangs on the floor — his little Morse code. Irena gives up her room for a baby; Olga gives up hers for an old woman, Anfisa. These networks are fine meshes thrown over the realistic surface of the play. The webs of character obscure — and enrich — the scaffold of action. And what is allusive about the play suggests the thematically symbolic. Where do people move? From room to room? (Is that why the first thing we see is a room within a room?) But two crucial moves, Irena and Olga doubling up in one bedroom and Anfisa moving out, are overshadowed by the movement, the literal displacement, of the soldiers going to two possible destinations: Poland (where we are still within the limits of the civilized and the credible) and Siberia (where we move into the realm of fear and fantasy).

The sense of danger, a hairsbreadth away from the cozy, becomes actual in the fire of Act III. People can really be forced out of their houses, they can be *made to move* by events beyond their power to predict or control. The fire presents us with a true Apocalypse, its victims huddled downstairs, lost souls wandering about, crying, the rescuers, inside and out, trying to keep the contagion from spreading. Blankets, beds, food are commandeered. Still the shadow of the flames races up the walls. We are in a disaster area, a battlefield. We are also in Olga's and Irena's bedroom. The disaster outside is the general counterpart of the specific horrors within. They have one thing in common: dislocation. For the burning houses are no longer truly houses, any more than the room is now either Olga's *or* Irena's. Natasha has invaded the place of privacy, the source of identity, and we get to know that because it is *after* this scene that Olga moves out to become headmistress and *during* it that Irena decides to marry the Baron and Masha to sleep with Vershinin. And these three decisions prepare us for a fourth: the removal of Anfisa from the household. That is not as simple a decision as it first appears, for Anfisa is the basic — and the last — link with whatever living tradition ties the sisters to their childhoods. The issue of Anfisa is the scale that balances the strengths and weaknesses of Olga and Natasha, the turning point of the act and the breaking point of the play. In a psychological terror scene, the fate of the Prozorovs is decided. Natasha's taking over of the house is played against the bigger landscape of the fire destroying the adjacent houses. But the small wreck and the large are equally devastating.

Each sister is given an opportunity for moral or emotional expansion and is finally enclosed in the limited world of the possible. Each outlasts a wish and is forced to go on living a life without any particular pleasure or savor. The sway of compulsion is important to the play because compulsion suggests what must be limited: to be compelled is the opposite of being able to make a free choice. And there are enough examples of the irrational in the air to make the fearful and the uncontrollable real: Vershinin's wife's suicide attempts, Andrei's gambling, the doctor's alcoholism, Natasha's temper, and Soliony, our capital case, because he brings about what we are most afraid of: death. The departed, the unloved, the disappointed — all these are pale imitations of true oblivion. Soliony is the darkest cloud of all.

Three Sisters is enigmatic — it would be hard to say just

how the last speeches should be played: sadly, bitterly, as a kind of cosmic, ridiculous joke? or realistically, as if in the face of hopelessness it were possible to conceive a Utopia? Only *Hamlet* offers so many unresolved possibilities. Could the doctor have saved Tuzenbach in the last act? Does he let him die to ensure his own continuing relationship to Irena? Is there a homosexual undercurrent in the relationship between Soliony and Tuzenbach? It was suggested in the Olivier–Bates version of the play. Are the trio of Irena's suitors — the doctor, Soliony, and Tuzenbach — an ironic or merely an instrumental little mirror-play of the sisters themselves, trio for trio? Is Vershinin's vision of the world to come just another more cosmic version of the never-to-be-attained Moscow of Irena's dreams? There are overtones and undertows. More clearly than in any of Chekhov's other plays, fantasy imbues consciousness with a strength similar to the power of dreams in the unconscious. The play teeters on an ambiguity: if coming to terms with reality is a sign of psychological maturity, philosophy offers a contrary alternative: in letting go of an ideal, the sisters may be depriving themselves — or being deprived — of the one thing that makes life worth living.

These positive-negative aspects of the play are not easily resolved. Ambivalence enriches the action but fogs the ending. The problems *Three Sisters* raises have been presented to us with a complexity that allows for no easy solutions. Yet the curtain has to come down, the audience depart. And Chekhov, almost up to the last moment, keeps adding complications. In spite of its faultless construction, or because of it, the play is full of surprises. Andrei's moving and unexpected speech about Natasha's vulgarity, for instance. He knows how awful she is, and yet he loves her, and can't understand why — an unusual, and far from simpleminded, admission.

The sisters long to accomplish the opposite of what they achieve, to become the contrary of what they are. Masha is most honest about this and most hopeless; she cannot console herself with the optimistic platitudes of Irena or shore herself up with the resigned puritanism of Olga. Irena is about to rush off to her brick factory and Olga to her schoolroom. Masha lives with and within herself — a black person in a black dress, beautiful, loving, without joy. *Three Sisters*, in spite of its ambiguously worded life-may-be-better-in-the-future ending, might properly be subtitled, "Three Ways of Learning to Live without Hope." It is a drama of induced stupors and wounds and its tagged-on hopefulness is the one thing about it that doesn't ring true. People use each other in the play sentimentally, desperately, and, finally, fatally; there is no reason to assume that, given the choice, they will ever do anything else.

What we hear in *Three Sisters* are the twin peals of longing and departure. They are amplified by human ineptitude, human error, human weakness. And behind them we hear the clangings of the extreme: the childish, the monstrous, the insane. The Brahmsian overcast of sadness that darkens the action — little outbursts of joy and gaiety always too soon stifled or abandoned — help to make what is essentially a terrible indictment of life bearable. Sadness is at least not hopelessness. A play of girlhood, it is a play of loss, but not only feminine loss, though that strikes the deepest note. The drums and fifes offstage, the batteries that occasionally go off, the gambling house and the office — male institutions and trimmings — are shadowy and have nothing of the power and the immediacy of preparations for a meal, the giving of gifts, the temperature of a nursery — the force of the domestic, whether frustrated and virginal, or fulfilled and turning sour. A play about women — men are strangely absent even in the moment of their presence — its author clearly saw what lay at its most profound level: helplessness — a real, social, or contrived trait associated with, and sometimes promulgated by, women. Social class and the accident of sex work hand in hand to defeat desire and ambition. Watchers watching life go by, a stately frieze longing for the activity of movement, that is the central image of *Three Sisters*. Not so much "If we had only known . . ." as "If we could only *move*. . . ." Temperament, breeding, upbringing fix the sisters to separate stakes. They go on, hoping for the best, getting the worst, which is, in their case, to stay exactly as they were.

J . HENRI FABRE

The Incomparable Observer

WHEN Shakespeare painted the settings of his plays in words, he described a world his audience couldn't see. Sometimes he did more; he described a world it couldn't know. The naturalist does something similar for us. Nature is everywhere; we stare at it blindly. The naturalist opens our eyes. Sometimes, even with our eyes wide open, we cannot see because we do not know. He opens our minds, too. Unlike the physicist or the chemist, the naturalist is committed to words; mathematics, and the disciplines that depend on it, may be important to his understanding of the world but not to his sharing of it. He must be an accurate observer who can describe precisely what he observes. But that is not enough. He must also be a good writer. Good writing never lies, but it doesn't consist only in telling the truth. The naturalist distinguishes science from literature while making their connection plain.

In the long tradition of nature writing — one that includes Linnaeus, Gilbert White, and Thoreau — a Frenchman who died in 1915 stands in a special position. Jean Henri Fabre, called by Darwin "the incomparable observer" and by Victor Hugo "the Homer of the insects," was born in 1823 in Provence, and, except for a sojourn in Paris to take his doctorate and a brief stint of teaching in Corsica, spent the ninety-two years of his life in southern France. Though Fabre's geographical range was narrow, the comparison to Homer is not inept; Fabre managed to make the seemingly mechanical world of the insect heroic. His life and work may be sampled in the recently reprinted *The Life of the Spider*, by Fabre himself (translated by Alexander Teixeira de Mattos), and *Fabre, Poet of Science*, a biography by G. V. Legros (translated by Bernard Miall).

Fabre came from a family of small farmers. Sent by his destitute parents to his grandparents at the age of six, so that he could survive, "he made for the flowers and insects as the Pieris makes for the cabbage and the Vanessa makes for the nettle . . . in ecstasy before the splendors of the wing-cases of a gardener-beetle, or the wings of a butterfly." At seven, trying to discover how light entered the human body, he closed his eyes and opened his mouth. Disappointed, he reversed the process. Fabre's endless curiosity about the world around him, his obsession with nature, had no precedent in his family; he seems to have been born with a predisposition for the natural world.

The experiment with light preceded experiments using a more or less similar method. Nothing was taken for granted; starting from scratch, and without recourse to the work of others, he depended as far as possible on empirical observation. In the intensity and single-mindedness of his labors, he became a local curiosity; riveted to one spot for hours, he watched some insect mate or moult or multiply. Eventually, he moved from the fields into controlled research. Though some of his experiments were to become famous, his first, "impossible laboratory" consisted of jam jars. A self-taught scholar, convinced that "one knows thoroughly only what one learns oneself," he was charmed while studying Latin by Virgil's descriptions of animals, and he taught himself Greek by comparing Greek texts with their Latin equivalents. He was to learn — and to teach — physics, the natural sciences, and mathematics. When he became a professor at the *lycée* in Avignon, he divided his spare time scrupulously between what he cared for (natural science) and what he was still ignorant of (higher mathematics). Natural science finally absorbed him completely. He brought to it a knowledge and love of languages, a thorough grounding in mathematics, and a prejudice against formal classification. The notion that nature existed only to be structured was repellent. He wanted to write about it with the knowledge of the specialist but in words anyone could understand.

In 1855, when he was thirty-two, he published his study on the Great Cerceris, a giant wasp — the first of his papers to get wide attention — and two years later came his memoir on beetles: the Sitaris and the Meloe, and their relation to wild bees. He was fascinated by the investigation of live forms ("a little animal proteid capable of pleasure and pain surpasses in interest the whole immense creation of dead matter"). In 1865, Pasteur, commissioned to find the cause of an epidemic that was threatening to destroy France's silk industry, consulted Fabre. Pasteur knew little about the silk-

THE INCOMPARABLE OBSERVER

worm and had never seen a cocoon. The relationship between the two men was touchy, and made touchier by Pasteur's request to see Fabre's wine cellar, which consisted of a demijohn of a local vintage. Pasteur may have been a snob, but Fabre was not an easy man himself. Outside a small, close circle that idolized him, he was uncomfortable. ("Good society I avoid as much as possible; I prefer my own company.") Antisocial, shy, a born solitary, he was gentle but had a violent temper. Like many dedicated people, he loathed interference, quickly took offense, and despised the trivial. His definition of it included opera and the theater. He could be heavy; dinners were eaten in imposed silence.

Fabre was eventually awarded the ribbon of the Legion of Honor and presented to Napoleon III, but his growing recognition did little for his pocketbook. He pieced out a living for his family (eight children, by two marriages) by teaching and tutoring and acting as custodian, at the Requien Museum, of a vast collection of flowers, herbs, weeds, and rocks, many of which he had gathered himself. At the *lycée*, the envy of his colleagues (according to Legros) soon found its occasion. One of the issues of the day was secondary education for women, and Fabre was invited to deliver a series of public lectures attended by both sexes. The lectures were popular, but the prejudiced devout and the narrowly pedantic were outraged, and Fabre's spinster landladies, joining forces with the local bigots, gave him a month to get out. He resigned his professorship, and it was only by borrowing from his friend and neighbor John Stuart Mill, who had retired to Avignon in despair at the death of his wife, that Fabre managed to survive. (How long Fabre lived in Avignon is a puzzle. On pages 61 and 91 of Legros's biography, it was twenty years; on page 80, it was twenty-eight. Legros, a friend of Fabre, has the virtue of intimacy but the disadvantage of hero worship, and he is inclined to rhapsodize when a clear fact or date is needed.)

Fabre moved to Orange, where he began to write textbooks for young people — *The Sky*, *Earth*, *The Plant*, and so on — that were cherished by a generation of Frenchmen. With what money he made, he realized a lifelong dream: he bought an isolated house in Serignan. As he attained the age of fifty-four, his career was just beginning its most fruitful period. In the remaining thirty-eight years, he did the major work that resulted in the publication of what stands as his monument — the ten-volume *Souvenirs Entomologiques*, of which *The Life of the Spider* is one.

The large garden of the house was composed of thistles, couch grass, and other weeds. To its owner it was

Eden . . . this accursed ground which no one would have as a gift is an earthly paradise for the bees and wasps. Never in my insect-hunting memories have I seen so large a population at a single spot. Here come hunters of every kind of game: builders of clay, weavers of cotton goods, plasterers mixing mortar, carpenters boring wood, miners digging underground galleries, workers in gold-beaters' skin, and many more.

Fabre lived in seclusion, and he made elaborate detours of several miles to avoid passing through Serignan. With a patience that would have exhausted almost anyone else, he continued to reveal a hidden world with a transparent clarity of vision and style. Here is Fabre on the bluebottle fly, the mature form of the maggot, as it emerges from the sand:

She disjoints her head into two moving halves, which, each distended with its great red eye, by turns separate and unite. In the intervening space a large glassy hernia rises and disappears, disappears and rises. When the two halves move asunder, with one eye forced back to the right and the other to the left, it is as though the insect were splitting its brain-pan in order to expel the contents. Then the hernia rises, blunt at the end and swollen into a great knob. Next, the forehead closes and the hernia retreats, leaving visible only a kind of shapeless muzzle. In short, a frontal pouch, with deep pulsations momentarily renewed, becomes the instrument of deliverance, the pestle wherewith the newly-hatched Dipteron bruises the sand and causes it to crumble. Gradually, the legs push the rubbish back and the insect advances so much towards the surface.

The cicada, whose metamorphosis is slow, exits from the soil after years of darkness; its larva

resembles a sewer-man; its eyes are white, nebulous, squinting, blind. . . . It clings to some twig, it splits down the back, rejects its discarded skin, drier than horny parchment, and becomes the Cigale, which is at first a pale grass-green hue.

Fabre can use an image that brings to mind the English poets of the nineteenth century. His cricket is "the brown violinist of the clods." He can be lucid as well. A spider, the banded Epeira,

turning her back on the game . . . works all her spinnerets, pierced like the rose of a watering pot, at one and the same time. The silky spray is gathered by the hind legs, which are longer than the others and open into a wide arc to allow the stream to spread. Thanks to this artifice, the Epeira . . . obtains not a thread, but an iridescent sheet, a sort of clouded fan wherein the component threads are kept almost separate. The two hind legs fling this shroud gradually, by rapid alternate armfuls, while, at the same time, they turn the prey over and over, swathing it completely. The ancient *retiarius*, when pitted against a powerful wild beast, appeared in the arena with a rope-net folded over his left shoulder. The animal made its spring. The man, with a sudden movement of his right arm, cast the net after the manner of the fishermen; he covered the beast and tangled it in the meshes. . . . The Epeira acts in like fashion, with this advantage, that she is able to renew her armful of fetters.

One phenomenon had always puzzled insect observers. When insects like the Cerceris wasp dragged their prey to underground burrows to feed their larvae, the prey seemed dead, yet there was no outward sign of decay for month after month. It was assumed that an embalming process had taken place. Fabre discovered that the prey was alive, not embalmed, and had been anesthetized by the venom of the predator: though the adult of the species lived on nectar, the newly hatched larva required live food. It turned out that the venom is injected only into the ganglia that control movement. With the skill of a surgeon, each predator stabs its prey in exactly the same place, and knows by instinct the nervous system of its victim as if it had been imprinted at birth. (No one has yet explored the psychological implications of this discovery.) If one stab is sufficient, it is always administered in the crucial nerve; no random stabs occur. And if the nervous system is complex, the predator uses its hypodermic needle the appropriate number of times in the appropriate number of places. A certain caterpillar, for instance, has nine nerve centers, one for each of its nine segments. Nine injections are necessary to immobilize it, and nine are administered. The venom can also be used to kill, depending on where it enters the body of its victim. Moreover, in the case of parasites, the interloper's egg is laid in the least sensitive spot each time, so when the larva begins to eat "the first mouthfuls are only feebly resented."

It was Fabre, too, who first saw how the newly hatched Narbonne Lycosa spiders disperse. Impelled by an instinct that asserts itself only once and then disappears forever, the young climb to the highest point they can reach. There, ejecting a tiny piece of thread, they become kites, ready to be picked up by the slightest breeze. Carried by the wind, like certain seeds, they land wherever. Spiders have been found two hundred miles from their starting point.

And wonders pile upon wonders. The spider weaves threads beaded with glue for entrapment, threads as dry as silk for its own resting place, a waterproof material for the egg cases, a fabric as fine as swansdown to protect the eggs. In a brilliant appendix to *The Life of the Spider*, Fabre analyzes the geometry of the Epeira's web. It is a "logarithmic spiral," the same spiral that is found in the shells of molluscs — a series of winding ramps around a central pole that spin closer and closer to their support without ever touching it. The bringing together of the abstractions of mathematics and the realistic observation that characterize Fabre's books is extraordinary, but no more so than a hundred metaphors whose exactitude and originality of language justify the subtitle of Legros's biography.

I do not know what Fabre's place in science will ultimately be, or even what it is right now. Work completed at the time of the First World War has surely been superseded in important respects. And Fabre is dated in many obvious ways: his moralizing, his occasional sentimentality, his more-than-occasional anthropomorphic personifications. His scientific stature is more seriously marred by his refusal to accept evolution as a final theory. He became one of its opponents not because of a narrow orthodoxy — his insistence on the spiritual nature of reality was pantheistic at best — or ignorance or naïveté. He distrusted generalizations and limited himself to conclusions that could be verified by direct observation and by experiment. He thought evolution a too comfortable all-embracing notion. Having found evidence of the power of instinct everywhere, and knowing it to be irreversible, he felt that Darwin's theory left too many mysteries unexplained. Fabre believed that "human knowledge will be erased from the archives of the world before we know the last word concerning the smallest fly." He and Darwin had enormous respect for one another, recognizing how passionately each was concerned with the truth. They corresponded for years, and when Darwin died Fabre was still trying to learn English in order to better understand the subtleties of Darwin's thought.

Fabre's virtues spring from the same source as do his limitations. Grounded in one part of the world for over nine decades, he was able to investigate the insect life within his radius with an unprecedented thoroughness. His work on the scarab beetle took forty years. At the same time, his fixity kept him a provincial. Yet Fabre did something without parallel. Using his marvelous eyes, uncovering the incredible (the cricket's one hundred and fifty prisms, which simultaneously set in motion the four dulcimerlike organs of the elytron) and the abysmal (the dung beetle eats steadily for two months, night and day, without stopping for a second), he approached nature with the openness and wonder of a child, even as he became steeped in the lore of the specialist. For him, the miraculous and the mysterious were not necessarily at war with the factual; despite Eden, knowledge did not supplant innocence but was its corollary. We turn to him not only to find out what something looks like or how it behaves but to learn again how much can be discovered by looking. He renews our original impulses toward the world. Translating that world, he proves over and over the importance of words in conveying perception. Accuracy and truthfulness relate the scientist and the writer, but the sense of discovering the new unites the naturalist and the poet. In the end, it is revelation rather than description that draws us to both.

&

Isherwood at Seventy-Five

It is almost fifty years since Sally Bowles shared the recipe for a Prairie Oyster (raw egg doused in Worcestershire sauce) with Herr Issyvoo in a vain attempt to cure a hangover. The time was the thirties, the place Germany, the book *Goodbye to Berlin*. Sally's subsequent transformations — from story to play to movie to musical to movie-musical — are ironic mirrors of the many roles her creator plays in his novels, for though he is the same person, he is, of course, never himself. How could he be, since he is the author of the very novels in which he appears? Christopher Isherwood has had many stand-ins: William Bradshaw (the original family name was "Bradshaw-Isherwood") in *The Last of Mr. Norris*, Herr Issyvoo in the Berlin stories, Christopher in *Down There on a Visit*, and even Christopher Isherwood in the openly autobiographical *Lions and Shadows* and *Christopher and His Kind*. Should we be suspicious of his many disguises, or trust him for abandoning them one by one?

Any biographer of Isherwood, asking himself that question, comes up against a formidable rival — his subject. At the age of seventy-five, he is still mining the events and conflicts of his own life in a continuing mixture of fiction and biography, subject always to future amendment. As the scrims lift, each succeeding work discloses a bit more, certifies a name, nails down a place, or transfers a character from the realm of fiction to the world of fact. Isherwood's mother, for instance, in the form of Mrs. Lindsay in *All the Conspirators*, undergoes a second recasting as Lily Vernon in *The Memorial*, emerges briefly as herself in *Lions and Shadows*, and receives a thoroughgoing evocation in *Kathleen and Frank*. Life to Isherwood, like the work that reflects it, is subject to revision.

As Brian Finney makes clear in his critical biography, this hovering between the first person and the third is not merely a matter of self-doubt, though there was plenty of that, and certainly not a question of a lack of talent. It is the result, rather, of a lifelong quest: taking up particular views at particular times, underneath them all, Isherwood was engaged in a continuous search for a truth to which he could commit himself. His uneasiness and insecurity — persisting until the age of thirty-five — seem surprising still because he comes across, even in the earliest of the books, with such clear-cut amiability. Yet two concerns of Isherwood run through Mr. Finney's book: the problematic nature of personality and, as its corollary, the feeling that, whatever personality may be, it is not enough. The question of viewpoint, in life and in literature, was crucial from the beginning. Isherwood, always witty, was never frivolous, and his career spans large distances: from left-wing rebel to an adherent of Vedanta, from a mother-dominated schoolboy to a spokesman for homosexual rights.

Isherwood's natural gifts were tainted by doubt and guilt from the start: the famous detachment was hard-won. Born into an upper-middle-class world of landed gentry in 1904 (a date surprising in itself, so strong is the flavor of youthfulness), his emotional life was scarred from childhood through his middle thirties by a protracted battle with his mother, whom he saw as hypocritical and enslaving. Family guerrilla warfare is peculiarly harrowing; the enemy can be loved while its values are detested. Mr. Finney sums up the situation: "Much of Isherwood's life and writing was determined by a compulsive reaction against selective aspects of his mother's personality"— a remark equally applicable to Flaubert and Proust, and not inappropriate to E. M. Forster. Whether the versions of Kathleen grew closer to the truth as they supplanted one another over the years, or approached an ideal Isherwood would always have *liked* to believe in, is impossible to say. The relationship was intense and ambivalent, and no proper counterbalance was available to level it: in 1915, Isherwood's father was killed in World War I.

At the age of eleven, Isherwood was shipped off to a preparatory school, St. Edmund's. W. H. Auden arrived in an autumn term, but he and Isherwood were not to become close friends until seven years later. Edward Upward enters the picture at Repton, the public school Isherwood attended after St. Edmund's, and, like Auden, he became a lifelong friend. Upward was the most influential person in Isherwood's early life; their relationship sheds some light on the seemingly impossible amalgam of snobbish public-school attitudes and left-wing convictions that now seems such an odd

characteristic of young English writers of the thirties. Isherwood, confused by his father's death, was obsessed with the
fear of being afraid, and dreamed up "The Test," some great
imagined challenge he might meet by performing a heroic
act. It would have a double function: it would rival his father's bravery and yet compensate for the loss of him. This
adolescent fantasy merged with another he shared with Upward: the creation of a legendary place, "Mortmere," peopled
with madeup characters and animals. Shadowy plots against
"the Enemy" were acted out in a no-man's-land in which
Beatrix Potter and Karl Marx would have been equally at
home.

Isherwood's tendency to make friends with "the Posho-
cracy" and Upward's inclinations toward the "ordinary"
were guarded over by "The Watcher in Spanish," a con-
science-keeper ever on the alert. By creating an entire imaginary world, one could control it. "Mortmere" was, on the
one hand, an act of the imagination, and on the other, protective and escapist. It was "writing" before you were ready
to go it alone; at the same time, it provided a subterranean
connection between an undergraduate daydream with paranoid overtones and the conspiratorial guardians of political
Utopias such as Soviet Russia, Nazi Germany, and Fascist
Italy. Except for the consequences, fear and power were the
big issues on the small scale and on the large. Isherwood and
Upward's fantasy was reassuring, their sense of power enhanced in the very act of mocking it. "Mortmere" had an
incidental value: it provided Auden with a good deal of the
imagery in the early poems.

The fear of cowardice, of never having been "tested" like
his father in World War I, haunted Isherwood for years, un-

til he freed himself from the set of values that defined cowardice in the first place. He was eventually to become a pacifist. At the time, he saw himself as a generic type, the young man of the thirties, rebellious, guilt-ridden, trapped in a dying culture gassy with obsolescent values. But Isherwood was automatically divorced from the typical young man of his time in many ways: the aristocratic connections, homosexuality, and, most of all, talent.

Talent is not in the power of the talented to choose. In a society as class-conscious as England's, what is one to do with genius and talent, which form aristocracies of their own? Isherwood was peculiarly special — a blend of qualities ordinarily incompatible: diffidence and authority, morality and wit. In the work (and one suspects in the man), deflation balances the tendency to mythologize. Even granted the license of intimacy and the bantering lovers'-quarrel aspects of certain friendships, Auden's description of Isherwood as "a strict little landlady" and "a Prussian drill sergeant" is harder to reconcile with the Isherwood we *think* we know than is the boyish but worldly author of the Berlin stories with the California Vedantist who, twenty-five years later, wrote *Ramakrishna and His Disciples*.

The greatest influence of all was to be Forster, and Isherwood's first novel, *All the Conspirators*, now reissued in paperback, is inconceivable without him. As Isherwood has explained, "One of the most revolutionary sentences to a working novelist was 'One may as well begin with Helen's letters to her sister,' the way *Howards End* begins. This was dynamite. . . ." An example of "tea-tabling," the reduction of high points of drama to matter-of-fact notation, the "use of understatement determines the tone and nature of Isherwood's first novel," according to Mr. Finney, and "profoundly affected his moral vision. By deliberately underplaying scenes and events . . . which the traditional Edwardian novel would have treated as significant, Isherwood was able subtly to undermine the conventional moral values. . . ."

Conventional moral values were detestable to Isherwood because they were untrue, and the hero of *All the Conspirators* can neither settle for convention nor face the truth. Written when Isherwood was twenty-one, it is really two novels uneasily joined: a talented piece of realistic fiction embedded in a lot of fancy literary footwork. The story of Philip Lindsay's two friendships, one with an artist, Allen, the other with Victor, an athletic young Englishman too typical to breathe, the novel is an adolescent *cri de coeur*, a case of family claustrophobia, and the first dramatization of Isherwood's mother-*versus*-son battle. What is modish in it — the stream-of-consciousness set pieces — is what is least original, but the low-keyed control of narrative, the sharp edge of character, and the drive of the action are notable. Currants, a "live-in" friend of Philip's mother, is an Isherwood original, the forerunner of the odd little characters he sees out of the corner of his eye. Something of her quality crops up again in Fräulein Schroeder. The natural mobility of *All the Conspirators* is forced to make detours around avant-garde clutter, yet it still has the ability to grip the reader fifty years after it was first published.

After Repton, Isherwood went on to Cambridge. He left it after a two-year stint and began the long period of wandering that ended up at the boy-bars in Berlin in the late years of the Weimar Republic, wanderings that were to be repeated on a grander scale after publication of *The Last of*

Mr. Norris. Auden was in Berlin in 1929 and had friends, and Isherwood — though he didn't stay long the first time — discovered a world utterly different from the repressive English one he disliked, and with it, the excitements of sex and new subject matter. Isherwood's talent, controlled but intuitive, was liberated by the atmosphere of crisis. He needed the documentary, and the documentary was, by definition, not a product of the imagination.

On the other hand, fiction is, by definition, a lie. The fantastic side of him, enchanted by the strange — the "Mortmere" side — and the side that desperately wanted to tell the truth: how were they to be reconciled in the service of the novel? In *Goodbye to Berlin* he found the perfect recipe. And aren't all those "Christopher Isherwoods" in the work that follows the bridge between the knowable fact and its imagined genesis or consequence? Collaborating with Auden on the plays fed his imagination from one direction, the nonfiction books from another. Isherwood never shared Auden's passion for music. But his interest in the extrasensory and the spiritual may correspond to Auden's interest in opera: each opens onto a world of magically expanded feeling.

Isherwood was more interested in life, low and high, than in slogans and programs. The role of the international spokesman, warning the world of the dangers of Fascism, a role partly made up by Auden in the early poems dedicated to Isherwood in which Isherwood occasionally appears, is off the mark. Isherwood offers too slanted a correction when he says, in *Christopher and His Kind*, "Berlin meant boys. . . ." It did, but it meant much more.

He was at work on *The Memorial* in this period, after abandoning one of his grander "Balzacian" epics whose outlines he described so amusingly in *Lions and Shadows*. Isherwood was not temperamentally suited to the novel of complex design. His talent flourished in smaller confines in which he was able to give the effect of something larger; the Berlin stories had the cumulative power of a novel. He is at his best with a narrator's developing perception of a single character, where revelation cuts both ways — as in "Sally Bowles," "Otto," "Mr. Norris Changes Trains," and *Prater Violet*, perhaps the best example of all. The four-part structure of *Down There on a Visit* repeats the device four times, but with a special effect: the author and the narrator dissolve into each other. And Mr. Finney's excellent chapter on the novel is an important effort to rescue it from undeserved neglect.

Isherwood's ability to make the unseemly and the ugly genial is a peculiar, even a singular gift, for Sally and Mr. Norris are, with the slightest twist of the moral lens, shabby in the first case, repellent in the second. The tone of sophisticated innocence in which each story is told not only clears the air but freshens it.

Forster was important in another way: Isherwood radiates a kind of compulsiveness in Mr. Finney's book, which, if I read correctly, was temporarily assuaged by sex but had as its real object work — the process of it and its accomplishment. Beyond either, it sought a form of peace that had to do with love, on the one hand, and the expansion of perception, the transforming of observation into observance, on the other. Being a homosexual and a pacifist, he was looking for a religious experience uncontaminated by dogma. In Swami Prabhavananda he finally met the kind of person in whom he could believe, that is, the kind of person whose *message* he could believe because the message had to be transmitted through a person, just as Isherwood's conception of style as a way of writing and a way of being was communicated through Forster. Swami Prabhavananda was unaffected and exemplary; his integrity did not crumble under "testing," Isherwood's subtle way of dividing the sham from the real.

The Swami and Forster had other connections, I believe. They were both enemies of the "undeveloped heart," and Forster, a skeptic himself, asserted a long-range and concealed effect: it is through *A Passage to India* that Isherwood, as well as the general public, first became aware of Hinduism as a subject worthy of serious study. Forster made Hindu tenets available by demonstrating them rather than expounding them in the novel, though Godbole (aptly named) in a few words illuminates some of the concepts. Forster exerted a triple influence on Isherwood — as a writer, as a man, and as a messenger bringing back news of the East. Forster's genius and integrity were unquestionable; he became the moral consultant of an age.

One forgets, until one rereads them, just how good Isherwood's stories and novels really are, and Mr. Finney's book leads you back to them. If something of the Ph.D. thesis clings to it, its concision and intelligence more than make up for it. Considering the multiple realities Isherwood presents, it is beautifully organized. One could easily write separate books on the English Isherwood, the Berlin Isherwood, and the American Isherwood. And the cast is a name-dropper's paradise. Mr. Finney, with the finest tact, steers clear of the anecdotal.

But there is an ever-present difficulty. Biographies of living writers examine the truth within the limits of discretion. With a homosexual writer, those limitations can become a barrier. Isherwood is open and frank in regard to the subject. That doesn't mean everybody else is. One suspects that certain sources will be made available only in the future.

Mr. Finney's difficulty only underlines a problem Isherwood faced as a novelist. What Isherwood has regarded as a lack of honesty in dealing with homosexuality seems, from a position of hindsight, actually an act of bravery: he communicated a position without having to elucidate it simply by being a good writer. The most honest of observers, he was obviously bothered by having to obscure the sex lives of his characters, including his own. The struggle with his mother — a matter of truth-telling and hypocrisy — must have come up, time and again, in his life as a writer. It is no wonder the battle was prolonged. As in the case of Forster, one doesn't have to be told where he stands; all one has to do is to read the novels.

If they vary in quality, they do not vary in talent. Isherwood has always striven for the generic — the characters represent something: a class (Mrs. Lindsay), a type (Otto or Paul), a historical divergence affecting personality (Bergmann). Sometimes material doesn't lend itself to this kind of treatment — *The World in the Evening*, for instance — and sometimes the material becomes too schematic —"A Meeting by the River." Isherwood has made his peace with the subject of homosexuality in *A Single Man* (fiction) and *Christopher and His Kind* (autobiography).

Mr. Finney's book is thorough and lucid, yet in talking or writing about Isherwood, one has the uncomfortable feeling that something not quite possible to say remains to be said; the element of charm is elusive. Born in the year Chekhov died, Isherwood resembles him in curious ways, and in more than being a fellow writer who once studied medicine: the warmth is implicit but not easily available — detachment gets in the way; the fusion of the subjective and the objective is original; and the lie is temperamentally the greatest sin in the moral register. Chekhov's voyage to Sakhalin Island bears a resemblance, not in kind but in motive, to Isherwood's trips to China and South America, and Chekhov's letters to Isherwood's autobiographical writing. In Isherwood's work, a magic potion of history and invention, the voice is clear, and, no matter how many times we hear it, it always seems to be speaking for the first time.

One Hundred Years of Proust

THAT a giant can be done in by flies is an old story, but that he could be mistaken for one is not. Marcel Proust was often just so mistaken in his lifetime, and he often still is. His life — at least a good part of it — lent credence to the error. Though he worked much harder than is generally supposed — the seven-hundred-and-forty-four-page *Jean Santeuil*, an earlier version of *Remembrance of Things Past*, was abandoned as early as 1900 — there is enough firsthand evidence to support the stereotype of the hothouse neurotic, snob, and social climber. But the mistake gets its strongest support from another source. Blurring the distinction between reality and fiction, Proust named the narrator and hero of *Remembrance of Things Past* Marcel, and from that moment on the confusion between his life and his work was fixed. The choice of name was deliberate — Proust had thirteen years in which to change his mind — but he might just as well have hung a sign saying "Reflections Inside" in front of a house of mirrors.

He once could have been considered a snob (though he dissected snobbery down to its ultimate fishbone) and a social climber (though he wrote the most devastating attack on society in literature), and this, added to the mix-up of the two Marcels, has resulted in a cloudy critical muddle. Over three thousand works in many languages (one of the two or three largest bibliographies of this century) trail after *Remembrance of Things Past* like a gigantic smoke screen, yet it is odd to note the peculiar condescension that often accompanies what appear to be salutes to his genius.

A recent one appeared on the front page of the *New York Times* Book Review, and I quote it because it represents a persistent view of Proust that survives all the adulation. Bearing the marks of time and study devoted to Proust as an act of homage, the article ended with "And perhaps one day soon we shall find ourselves pleasantly immobilized, comfortably hammocked or mildly ill; one day when the guns are gone and the looters are out of the suburbs; when all the threats have been withdrawn, and time lies as empty in our hands as an office present, then perhaps — I won't say we shall read Proust again — but then, perhaps, we may make a start."

This notion of Proust as irrelevant or frivolous, as a kind of dessert, is not supported by *Remembrance of Things Past*. For Proust was a moral and political writer, and the widely held view that he was some sort of society columnist who watched over the disintegration of France's aristocracy as court chronicler is at best simplistic and at worst a distortion. In *Remembrance of Things Past*, the great political and social scandal is the Dreyfus trial, with its stench of anti-Semitism and military duplicity. Because of both, the Dreyfus trial sheds light on every modern political crisis of the Western world, from the burning of the Reichstag to the publication of the Pentagon Papers. Proust examines the Dreyfus case with a thoroughness and an objectivity in regard to the stupidity displayed on both sides that are all the more remarkable in view of his personal commitment to Dreyfus. Proust's ability to examine men and issues with the dispassion of true judgment is not a fashionable ability at *any* time, but he performed a task that time makes necessary in the long run.

Without the benefit of years of hindsight, Proust understood the human and social forces that led to the First World War, and his portrait of the cravenness, vulgarity, and pettiness, the inner corruption of people who held power in their hands is icily cold and crystal clear. His depiction of Norpois, the diplomat, is cruelly instructive. Where else could one turn in fiction to find so damning a picture of self-interest, lack of political principle, and their consequences? Just as it was only one step from Neville Chamberlain and the Munich Pact to the invasion of Poland, it is only one step from Norpois to the aerial bombardment of Paris. It is a step Proust explicitly takes. Proust's skill in dealing with every class and type of character would stamp him as a first-rate social novelist in the old-fashioned nineteenth-century sense even if *Remembrance of Things Past* made none of the other claims it makes — to literary experiment, profundity of thought, psychological originality, and philosophical speculation. And it contains in its first two volumes the most accurate and evocative re-creations of childhood and adolescence I know. If one substituted Mann or Joyce in the sentence I quote from the *Times*, there would be letters of outrage. In short, though Proust is rarely under direct attack, he always needs to be defended.

And not only from the charge of preciousness. Another view flourishes right alongside the first: that of the task to be got through, the labor constantly postponed because its demands are too formidable. These twin, conflicting misconceptions — that Proust is not worth reading because he is effete, that it is one's duty to read him because he is major — have kept more than one reader from picking up *Swann's Way*. Every other important writer of this century is read for pleasure or has been made into a movie; there are even those once so unimaginable screenwriters Lawrence, Mann, and Joyce. Only Proust still bears the stigma of the unapproachable, even though *Swann's Way* is read in modern-novel courses as if it *were Remembrance of Things Past*.

Proust presents a unique problem. The original French edition was not published in its entirety until 1927, five years after the author's death. Many readers who enjoyed *Swann's Way* in 1913 weren't around to attend the terrifying party the Princesse de Guermantes throws in *The Past Recaptured*. How could they have ever dreamed that the Princesse, in this final volume, is none other than hideous Mme. Verdurin, twice remarried? Were those readers interviewed on their deathbeds, their notion of Proust would be similar to that of the many readers who are under the misapprehension that one volume of the novel is the novel itself or who have stopped somewhere along the line. The impossibility of containing what is a single work between the covers of a single book tends to obscure not only the various views of it but even various memories of it.

Only one thing is worse than getting the wrong attention, and that is to be ignored. On the occasion of Proust's centennial, the one book the American publishing community could muster that attempts an overall evaluation is imported from England — *Marcel Proust 1871–1922: A Centennial Volume*, ten essays on facets of Proust, with photographs and reproductions, and an introduction by its editor, Peter Quennell. A strange combination of gift book and serious critical study, it oddly misfires on both counts. Anyone interested in Proust would want it, anyone interested in literary gifts would have to consider it, but there are other gift books, even literary ones, less limited in scope and more lavish. And the essays have a tendency to stop just when they are developing their themes, as if the writers were afraid of going too far or had just become aware of how far there was to go. The result is that they often seem too detailed and specific for the general reader and not thoroughgoing enough for the specialist.

As far as I can make out, there are four kinds of Proust criticism:

(1) *The guessing game:* Questions like "Was the Duchesse de Guermantes really the Comtesse Greffülhe or was she really the Marquise de Chevigné?" are posed and answered, but not definitively, for they are asked over and over again. A good deal of what passes for Proust criticism consists of pretending that *Remembrance of Things Past* is a *roman à clef.*

(2) *The counting house:* (a) How many laundry images did Proust use? (b) How many times does the word "disappear" appear?

(3) *The construction gang:* Though Proust wrote the beginning and the end of his novel first, the ever-expanding accor-

dion of what came between has led to three differing views: (a) *Remembrance of Things Past* is a perfectly formed work, and all the additions Proust made to it serve only to prove how tightly shipshape it was right from the start. (b) It's a mess, but a beautiful one, and its very messiness allows for all those wonderful digressions by which we define the word "Proustian"; that is, when it isn't being confused with the word "reminiscent." (c) It is a compromise. It was superbly conceived, architecturally, as a three-volume novel, but two unforeseen events threw it wildly out of gear: Proust's relationship with his chauffeur, Alfred Agostinelli, and the First World War.

(4) *The real thing: Remembrance of Things Past* is the story of a man in search of a vocation. Primarily concerned with memory, and particularly involuntary memory, it is a book in which the idealizations of youth are destroyed by time, only to be triumphantly resurrected in art. Critics who write about it as a work of art, and of its connection to life, past and present, include Samuel Beckett, Roger Shattuck, Leo Bersani, Germaine Bree, and Georges Prioué. None of them is represented in Mr. Quennell's collection.

It *does* include such first-rate writers as Elizabeth Bowen and Anthony Powell, two very different masters of style. Miss Bowen tackles the character of Bergotte, Proust's novelist — one of the trio of artists who provide continuing motifs in the novel. Her essay is meticulously organized and wonderful to read, but it throws the collection out of kilter because the two other members of the trio — Elstir, the painter, and Vinteuil, the composer — are not treated in separate essays. A general and informative piece by I. H. E. Dunlop, "Proust and Painting," good as it is, doesn't plug up the gaping holes. The lack of a chapter on Proust and music is particularly damaging. Vinteuil — as a character, as the composer of the Sonata, as the father of a lesbian daughter whose friend, the very cause of his early death, pieces together his Septet, assuring his immortality — is so obviously one of the cornerstones of the book that the omission of an essay on him is inexplicable.

In "Proust as a Soldier," Mr. Powell repeats an anecdote. Asked "What event in military history do you most admire?" Proust wrote, "My own enlistment as a volunteer." The idea of Proust as a soldier is as alien to his "legend" as the notion of Ronald Firbank as a Marine sergeant, yet the facts are there, and Mr. Powell traces the effects of Proust's one year in the ranks on the military events, characters, and scenes in *Remembrance of Things Past*. Mr. Powell plays a version of "the guessing game," but he plays it with authority and style, going after facts rather than surmises:

> Captain de Borodino . . . is one of the characters in the novel drawn from life. His prototype was Captain Walewski, a Company Commander in the 76th, a grandson of Bonaparte by a Polish lady, an affair well known to history. As it happened, the Captain's mother, in addition to his grandmother's imperial connections, had been mistress to Napoleon III. That such a figure, with origins, appearance, and behaviour all crying out for chronicling, should turn up in Proust's regiment illustrates one of those peculiar pieces of literary luck which sometimes attend novelists. Borodino represents the most extreme example of "putting in" — that is to say, no doubt whatever exists as to his identity, owing to the exceptional nature of his background.

An essay on the Faubourg Saint-Germain quotes an illuminating remark of Proust to the Duc de Guiche: "The

274

Duchesse de Guermantes resembles a tough barnyard fowl whom I formerly took to be a bird of paradise — by transforming her into a puissant vulture, I have at least prevented the public assuming that she was just a commonplace old magpie." A valuable study, by Sherban Sidery, of Proust's "Jewishness" brings up a simple point not often made: unlike his creator, the Marcel of the book is neither Jewish nor homosexual, those attributes being assigned to other characters. In a discussion of the influence of other writers on Proust, Baudelaire and Balzac are seen as his opposing magnets, but only brief mention is made of the *Arabian Nights* and none of Saint-Simon, two well-established influences on Proust. After "The World of Fashion," and a note by Francis Steegmuller on "Proust and Cocteau," it is left to Pamela Hansford Johnson to explore the larger themes of the novel: memory as the only preserver of time, art as the only preserver of memory. In ten pages, she does a fine if understandably breathless job, and redresses the notion of Proust as merely the portraitist of a vanished world.

When Illiers — the town Proust transformed into the fictional Combray — was officially renamed Illiers-Combray this past spring, more than the interests of poetic justice were served. In a very particular way, the gesture, blending nature and art, echoed the work in whose honor it was made. In *The Past Recaptured*, passages from the Goncourt brothers (it seems) confront the reader, who at first thinks they're genuine. It takes some time to realize they are a pastiche — as much time, I'd say, as it takes to realize that the final Guermantes party is not a masquerade. Marcel, who has been away from Paris for years, is under the impression that it is. It slowly dawns on the reader, as it does on Marcel, that he is not attending a costume party: the partygoers have simply grown old; they are transformed, all right, but only by time. Just as nothing could be farther from Marcel's mind when he talks about time than the little world of it represented by the French aristocracy, nothing could be less like his idea of literature than the inspired reportage of "The Goncourt Journal" — so like, so *unlike* what he plans to do. That *Remembrance of Things Past* should be judged in the same light is profoundly ironic, for Proust, as a warning against the judgment, included a species of what he was *not* writing in the very book he wrote.

In *Remembrance of Things Past*, characters who actually lived — the Princesse Mathilde, Celeste Albaret — are minor and dwarfed by the reality of the created ones. Though Françoise is primarily based on Celeste Albaret, both are included. In Proust, the reporter and the fabulist are entwined. He was one of the first writers to see the relation between the document and fiction, and the psychological truth implicit in the relation. Most people's lives are questionable documents in which illusion and fact are interchangeable, in which love and status, say, as in the case of Swann, may be real personal and social powers but — from a viewpoint only one turn of the screw away — also ridiculous shams and pretension.

And Proust had something else in mind. One of the profundities of art is the form working itself out, in the same way a musical theme is sounded, developed, and concluded. In Proust, it is not the content of the motif but its function that is the point. He explicitly makes a distinction between Swann's experience of Vinteuil's Sonata as remembered emotion and Marcel's experience of Vinteuil's Septet as form itself. That distinction ultimately separates the nonartist from the artist. Human interest and philosophical drama aside, *Remembrance of Things Past* can be conceived as an aesthetic object, in which certain colors, tones, notions are planted, allowed to grow, expand, alter, and resound. It uniquely combines some of the characteristics of painting and music, and propounds — and is an example of — the notion that the function of the artist is to add forms to nature as well as to hold a mirror up to it. It is the peculiar quality (and difficulty) of *Remembrance of Things Past* to have met the conditions of the novel in the way, say, a masterpiece like *War and Peace* meets them, and yet to be something else again, more like a gigantic poem or a cabalistic exercise whose characters become phantoms of ideality. Because they do, they must at some point appear solidly real. Proust is a realistic writer, but for a purpose that has little to do with realism. He is like a magician who makes a live rabbit disappear. It is all too easy to forget that the reason the rabbit is there in the first place is to prove not that rabbits are real but that magic is powerful.

Since viewpoint is of the essence in Proust, a viewer — Marcel — is included along with the view. And Proust had a good reason for naming his viewer Marcel. As the fictional Marcel discovers his vocation and becomes a writer — a discovery that, after thousands of pages, takes place at the last minute — we realize we have just read the work he is about to undertake. At that point, Marcel becomes Marcel Proust.

ACKNOWLEDGMENTS

Walt Whitman: A Candidate for the Future, reprinted by permission of The New Yorker Magazine, Inc. Copyright 1981 by Howard Moss. First published under the title "A Candidate for the Future" in *The New Yorker*.

Constantine Cavafy: Great Themes, Grand Connections, reprinted by permission of The New Yorker Magazine, Inc. Copyright 1977 by Howard Moss. First published under the title "Great Themes, Grand Connections" in *The New Yorker*.

W. H. Auden: Goodbye to Wystan, reprinted by permission of The New York Times Company. Copyright © 1975 by Howard Moss. First published under the title "Goodbye to Wystan" in *The New York Times Book Review*.

Elizabeth Bishop: The Canada–Brazil Connection, reprinted by permission of the University of Oklahoma Press. Copyright 1977 by the University of Oklahoma Press. First published under the title "The Canada–Brazil Connection" in *World Literature Today*.

James Schuyler: Whatever Is Moving, reprinted by permission of The American Poetry Review. Copyright 1981 by Howard Moss. First published under the title "Whatever Is Moving" in *The American Poetry Review*.

The Poet's Voice, reprinted by permission of The New Yorker Magazine, Inc. Copyright 1978 by Howard Moss.

The First Line, reprinted by permission of The American Poetry Review. Copyright 1978 by Howard Moss.

From a Notebook, reprinted by permission of The American Poetry Review. Copyright 1979 by Howard Moss.

The Poet's Story, reprinted by permission of Macmillan Publishing Company, Inc. Copyright © 1973 by Howard Moss. First published in *The Poet's Story* edited with an Introduction by Howard Moss.

Eudora Welty: The Lonesomeness and Hilarity of Survival, reprinted by permission of The New Yorker Magazine, Inc. Copyright 1970 by Howard Moss. First published under the title "The Lonesomeness and Hilarity of Survival" in *The New Yorker*.

Eudora Welty: A House Divided, reprinted by permission of The New York Times Company. Copyright © 1972 by The New York Times Company. First published under the title "The Optimist's Daughter" in *The New York Times Book Review*.

Jean Rhys: Going to Pieces, reprinted by permission of The New Yorker Magazine, Inc. Copyright 1974 by Howard Moss. First published under the title "Going to Pieces" in *The New Yorker*.

Elizabeth Bowen: Interior Children, reprinted by permission of The New Yorker Magazine, Inc. Copyright 1979 by Howard Moss. First published under the title "Interior Children" in *The New Yorker*.

Elizabeth Bowen: 1899–1973, reprinted by permission of The New York Times Company. Copyright © 1973 by Howard Moss. First published under the title "Elizabeth Bowen: An Obituary" in *The New York Times Book Review*.

Sylvia Plath: Dying: An Introduction, reprinted by permission of The New Yorker Magazine, Inc. Copyright 1971 by Howard Moss. First published under the title "Dying: An Introduction" (from the title of a collection of poems by the late L. E. Sissman, courtesy of the author) in *The New Yorker*.

Katherine Mansfield: A Pinched Existence, reprinted by permission of The New York Times Company. Copyright © 1980 by The New York Times Company. First published under the title "A Pinched Existence" in *The New York Times Book Review*.

Jean Stafford: Some Fragments, reprinted by permission of Shenandoah. Copyright 1980 by Howard Moss. First published under the title "Jean: Some Fragments" in *Shenandoah*.

Anton Chekhov: Hingley's Chekhov, reprinted by permission of The New York Times Company. Copyright © 1976 by The New York Times Company. First published under the title "Hingley's Chekhov" in *The New York Times Book Review*.

Anton Chekhov: Three Sisters, reprinted by permission of The Hudson Review, Inc. Copyright 1977 by Howard Moss. First published under the title "Three Sisters" in *The Hudson Review*.

Christopher Isherwood: Isherwood at Seventy-Five, reprinted by permission of The New York Times Company. Copyright © 1979 by The New York Times Company. First published under the title "Isherwood at 75" in *The New York Times Book Review*.

J. Henri Fabre: The Incomparable Observer, reprinted by permission of The New Yorker Magazine, Inc. Copyright 1972 by Howard Moss. First published under the title "Fabre" in *The New Yorker*.

Marcel Proust: One Hundred Years of Proust, reprinted by permission of The New Yorker Magazine, Inc. Copyright 1971 by Howard Moss. First published under the title "One Hundred Years of Proust" in *The New Yorker*.